A Lost Paradise

SAMUEL CHOTZINOFF

A Lost Paradise

EARLY REMINISCENCES

In life there is really no great or small thing.

All things are of equal value and of equal size.

OSCAR WILDE, De Profundis

ALFRED A. KNOPF

NEW YORK

1955

L. C. catalog card number: 54–7202

© Samuel Chotzinoff, 1955

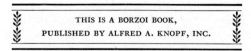

THIS IS A BORZOI BOOK,
PUBLISHED BY ALFRED A. KNOPF, INC.

FIRST EDITION

A shorter version of the chapter entitled "Mr. Harris" appeared originally in THE NEW YORKER, and a section of the chapter entitled "The Fountain" appeared originally as "East Side Boyhood" in HOLIDAY.

For ANNE *and* BLAIR

Contents

A Lost Paradise

The Healing Earth

WHEN, through the proddings of that species of vanity which makes some people believe that their lives have had a special significance and are therefore worthy to be recorded, I undertook to write these memoirs, I was disconcerted to discover that my family (and I, too, for that matter) had kept no records. Neither births, deaths, nor marriages had ever been inscribed in Bibles or other sacred books. I should not have wondered at this, having been told as a child that it is forbidden to deface God's utterance or the chronicles and opinions of holy men. But I had hoped to find the information I was seeking set down in journals, diaries, letters, and on the flyleaves of profane books. I should have known better; indeed, I did know better. For in so orthodox and so poor a Jewish household as ours there were no journals, diaries, or letters that survived their perusal, and no profane books.

I cannot recall ever seeing legal documents of any sort around the house except my father's identification papers as a Jew and a legal resident of our home town of Vitebsk, on the Dvina River, in the "government" of Vitebsk. And I became acutely aware of this sinister paper only because at alarmingly frequent intervals it was held by the local police to be *not* in order. Since no one ever tampered with this document, it was difficult to understand how anything could ever be wrong with it. The discovery of its irregularity always occurred in the dead of night and was heralded by a great knocking on the door, which aroused the entire family and even the neighbors. While the rest of us hovered trembling with fear in the background, my father, looking fatalistically resigned in his long underwear, would admit the two policemen (they always came in pairs) and automatically and without inquiring into the reason for their untimely visit produce his papers. And while the two pretended to scrutinize the documents (the Russian police in general never learned to read), my father would dress himself with the celerity of an actor making a quick change in a farce that was enjoying a long run. The three would then depart for the station house, whither my mother, her toilette taking longer than my father's, would follow soon after, in her hand the two rubles she would by then have borrowed from neighbors who had also been aroused by the clamor. And having, after many lengthy formalities, paid the fine for the alleged irregularities the identification papers revealed to the cursory scrutiny of the sergeant at the desk, my parents would return home and the family would resume their interrupted rest.

Important family events were remembered and placed as to time by the concurrence of noteworthy happenings in the outside world. Thus it appeared that I came down with the measles the day after the great fire broke out in the Governor's Mansion on the "other" side of the river. That, by backward computation, would fix my age at the period of my

malady at around three. Similarly, I received my first haircut
—deemed a solemn occasion in the life of a Jewish male—
during the great drought which lasted a month, the reluctant
heavens finally succumbing to the pressure of a series of special all-night prayers by the town's most pious Jews. Fires
were, perhaps, the greatest aid to memory, for there was
hardly a conflagration, great or small, that was not associated
with a birth, death, marriage, or family event of even minor
importance. Other outside happenings also served as memory
posts, some tragic and some tragicomic, such as the death of
the pampered young son of a close neighbor, who succumbed
after consuming four dozen oversized latkes (potato pan-
cakes) which his doting mother, unable to deny him, had
fried and served up to him. By a rare coincidence it was on
that very day that my great-aunt Shprinze ran away with a
"goy" and was never heard of again. And any reference to
the unhappy fate that overtook our neighbor's hedonistic
child brought with it a reminder of the shame to her family
caused by my great-aunt's elopement.

Owing to the absence of recorded data, the ages of the
members of our family remained approximations. We were
"about" so many years old, having been born "around" the
beginning, middle, or end of whatever year and month some
memorable external event had taken place. Along with wars,
pestilences, pogroms, the accession of tsars or their deaths,
either natural or by assassination at the hands of what my
father called "godless terrorists," the more important Jewish
holidays helped to identify and place in some sort of chrono-
logical order the high points of our family history. Some of
us were born on the eve of such holidays or even on the very
day. Such birthdays were the more easily catalogued and
remembered. My mother herself had been born so close to the
first day of Passover (and in the year of the Great Plague, at
that!) that my grandmother, overanxious to put her house in
a kosher state for the holidays, left her lying-in bed prema-

turely and set about scouring and dusting, and in consequence
suffered poor health for the rest of her life.

My mother "thought" that her marriage to my father might
have taken place "around" the time of the pogrom in Su-
walki. And on investigation many years later I found that
tragic event to have taken place in 1888. And since there was
a recollection that I was born one year later, 1889 was clearly
the year of my birth. My mother had been married twice
before (this I also learned many years later), and both marriages had ended in divorce. The divorces, my mother later
assured me, were obtained by her on the grounds of inebriety,
certainly a remarkable coincidence, it seemed to me, in the
failings of two husbands otherwise different in temperament
and character. Habitual drunkenness served not uncommonly
as grounds for divorce, though it did not have the major
importance of sterility in women, failure to produce a male
child, or impotence in men. Still, while the charge of drunkenness may have been acceptable to the rabbi who sat in judgment, I find it hard to believe that my mother would have
resorted to the extremity of divorce for so human a failing.
Furthermore, she had borne each of her husbands a girl, and
the welfare of the two little children was a consideration that
must have counted against the solution of her domestic problems by divorce. My mother was strong-minded and strong-
willed, ready and even eager to adjust herself to the frailties
of those she loved. Where her emotions were involved she
could summon endless reserves of patience and endurance. It
is highly probable, therefore, that her emotions were not involved in her first two marriages. And rather than live out
her days *unloving*, to her a more depressing condition than
unloved, she would suffer the obloquy of a twice-divorced
woman in order to retain at least the hope of some future
emotional fulfillment.

Whatever her motives, her determination to keep herself
free at all costs for some problematic destiny was highly un-

conventional for those times. To give it respectability she required the sympathy and approval of some powerfully placed and greatly respected person in the town and neighborhood. She did not have far to look. Her own father, Reb Shnayer Tresskanov, was the most idolized, the most respected savant in Vitebsk and within a radius of at least seventy miles. What was more, my mother was his favorite among his six children. She had always known it, though he had shown to the world the conventional preference of Jewish fathers for their male offspring. She understood him, not perhaps rationally, but instinctively, and she loved him devotedly, even while she wondered at the extremes of piety and generosity his mystical nature drove him to. Abhorring the very idea of favoritism, he was secretly indulgent to my mother and prone to overlook lapses of propriety in her that he would not tolerate in his other daughters. Many years ago, when the crinoline came into fashion among goyim, it was tacitly assumed that it was no proper garment for well-brought-up Jewish girls and women. Walking one day in the public park, my grandfather came face to face with his eldest daughter, Rivkeh, then a pretty girl of eighteen. He could hardly believe his eyes! Rivke was clad in the billowing, irreligious, goyish abomination, the crinoline! My grandfather seized his daughter by her wrists and commanded her to remove the offending garment instantly. Adamant against her plea to be permitted to return home, there to discard her dress and never to wear it again, he insisted on its immediate removal in plain view of the crowd that had collected around them. The crinoline finally fell to the ground, and the sobbing Rivke, stepping out of it clad only in a petticoat, made her escape. My mother contended that had she herself been the culprit, her father would have spared *her* the humiliation he had not hesitated to inflict on her sister.

In her divorce proceedings my mother undoubtedly had the support of her father. The rabbi who tried both cases must

call on the tailor. This would be recognized as a deliberate piece of condescension and would so gratify the latter as to dissipate any idea of the proposed alliance being disadvantageous to his son, in the event that rumor and gossip relating to my mother had already reached Ula. To keep the tailor forever at a safe remove, the widower and his six children were to be invited to take up residence with the new bride in Vitebsk in a house that my grandfather would purchase for the couple, himself to make a substantial down payment and the groom to undertake the payment of the rest of the sum in monthly installments.

The shadchen's plan was approved and duly carried out. My grandfather was no snob, though he was not above the prejudices of his time. He carried off his visit to the elder Chatianov with quiet dignity and a naturalness that both impressed the tailor and put him at his ease. Nor did the visitor attempt to evade the subject of his host's embarrassing profession. On the contrary, he introduced the subject early at their first meeting and expressed a wish to examine the shop and see for himself the place from which the elite of Ula were outfitted. My father and mother were ceremoniously introduced to each other. The shadchen, being present and acting as chaperon and manager, reported the meeting to my grandfather as having been successful, even more than he had hoped. The shadchen was a great believer in a man and a woman getting a glimpse of each other before the marriage ceremony. Such a meeting, if immediately rewarding, might at once lay the foundation for a happy future; and if momentarily disappointing, it at least gave the couple time to adjust their former hopes to the reality they would face on their wedding day and after. My father was sufficiently pleased with the face and figure of my mother to admit as much later to the shadchen, and to confide, in a burst of confidence, that he had had his first glimpse of his late wife when he lifted her veil at the marriage ceremony. He was then only seventeen and the bride was ten years his senior. The shadchen surmised that there must have been other elements of disparity which my father quite properly refrained from mentioning. As for my mother, the shadchen reported that she had been much taken with my father. Through long experience in such delicate matters the shadchen prided himself on an ability to penetrate the craftiest dissimulation. He was now ready to swear on the heads of his children that my mother loved the widower at first sight.

The wedding followed duly. The house in Vitebsk was purchased and furnished by my grandfather and the family moved in. My father's six children ranged in age from the year-old Sarah to Albert, a youth of about nineteen or twenty. In between were Hodde (renamed Gertie in America), seventeen, Leyke (Lea), fourteen, Zalman (Solomon), eight, and Lebbe (Louis), five. My mother at once gave herself up fully to the duties of a wife and mother. Her energy and vitality were inexhaustible and she marketed, cooked, washed, swept, and mended from earliest morning to bedtime. With the assistance of my grandfather my father established a *cheder* (Hebrew school) in an untenanted house at the end of town. The pupils were few at first, but grew in number as my father began to be talked of as a strict disciplinarian and a specialist in the treatment of pampered or backward children. My grandfather contributed to the success of the cheder by not neglecting to put in a word about the solidity and extent of the learning of his new son-in-law where it would be most effective, with fathers of prospective pupils. Albert and Zalman, the two elder boys, were apprenticed to a carpenter. They received no pay, but were guaranteed their midday dinner. Lebbe joined the pupils in his father's cheder. Hodde being of a marriageable age, my father considered it best for her not to engage in remunerative labor, but to stay at home to await her destined suitor, she in the meantime assuming (voluntarily, as he stipulated) some of the lighter chores of the household; nor was the younger Leyke to overtax her

where she guessed her husband had taken refuge. She improvised a bed for the two girls on the kitchen floor, and when they fell asleep she put on her shawl and left the house. By midnight she was at her father's house in Serotchaya. He had not yet retired, and the two conversed earnestly for a long time. Before she left for home, it was agreed that her father should visit the cheder early next morning and do his utmost to placate her husband. When she reached her own house, Mayshe Baer had not returned. As she surmised, he had chosen to spend the night in his cheder stretched out on one of the benches.

The next morning her father appeared, bearing the best of news. He had just come from the cheder and found his son-in-law still smarting from my mother's treachery and the discomfort of his makeshift bed. My father had demanded a speedy divorce to wipe out the shame of a deception that would in any case make him the laughingstock of the entire city. My grandfather pointed out that not the deception but the divorce would make him a laughingstock, since the divorce would be the proof that he had been hoodwinked by a clever woman. But there was a way to save both his own self-esteem and the respect of Vitebsk, and that was for Mayshe Baer to welcome the two little girls openly as if he had always known about them and they had now merely returned from a protracted visit to their grandparents in the country. This sensible advice my grandfather had enforced with learned quotations in Hebrew and (to my father) obscure commentaries of ancient rabbis bearing on human frailty and the advantages accruing in heaven to him who pities and forgives. Of course Mayshe Baer had finally given in. Only an idiot, my grandfather said, could fail to appraise the ridiculous position intransigence would force on him, and Mayshe Baer was anything but a fool.

My grandfather now cautioned my mother against exploiting her victory. She must be tender and understanding, silent and submissive. It would be wise, he thought, if she herself repaired to the cheder at lunch time and took her husband a bit of food and a towel to wipe his hands on after his matutinal ablution. Above all, she was not to reveal her father's visit to her or pretend to any knowledge of the scene at the cheder that morning. As her father prepared to return to Serotchaya, my mother threw her arms around him in gratitude for his successful intervention. He kissed the top of her head and asked her why she had made only a partial confession to her husband about the parentage of her children. But before she could reply, he laughed and told her that she did right in admitting to only one previous husband. There are times, he said, when it is wiser not to strain a man's power of endurance, and to confess only one thing at a time.

I was born punctually nine months after the marriage, becoming my father's fourth son and my mother's first. No noteworthy event occurred at the time to highlight the date. But my maternal grandmother had died the month before, and her death, though for a long time expected, had seriously affected my grandfather and, soon after, the well-being of his children. At any rate her death and her funeral, a ceremony attended out of deference to my grandfather by all the rich and poor Jews of Vitebsk and the peasants of Serotchaya, gave my birth an approximate date. In the weeks preceding my birth my mother made daily trips to Serotchaya on foot to do what she could to comfort her father, whose grief seemed to bear no relation to his great piety and was a clear denial of his frequent assurance to the bereaved and afflicted he used to visit that God was merciful and wise and always knew what He was doing. Each morning at seven after breakfast, when she had given my father and Lebbe their bundles of lunch and sent them off to cheder, she would set out for her father's farm. She would return home in time to clean up the house and cook the evening meal. After supper there were washing and mend-

path, and soon she came upon the small, still fresh mound she had been seeking. Too much time had already been lost! She threw herself passionately on the grave, and as she did so, the bottle flew out of her hands and hit the ground. She retrieved it instantly, but the fall had decapitated it and the precious liquid now stained the grave. There was no time now to appeal to her mother. She scrambled to her feet and, clutching the jagged bottle, fled at top speed through the narrow lanes, out of the cemetery gates, and through the shuttered, echoing streets. For a moment she had considered returning to the apothecary's, but she abandoned the idea when she remembered the doctor, who must certainly have arrived at her home by now.

When, breathless, she reached home, the doctor was there sitting beside the cradle and writing a prescription on a little pad on his knee. He took no notice of my mother or of my father and some of the older children who stood respectfully at a distance. Nobody, under any circumstances, ever addressed the doctor first. And now my mother stared mutely at my crimson face in the cradle and waited motionlessly for the doctor to finish writing. He took a long time. When he was through, he folded the paper leisurely and said, without looking at my mother: "You are a foolish woman. An apothecary knows nothing of medicine. He can only do what he is told by a doctor. What did he give you?" My mother handed him the broken bottle. Still without looking at her, he held it to his nose, glanced at the label, and tossed it on the floor, where it smashed to bits. He rose to go. "But God takes care of the foolish," he said at the door. "That medicine would have *killed* your child! Go back now and have that idiot fill *this* prescription." My mother seized the doctor's hand and kissed it reverently. This the doctor suffered patiently and indifferently, like royalty, which indeed he symbolized to his poorer clients. When he made a call in winter he would throw back his fur-lined overcoat, certain that some member of the family would stand behind him waiting with outstretched arms to catch and hold it up at arm's length for the duration of the visit. He disdained all forms of greeting as tending to encourage familiarity. My mother hastened to open the door for him and he left the house silently, his eyes on the ground.

My oldest brother was immediately dispatched to the apothecary, and my father, on learning the details of the miraculous mishap at the cemetery, agreed that my life had been saved by the direct, though unsolicited intervention of my grandmother. He urged my mother to lose no time in thanking her. And my mother, losing no time, put on her shawl again and went back to the cemetery, where she stretched herself prone on her mother's grave and remained a long time, thanking her and weeping tears of gratitude and joy.

After that happy catastrophe of the medicine bottle my mother sought her mother's grave directly anyone she loved was threatened by calamity or disease, confident that the beneficent shade would not fail her. It did, however, fail her once. A year after I was born, my mother gave birth to another son, an ailing infant who died after some weeks of a feeble struggle to survive. As the child grew worse, my mother increased her visits to the cemetery both morning and evening, but to no avail. She went again the day after the baby's funeral, but it was not to reproach her mother. Instead she implored her to be increasingly watchful over me. For it was now clear to her that for some reason best known to herself her mother desired that I should remain an only son. After all, I had been saved and my little brother had been allowed to perish. I must be, then, my grandmother's special charge. But since the dead were known to be, at times, as forgetful as the living, it was only prudent to remind them, occasionally, of certain obligations they had assumed. My

mother maintained that except for the unfortunate lapse in
the case of my infant brother my grandmother never wavered
in her protection of persons dear to her daughter. My mother
would recall the anxious days when her own daughters,
Hannah and Mirele, came down with typhoid. They were
critically ill for a long time, their heads having to be shaved
and the room kept in semidarkness. I, who was four or five
at the time, laughed to see them without hair, but I was
obliged to stop up my ears to shut out the sound of their loud
and quite incoherent prattle. For, notwithstanding the doctor's
frequent visits, they were often out of their heads. At length
my mother in desperation sought the familiar grave in the
cemetery. After some agonized visits the girls' fever abated
and they presently rested cool and silent. The doctor, for
once deigning to speak, said that *he* had steered them safely
past the crisis. My mother kissed his hand and thanked him.
But in her heart she knew better.

When I was five years old, I became a pupil in my father's
cheder. I had learned the alphabet at home in order to qualify
for the youngest group. Though my mother often complained
about my being around all day trailing at her skirts and getting
in her way, she pleaded for another year of indolence for me.
But my father was adamant; and each morning at seven we
set out for cheder, I holding his hand as we walked or, growing fatigued, trailing behind him, with the bundle of food for
our lunch which my mother had prepared and given me under
my arm.

My father's cheder was now well established in the town.
In the six years he had lived and taught in Vitebsk he had
earned a reputation for probity and discipline, if not for
erudition. He began to be looked upon as an authority on the
upbringing of boys, more especially of intractable ones; and
parents came to the cheder to consult him about aspects of

their children's behavior which would ordinarily be outside the concern and jurisdiction of a teacher of Hebrew. We soon learned that the purpose of these seemingly friendly parental calls was in every case punitive.

I remember how surprised I was when the parents of one of the best-behaved and most studious boys called unexpectedly one day toward lunch time. My father, after greeting them affably, sent us out of the room. When we were reassembled we could see by the cold, determined look on my father's face and the uneasiness of the visitors that my father, after hearing and judging the complaint, had recommended severe punishment, to be administered by himself as a disinterested outsider. In cheder the boy had always been a model of behavior, but, obviously, he was not so at home. His guilt was now evident, for he began to look furtively around the room as if for an avenue of escape. My father called to him in a voice that I had often heard at home, a cool, impersonal voice, as deceptive as the dull whiteness of molten steel. The boy, disregarding my father's command, ran to his mother instead, who herself made a protecting movement toward him; but her husband barred her way. My father seized the distracted boy with one hand and with the other undid his own leather belt. He then shoved the boy face down across his knee. As he wielded the belt, my father's face grew white with rage. The rhythm of his strokes imparted a corresponding rhythm to his speech: "So!—You are good in che—der— and—bad at—home!—So!—You thought—you would never —be found—out!—This will—teach—you. . . ." The boy's mother murmured softly: "Enough—enough . . ." My father kept on administering his strokes with restrained, deliberate fury. At last the boy's father interposed: "Enough, Mayshe Baer—enough. We are *satisfied*." My father dropped the boy to the floor and replaced his belt. The boy's father led his sobbing wife from the room. "Thank you, Mayshe Baer," he

to be sharper with her own), he would call them his "or-phans" to their faces, to my mother's embarrassment and confusion.

Faced with sudden danger, I had lied to save myself; for I had *not* seen my mother hit Sarah with a broom. And I was saved, I could see, at least for the present. My father said: "*Takké?* (Really?)," and then repeated the word. It was his favorite expression, and it served many purposes. Unlettered as he was except for a literal knowledge of the Bible and a few commentaries in Hebrew, it was for him a basic word, whose meaning could be altered by mere intonation. By raising or lowering his voice, by stress or lack of it, by coldness or intensity of delivery it could indicate a simple query (*takké?*), indignation (*takké!*), naïve perplexity (*takké—?*)—indeed, every variety of incredulity or the coldly savage acceptance of a challenge. I now understood perfectly the implications of his reiterated "*takké!*" The first was simple incredulity, the second an outburst of lacerated pride, with savage overtones of terrible retribution that would be shaped and carried out in due course. Then he fell silent, his forefinger still pressing the fatal word in my book. He stared into space over the heads of the boys, and his face flushed and went white al-ternately as waves of anger washed over him, and at each recession thoughts of revenge rushed into the vacancy; at least the determined, brutal expression of his features seemed to me the plastic embodiment of vengeance. He had quite for-gotten me and whatever reprimand he had designed to put me in my place. He seemed lost to any consideration but that of the enormity of my mother's treachery and of the epic punishment he would devise. After a while he became con-scious of the boys in the room and he got up and moved to the table for the advanced students. Outwardly he looked himself again, and he conducted the lesson with his usual impersonal efficiency. But I knew that he was pigeonholing his wrath and his ideas of vengeance for the rest of the day.

Later, walking home behind him, I became aware of the new danger that awaited me when we reached the house. For, of course, my mother would deny the accusation and her stepdaughter would bear her out. I thought of my mother and how much I loved her, and I wondered at myself for having planned to hurt her. She would never believe that I had *meant* to hurt her. I must tell her, I must make it clear that in doing what I did I hadn't thought of her at all, but only of *myself*. I must tell my father right away, and then perhaps my mother need never know. As for myself, the worst my father could do was to beat me. At the moment I felt I could face anything but my mother's bewildered, reproachful look. I hastily overtook my father and seized his hand, which, to my surprise, he suffered me to take. And as I ran beside him to keep pace with his rapid strides I confessed to the lie. He did not believe me at first, and dropped my hand in anger. But when I told him that he could learn the truth from Sarah herself, he said nothing more and I took his hand again. Once he paused to ask me why I had lied to him in the first place, and I, lying again, said I didn't know. But I implored him to say nothing about my sin to my mother. He did keep my secret, perhaps for reasons of his own. And after several weeks had passed and I grew more certain that he would not give me away, I promised myself as an act of atonement to make a full confession to my mother at the earliest favorable moment. Many opportunities presented themselves, but none, in my opinion, was favorable. And in time the incident itself passed out of my mind. In cheder my status remained unaltered. My successful maneuver had increased my prestige with the boys, and I continued to be the object of flattery and the recipient of unsolicited, yet none the less welcome, gifts.

The situation at home as it presented itself to a boy of six without any knowledge of the true relationship of the protagonists or of the nature of the passions involved was often baffling, but almost always dramatic. I felt that tensions were

intermittently at play in the overcrowded house, and I grew
to anticipate the periodic, open clashes with a certain pleasurable horror, as later, when I began to attend the theater, I
would look forward with a like emotion to the denouement
of a tragic play. My earliest recollection of the charged atmosphere of my home is that of an interminable game played
by apparently evenly matched forces, now one side triumphant, now the other, myself a passionate spectator absorbed
in the battle, favoring neither side; indeed, often inclined
through love of mischief or out of what I thought self-interest
to play one side against the other. But soon after, as my years
and sensibility grew, I realized that my sympathies and interests lay with the side I loved best, the side of my mother
and my half-sisters, Hannah and Mirele.

Those two still unwanted girls, young as they were, had
been diplomatically put to work at a tobacconist's to package
cigarettes for a few kopeks a day. This meagerly rewarded
employment provided my mother with a defense against her
husband's frequent charge that the girls were eating him out
of house and home. Hannah and Mirele were attractive and
sensitive. They differed, however, in temperament. Hannah,
the elder of the two, was patient and long-suffering, always
eager to avoid battle with the women of my father's faction.
Mirele was high-spirited and impetuous, eager to engage the
enemy and highly proficient in counterabuse and invective.
The two clung to each other and to my mother and me,
though they often quarreled with each other and pulled each
other's hair, so that it seemed to me they must remain bitter
enemies thereafter. But they always made up quickly, did
little offices for each other, and were inseparable. And they
showed plainly that they loved me.

My position in the house was unique. Though I belonged,
naturally, to my mother's camp, I was, through my father,
also a member of the opposite faction. I was, in fact, inviolate.
My father's other children perhaps envied me my pleasant

status, but they were never hostile and very often friendly. My father seemed to like me; at least he was less aloof and impersonal with me than with his other sons. As for my mother, whose affection I craved most, I thought for a long time I had no rival there. There was, of course, my father. I cannot say how I became aware of the danger from that quarter to my supremacy in my mother's heart. There were no visible signs in the demeanor of my parents to each other that I might construe as danger signals. Their life at home was a long truce, frequently and rather unaccountably interrupted by skirmishes and great battles. During these my father rather monotonously concentrated on three charges: my mother's now historic deception, her hatred of "his" children, and her household extravagance. The first left my mother mute, but against the other two she defended herself passionately. The third did, indeed, defy proof. The family was large, the income small. Yet my mother could point to the general "decent" look of the house and to the plain fact that no one ever complained of hunger. My father could bring up the matter of my first pair of shoes, which my mother had ordered from the traveling cobbler during his autumn visit, as an extravagance in a household operating on an economic plane so low as to deny footwear to all but the three oldest children. But my mother countered with the claim that since her arrangement with the shoemaker called for payment at some unspecified future time, there had occurred no actual transaction at which money had passed. That being the case, a charge of extravagance on that score was obviously absurd. The second charge she always denied with a great show of moral indignation and contempt for a mind that could so misread the humanity and the nobility of her nature.

Learning was for my mother in the highest degree estimable, and the learned were the only true elite. She had instilled this belief in her two daughters and in me. And we, developing in our youth, and quite on our own, a feeling for

the æsthetic, in turn were able to communicate our enthusiasm
for art to her and make her a sympathetic though vaguely
comprehending ally in our battle against the philistinism of
the larger side of our family and, later in life, of the larger
side of the world.

For my mother the world separated itself into the learned
and pious (not the academic, but the mystically pious) and
the mass of people, whose only problem was that of existence.
In her father she was privileged to observe at close range the
operation of learning and piety as a moral and as a humanitarian force. Being of a practical turn of mind, she sometimes
considered her father's selflessness extreme to the point of
foolishness. Yet its very extravagance was a proof to her of
the power of the word of God when it was accepted *literally*
as a way of life.

Judged by these lofty standards, her husband could not
qualify for either category. His learning was elementary, his
piety merely doctrinaire. He appeared to be unaware of the
interdependence of learning and life. She could not escape
being aware that spiritually there was a gulf between her
husband and herself. She did not blame him. He had not had
the good fortune of a cultural past. And without such a herit-
age one becomes a prey of elementary moods, passions, and
prejudices that only culture can channel, curb, and modify.
He was never able to view himself dispassionately. She had
never known him in moments of rage to pause and exclaim
in self-criticism, as she was wont to do in like circumstances:
"May God forgive me!" But if those were her thoughts, she
never spoke them. And while she openly adored her father
and refrained from any public demonstrations of affection for
my father, there were no visible signs of discontent and unhappiness on her part.

Indeed, during the periods of truce a palpable contentment
would descend on the house. At those times—usually born
of the temporary absence of economic and domestic irritations

—my mother went about her chores with an air of satisfaction that I found, curiously enough, disturbing. It embraced not only her daughters and me, but also the rest of the family. It was as if she had decided to renounce her feeling of superiority to her husband and stepchildren and to welcome them to her own social level. When my father returned from cheder, she would come out to the courtyard to greet him, her face newly scrubbed, her own hair slightly wet from combing, parted carefully in the middle and done up in a bun at the back. (My mother had resisted all pressures to make her cut off her hair and wear the traditional *"sheitel"* [wig].) The soup, which we ate last, would be scalding so that my father should have no cause to complain. After supper my mother and father would converse amiably and retire early, often leaving the dishes to be washed by the girls. Once my father created a sensation by commanding his two elder daughters to clean up! There might even be a temporary rapprochement between the opposing sides. My youngest sister, Golde, was born during one of these harmonious stretches. My father showed an unusual solicitude for the health of mother and child, and the other children greeted the new arrival in a friendly spirit.

Because of its long duration, that particular interlude became historic for me. It was packed with exciting events and experiences, made possible by my father's placid frame of mind and apparent friendliness toward me. Walking to and from cheder, he talked to me about the Tsar, about God, and about the miracles attributed to celebrated Chassidic rabbis. The Tsar, according to my father, found his vast riches rather a nuisance than a pleasure. I laughed to hear that he owned so many shirts that for appearance' sake he felt obliged to don a new one every hour of the day! God sat in the heavens, benign or vengeful, in keeping with the behavior of the people on earth. And His memory was *stupendous*. He forgot *nothing*, as many wrongdoers (that is, those who failed to observe the Sabbath or missed a prescribed prayer) found to their dismay

on Judgment Day. The celebrated Chassidic rabbis all enjoyed supernatural powers. One of them, walking with someone just as we were doing at the moment, might suddenly
disappear into thin air. His astonished companion would continue to hear the rabbi's voice uttering words of great wisdom.
A second later the Chassid would choose to become corporeal
again. When I gasped at this intelligence, my father smiled
and looked pleased. But he said such an occurrence was really
not to be wondered at, as these exceptional persons were on
speaking terms with God. I saw his point, but it did not lessen
my wonder.

He took me one unforgettable Sunday to a large field on
the outskirts of the town where a great celebration of something (I can't remember what) was in progress. Thousands
of people were assembled, some seated in a grandstand (the
Governor of the province of Vitebsk was the guest of honor),
but most standing around in large groups. I heard the music
of a brass band and watched ladies in spangled tights walking
across wires strung at perilous heights. The climax of the
celebration was a balloon ascent, followed by a parachute
jump by a famous acrobat-comedian. I had never seen a balloon, and I could hardly contain my excitement as I watched
the enormous bag rise from the ground and soar into the sky.
There were two men in the basket under the balloon, and
one of them climbed over the edge and onto a trapeze that
swayed underneath. He was the celebrated acrobat-comedian,
and he performed acrobatic feats that were both hazardous
and comical, and the crowd gasped and laughed alternately.
When the balloon had become a tiny ball in the sky the acrobat-comedian, who now looked no bigger than a twig, ceased
his antics and made ready to jump. His companion leaned
over the side of the basket and handed him the parachute.
My father had explained to me the function of this instrument, telling me to watch closely for the moment it would
open and bring the man slowly and safely to earth. With the

parachute in one hand, the other grasping the wire of the trapeze, the little figure stood poised for a long while looking down on the sea of faces turned toward him. Then, with a great warning shout, which we could all hear plainly, he leaped into the air. Straight down he plummeted. I strained my eyes to look at the parachute. It refused to open. Suddenly the figure turned head over heels, then fell like a stone with a tremendous thud on the roof of a cowshed a few feet from where I was standing. There were horrified cries of "Save him! Save him!" but he had rolled to the ground and lay bloody and inert, the cord of the parachute clutched in his hand. A moment later men ran up and carried him away. But I had looked closely at him and was bewildered and troubled by the sight. It seemed impossible that the little gesticulating figure I had seen posturing on the rim of the balloon basket had in an instant become the silent, *careless* bundle that lay at my feet. There seemed to be no *relation* between them.

I had known before about death. A playmate had failed to appear on the street for several days, and in explanation I was told that he had died. From a window I watched his funeral go past my house. I had felt a sense of deprivation. But there was also a sense of continuity between the friend I had played with and the *unseen* boy in the pine box that was carried past my house. He would go on resting, silent, but in spirit accessible to his friends and relations, like my grandmother in the same cemetery on the edge of the town. There his mother would probably pay him frequent visits and converse with him as my mother did with my grandmother. This was not the same Death I had seen in the field. But only one of them could be the *true* Death. And because I could not accept and live with a Death so final as the brutal and ludicrous one I had just witnessed, I *chose* not to regard it as Death at all. I chose to forget its horror and remember it as part of the entertainment of an exciting day.

Soon I was duplicating in our back yard for the boys of the neighborhood the entire "show" of that Sunday afternoon, the tightwire-walking and the parachute jump, the last being negotiated from the slanting roof of our house. As I made the leap clutching a folded umbrella in my hand, I yelled: "Save him! Save him!" And on landing on the ground on my feet I collapsed in a ludicrous, ungainly heap and lay motionless, while my audience clapped and shouted with delight.

CHAPTER TWO

Mr. Harris

W<small>HEN</small> I was a boy of eight or nine, at the beginning of the century, I would often accompany my mother to the offices of a charitable organization that looked after the welfare of Jewish immigrants arriving in New York from overseas. The offices were on East Broadway near Pike Street, only a long block from the tenement at East Broadway and Rutgers Street in which I lived. The organization sent its representatives to meet incoming boats. They would circulate among the steerage passengers, assist those who had not been met by friends and relatives, do what they could to find them temporary lodgings, and take them back to the society's offices while they traced their relations or *landsleit* (fellow townsmen). The society was also prepared to advance the purchase price of steamship tickets to people who desired to bring members of their families to America, but who did not possess the necessary cash. The arrangement required no deposit of collateral, but the society investigated the ability of the borrowers to meet the small weekly payments (without interest) toward their liquidation of the debt. My mother, over a period of years, made several such deals with the society. The relatives she helped transport from the Old World to America put no further strain on the generosity of the society. My mother always met them at the pier—and installed them in our three-room tenement, where they resided for weeks and months, and even for years. My mother's trips to the society to purchase steamship tickets or to pay the installments due on them never ceased.

Young as I was, I took an interest in the humane objectives of the society (I never knew the society's full title), and always gladly accompanied my mother to its offices. There we were always sure to find sad and bewildered immigrants sitting on dilapidated suitcases and wicker trunks in a large, unfurnished room reserved for them. The relatives and friends they had expected to find on the pier had failed to show up. My mother would interrogate the more dejected arrivals. Sometimes she would invite one of them to spend a few days with us in our generally overcrowded apartment. The bewildered but grateful guest would shoulder his wicker trunk; my mother and I would carry what suitcases he had; and thus laden we would arrive home, where the stranger was welcomed by the rest of the family and given what accommodations were available. If, as sometimes happened, there was no available floor space for him to lie down at night, my mother would canvass the resources of friends and neighbors, always with satisfactory results.

It was quite natural for our family to enter into the plight of the bewildered immigrants and to value the kind efforts of the society. For, only three years before, we, too, had arrived friendless in a strange country and had been met by an agent of a society, though not this one, who spoke our language and attended to our needs. To ease the anxieties of our occasional house guests, the story of our own vicissitudes was often told them by my mother or father, or by both in friendly rivalry, with eager interruptions and reminders and, I now believe, embellishments that were often more picturesque than truthful. But I was able to corroborate the essentials of the story, for I had been both an actor in it and an eyewitness. As for the embellishments, I accepted them as a legitimate device to ensure the continued attention of our audience. In truth, our listeners, understandably overwrought and distrait, usually responded more warmly to the fabrications, which took the form of comic relief, than to the realistic details.

When my father was the narrator, he would begin the tale at the point where he and his wife and children left their native Russia on the way to the New World, a continent which consisted, for him as well as for most immigrants, only of the United States. (I was surprised later to learn of the existence of Mexico and Canada.) But when my mother told the story, she would begin with a description of our early life in our native city of Vitebsk, recall her own girlhood and marriage, and lead up, by slow and interesting stages, to the moment of our departure. I preferred my mother's sentimental, rambling narration because it gave color and dimension to my own increasingly fuzzy memories. I loved to hear her speak of her father's little farm, a few miles from Vitebsk, where she and her numerous brothers and sisters were brought up, and of her father, a saintly man whom she loved next to her own children. I had loved him too, and my memories of him were still fresh. Several times a year he would come to town to spend the Sabbath with us. I would be told in advance that he was coming and would be out on the street waiting for him. He would always walk the three miles from his farm to our house, and I would catch sight of him in the distance, his tall figure slightly bent, walking slowly with the aid of a stick and carrying in his left hand three or four large apples tied in a colored handkerchief, which he invariably brought me as a gift. When I came up to him, he would hand me his stick and handkerchief, place his arms on my head, and bless me, after which he would press me to him hard and kiss me many times, and I would smell the sweet aroma of snuff which clung to his hands and his long, shiny double-breasted coat. He had the most elaborately curled earlocks of any old man I had ever seen, a long, thin face, prominent nose, and high forehead, and small twinkling eyes. When he sat, it was always bolt upright, supporting this position with rigid arms and clenched fists resting on his knees. I have a photograph of him sitting thus, with his eldest son, Solomon, standing behind him. It is an old daguerreotype taken on the occasion of Solomon's *bar mitzvah*, or coming of age, when he was thirteen. At the time we left Russia, my Uncle Solomon was a man of forty, a well-known rabbi and scholar, with a wife and many children. Yet his future greatness had been foreshadowed at the time the photograph was taken. Even at that tender age he had proved himself so precocious a scholar that his *bar mitzvah* attracted learned men and rabbis from places as distant as Dvinsk, a two-hour trip on the Dvina from Vitebsk. An even finer recognition of my uncle's precocity came with my grandfather's announcement during the large repast that was served after the *bar mitzvah* ceremonies that the young Solomon was already affianced to the daughter of the Dvinsk rabbi! The marriage would of course have to wait until the groom reached the mature age of seventeen. But, for the moment, the double ceremony made the extraordinary youth the hero of the neighborhood.

Such detailed bits of family history brightened my mother's narration of our flight from Russia. At some point in the story, my father might become impatient with what for him was merely feminine discursivness. Then he would, without apology, proceed to take over in the interest of veracity and realism. He usually began with the day he, and presumably

to speak rapidly about his sorrow and approaching loneliness and the inscrutable intentions of Providence. He spoke in long, rolling phrases, interpolating poetical quotations, some of which I had myself encountered in the Book of Genesis, which I had studied in cheder. I can remember snatches of sentences addressed toward my mother and, I thought, toward me as well: "The Almighty will guide you safely over the great waters. . . . Lord, take them under Your mighty wing. . . . These dim eyes will not see them again. . . . But the Eternal, the Ever-Watchful, will not let them out of His sight."

We then left on foot for the wharf, our baggage having preceded us there by cart. We had said good-by to everyone. But my grandfather insisted on accompanying us, and his slow pace retarded our progress. I was impatient to see the paddle-boat that was to bear us away forever, and would have run ahead; but my mother held my hand firmly as we walked, and it was a long time before we sighted the pier and the boat with its enormous, gaily painted paddle-wheel. When we reached the pier, my mother suddenly flung her arms around my grandfather and clung to him, weeping, for an embarrassingly long time. She then as suddenly disengaged herself and, without once looking back or waving, made her way to the boat and disappeared into its interior. The rest of the family followed, but remained on deck and waved to the old man, who stood rooted to the spot where my mother had left him, oblivious of our gestures, for he did not wave back. The whistle blew and the gangplank was removed. A towpath ran parallel with the river for some miles. When the boat began to move, my grandfather suddenly came to life. He started walking—and, as the boat picked up speed, running—along the path, trying to keep us in sight as long as he could. I watched the hurrying, stumbling figure grow smaller and smaller, and at last dwindle away.

We paddled lesiurely down the Dvina and reached Riga

on the third day. There we transferred to a boat that would
take us to Stettin, where we were to board the ship that
would carry us to America. As the boat pulled out of Riga
we had our last glimpse of our native land. To my surprise,
we were all taken down to the hold of the ship and locked
into a storage room for coal next to the ship's engines. But
my father had been told beforehand to expect a temporary
concealment during the period when the police came on board
to make their routine inspection of the passengers' passports.
As we had no passports, we were to remain hidden in the coal
room until the police had gone and the boat had put out to
sea. We sat silent and fearful on the dusty floor for a long
time. At last we heard the sound of the engines starting up,
and presently we knew from the creaking all around us that
we were moving.

The time must have been about dusk, for my father now
signaled my brothers to evening prayers. They all turned to
the wall on their left and began to pray, swaying back and
forth and softly beating their breasts the while, as they always
did at evening prayers. A moment later the boat pitched
headlong into the turbulent Baltic. The coal suddenly shifted
to the side where we were huddled. The floor receded from
under our feet, and my father and brothers wavered and fell
to the floor. I was seized with a dreadful nausea, and retched
and vomited until, half dead, I fell into a sleep like a coma.
Sometime later we were released and helped on deck; and
there we spent the night, on the floor, on stools, and on pieces
of luggage, for nothing would induce any of us to brave the
airless terrors of the interior of the ship.

We reached Stettin, in Germany, the next morning and
boarded the ship for America. This boat was disappointingly
small, being not very much larger than the one we had quitted.
There were any number of big ships moored to piers and
anchored in the bay, and I assumed they were bound for more
distant places than New York. I remembered the vision of

"great waters" my grandfather had conjured up, and I wondered if our modest vessel could make a dignified showing in them.

We had a small cabin with a porthole to ourselves. Three tiers of bunks lined the walls. Our baggage had already been dumped in the middle of the room. My mother extricated the canvas bag containing the indispensable *kuchlech*. But now again, our boat ran into heavy seas soon after we sailed, and the *kuchlech* remained untouched. We crawled into our bunks and remained there fully dressed for two days, groaning, vomiting, dozing, and taking no nourishment except water and some oranges a sailor brought us each morning. On the morning of the third day the sea began to quiet down, though sheets of rain still beat against the porthole. We felt better and climbed out of our bunks feeling hungry for the first time. We were about to attack the *kuchlech*, which my mother began handing around, when two sailors appeared and conveyed to us in German and in dumb show that we were about to land.

It seemed hardly possible that we had made the crossing in so short a time. There was no time for speculation, however, for some of our luggage had to be repacked. By now the porthole showed not only rain, but also dim outlines of buildings quite close to the ship. The motion of the vessel subsided and presently ceased. The two sailors reappeared and began gathering up our belongings. We followed them out to the deck and down a gangplank, emerging on a large roofless wharf. The rain had slackened to a drizzle, and a thick mist disclosed shadowy outlines of tall buildings. Our luggage was piled in one heap. I clambered up to a perch on the top of a huge bundle of bedding, and the rest of the family grouped themselves around the luggage. A number of people had disembarked, and these, carrying valises or steamer trunks on their shoulders, walked quickly past us and disappeared. A whistle blew, the gangplank was removed, and the ship moved slowly away, soon melting into the pervading mist. We were quite alone on the eerie wharf.

This, then, was America! At the moment it was decidedly disappointing. And where was my father's cousin from Passaic? Perhaps he had not heard about our record-breaking journey. But he had heard, for a man suddenly emerged from the gloom and with open umbrella in his hand was advancing on us. My father ran to meet him, and the rest of us waited breathlessly. Strangely enough, they did not embrace when they met. They talked long and earnestly. At length, my father turned and walked slowly toward us, the man right behind him. My father's face was white. "This is *not* America!" he at last brought out. "We are in *London!*"

The effect of this disclosure on my mother was stunning. Unexpected happenings threw her instantly into a "state," in which she wept, lamented, and ran the gamut of unbridled agitation. But she always recovered quickly, her practical nature reasserting itself automatically to face the challenge that life perpetually presented to her. Crises were only to be expected, but their extraordinary frequency in her life put on them the stamp of naturalness, like rain and snow and the change of seasons. I was therefore hardly surprised to see her, a moment after she had extravagantly given vent to her feelings, take charge of the strange situation, brush my father aside, and ply the stranger with questions. For myself, I was old enough to appreciate the gravity of our predicament. I knew that my father had only a few rubles when we left Russia and that most of these had been spent by the time we boarded the ship that had now so unceremoniously disgorged us. Yet, though I was very familiar with the name of New York, I had never heard of London. To be in unknown London was, in its way, as exciting as to be in the dark interior of Africa, of which I *had* heard. I sensed the possibility of adventure in London as, unmindful of the drizzle, I sat elevated on our only earthly possessions and followed the course of my mother's inquiries.

The man, who spoke in Yiddish, introduced himself as a representative of a British Immigrant Aid Society, a wholly charitable organization, whose purpose was to offer aid and comfort to friendless Jews arriving from foreign ports. He showed no surprise at our situation. He told us that we were the victims of unscrupulous travel agents in Russia who had sold us tickets to London while charging us for passage to New York. Ours was not an unusual case, and his society was prepared to look after us temporarily until it could locate our friends or relatives or fellow townsmen now residing in London. He then left us for a while and soon returned with a man trundling a pushcart. Our belongings were loaded on the cart and, led by the Samaritan, we left the wharf. (It was Tilbury Dock, I learned later.) After walking through miles of ghostly streets, we reached the dwelling that had been prepared for us or for unfortunates like us.

Before the man from the society left us, he explained the British monetary system to my mother and then put ten shillings in her hand. This sum, he assured her, would take care of us for a week in a section of London where food could be bought cheaply on the streets, practically at one's doorstep. Indeed, our dead-end street, as well as the entire district around it, proved to be one great outdoor market.

Our accommodations were two rooms in a two-story, dingy old house in a dead-end street off Commercial Road. Some rickety chairs, a table, two iron cots, and a small kerosene stove were all the furnishings. My mother, after disposing our belongings to the best practical advantage around our apartment, went out shopping. She returned with bread, herring, sugar, tea, and cottage cheese, and with grave doubts about the integrity of our benefactor, whose optimistic evaluation of the cost of living in London's ghetto she had discovered to

rapid calculation, "about forty-eight or fifty, wouldn't it? What did he look like? But of course he'd be quite changed after all these years. Was he heavy-like? Thin? What color hair? Eyes?"

My father's information on all these points was inconclusive, but that didn't faze my mother.

"It doesn't matter," she declared, "and anyway it can't be helped. Now let's see—what did Mr. Horowitz do in Vitebsk?"

Mr. Horowitz had worked at odd jobs in Vitebsk. No clue there.

"Did he have any money?" It appeared he couldn't have had.

"Well then," my mother said, "since he had no money when he came here, he must have been obliged to go to work!"

At this point my father advanced the dreadful possibility that, for all he knew, the man might be dead. This my mother brushed aside as irrelevant to the execution of the plan she had by now formulated in her mind.

"Now, as a Jew, Horowitz would naturally live and work among Jews, wouldn't he?" My father agreed, and my mother pushed on to the heart of her plan. "People go to work in the early morning and they return home in the evening, don't they? Now, if Mr. Horowitz is alive—of *course* he's alive, a man of fifty—and if he is working—you agree that he *is* working—then he will be going to work at seven o'clock tomorrow morning somewhere in this very part of London, and at seven at night he will be returning to his home somewhere around here!"

I could hear her rise and walk across the room with decision, as if she had definitely disposed of the vexing question of our future in London.

"And now let's get some sleep," she said.

My mother spent the next day exploring the Whitechapel district, asking questions of storekeepers and pedestrians, watching the flow of traffic in the larger thoroughfares, and noting when and where it was heaviest. That night she discussed her strategy with my father, or rather she apprised him of it, and on the following morning at seven they took up positions on each side of Commercial Road at its junction with Leman Street.

"Watch out for men who look about fifty—a little younger or a little older," my mother told my father as they separated to take up their posts.

I accompanied them for a lark, for the discovery of Mr. Horowitz seemed a very remote possibility even to an imaginative child of six. When, an hour later, the stream of pedestrians had thinned out to a trickle, and my father, relinquishing his post, crossed over to join my mother for their return home, I felt that the quixotic adventure definitely had been proved a failure. My father had accosted only one likely prospect, and my mother had seen none who might conceivably be Mr. Horowitz. We walked home in silence, and I wondered what new scheme my mother would evolve now that Mr. Horowitz had proved nonexistent. But toward nightfall, as I played in our street with a new-found friend, I saw my parents leave the house and walk toward Whitechapel. I abandoned my playmate and joined them. At the corner of Commercial Road and Leman Street, they again took up their positions of the morning, and again for an hour scrutinized the hurrying passers-by, again without success.

Once my mother ran after a middle-aged man, caught him by his sleeve, and said: "Excuse me, you look so familiar. Did you ever live in Russia?"

The man, obviously astonished, stopped in his tracks, looked my mother over, and said: "Why, yes."

My mother then led him aside, away from the stream of fast-moving men and women. "Your name isn't—Horowitz?" The man shook his head and asked why. My mother made some hurried excuse, and he went on his way.

My father had accosted no one. At eight o'clock we again returned home. My mother busied herself with the evening meal while my father read his Talmud.

Days and weeks went by. Each Monday the man from the Aid Society appeared and placed ten shillings in my mother's hand. Our meals seemed never to vary. It was always herring, potatoes, bread, cheese, and tea. My father found himself a synagogue of the proper denomination, where he went three times a day, and my mother was endlessly engaged in shopping, cooking, scrubbing, and washing. But every morning and evening except Saturdays and Sundays they would both be at their posts in the London ghetto, patiently scanning the figures and faces of men hurrying by, occasionally stopping one and after a brief colloquy turning away to search for other possibilities. I soon lost all interest in the game and joined my parents only when I had nothing better to do.

A letter had been dispatched to our cousin in Passaic, apprising him of our recent misfortune and present predicament, and a reply came back expressing sympathy for our plight, but containing no constructive suggestions for its alleviation. In truth, there was nothing the man could do to help us, as it was unlikely that he possessed or would wish to part with a sum large enough to pay our passage to America. Furthermore, his kinship to us was not close enough to justify any great sacrifice on his part. There were certain things one could reasonably expect of a first cousin, but not of a second. The moral obligations of relatives were well defined among us, and people did only what they were expected to do. He did, however, urge us to "look around" and keep him posted. His offer of a temporary home in Passaic still stood.

As she grew more familiar with the neighborhood of her search, and to avoid being thought queer by the people in the shops, who were sure to wonder at her persistence, my mother shifted her operations to adjoining streets and avenues. She was "working" one of these side streets one evening. I had come along for the walk. The crowds had tapered off, and my father was signaling us from the opposite corner that it was time to go home. At the same moment a man in a gray bowler hat brushed past us. My mother looked at him and shot out a restraining hand. I had seen this happen many times during the past six weeks, and I tugged at her skirts, impatient to be off. But my mother's routine question had already stopped the man.

"Yes," he replied, "I come from Russia. Why do you ask?"

My mother disengaged her skirt from my grasp and went very close to the man. "Excuse me," she persisted, "perhaps from Vitebsk?"

The man regarded her wonderingly. "Why, yes," he said, "I come from Vitebsk."

This was, indeed, progress of a sort, and I began to share the excitement that I read in my mother's face. Many men she had accosted had acknowledged Russia as their birthplace, but none had even spoken the magic name of our native city. Still, any number of Vitebsk men might be living in London. Why should this man in the bowler hat be the one man we were seeking? Before I could wonder about him any further, my mother had breathlessly put to him her final question.

"Why, no," he answered quickly, "my name is Harris." He started on, but after a few steps he suddenly turned and came back to her. "As a matter of fact," he said slowly, "it *was* Horowitz. But that was a long time ago, in Vitebsk. When I came to London, I changed it to Harris. Why do you ask?"

Without a word my mother clutched him to her heart. The man endured the embrace with equanimity, for my mother was then in her early thirties and quite handsome. My father, hoping that the miracle had finally occurred, now crossed the street on the run and, without seeking to know more, shoved my mother aside and in his turn embraced Mr. Harris. I ran home alone to be the first to bear the good news to my brothers and sisters. A few minutes later my parents arrived with the now radiant Mr. Harris in tow. For Mr. Harris, on learning our identity and the nature and extent of the hunt that had been conducted for him, marveled at my mother's ingenuity and persistence, and expressed himself as very pleased to find himself so suddenly provided with a set of kinsfolk, "ready to wear, so to speak," he said.

After listening to a long and quite detailed recital of our unfortunate history since we had left Russia, Mr. Harris at my mother's urging told us of his life in London. Fortified with a glass of tea, he began his tale with his five shillings a week apprenticeship in a hat factory off Whitechapel Road twenty-five years before, and finished it with his present ownership of the selfsame establishment, now double in size and importance. He was a widower and childless, and it was only because he had no home ties that he kept workman's hours. Otherwise, the chances of his being on the streets in the morning and evening rush hours would have been slim indeed, for truth compelled him to confess that he was very well off and was in a position to retire altogether from work if he chose. He regarded the evening's encounter as providential for all concerned, but more especially for him. For, while he had many friends in London, he had thus far not discovered any relations.

Before another hour had gone by, Mr. Harris had planned our future. My older brothers would be employed in his hat factory; he would find jobs for my sisters; and the younger children would be sent to school. He would also find an apartment suited to so large a family as ours, and my mother was to serve notice on the Aid Society that we should henceforth be self-supporting. But at the moment Mr. Harris desired to show the menfolk his factory, which was near by. I begged hard to be taken along, and after our frugal supper, which Mr. Harris shared, and, for a rich man, appeared, much to our surprise, to enjoy, the four males of our family followed him out of the house and through a maze of streets and alleys to his factory.

This was an imposing structure, two stories high. It was shut for the night, but Mr. Harris rang a bell and a night watchman let us in. We were led through rooms full of sewing machines, and then into Mr. Harris's private office, a large room with a magnificent rolltop desk and showcases with glass doors lined against a wall, in them a most bewildering variety of caps and hats. Mr. Harris enjoyed our pleasure in what we saw and insisted on fitting us all out with headgear of our own choosing as his initial gift to the family. My father and brothers expressed a preference for top hats, or stovepipes, as Mr. Harris jokingly called them. I was urged to choose a velvet cap with ear muffs to match, and indeed the one showed me looked so rich and sleek that I was tempted to accept it. But the desire to be considered grown-up was strong within me, and I pleaded so hard for a "stovepipe" that Mr. Harris at last gave way and we left the shop uniformly outfitted. There had been some difficulty in fitting a head so small as mine, and the smallest "stovepipe" in the shop, which became mine, fell short of the snugness with which the other hats rested on the heads of my father and brothers. But though I could have felt more comfortable, I was proud of my hat.

On our way home, people in the streets stopped to stare at us, and as we turned into Black Lane, I prayed that my mother and sisters would be looking out of the windows and would see us as we marched in single file down the narrow sidewalk. Sure enough, they were looking out of windows and could hardly believe their eyes when they saw us. So ended in triumph a day that began as fruitlessly as all those we had doggedly lived through since being so unceremoniously dumped out on Tilbury Dock.

Mr. Harris was as good as his word in all respects. A few days after our memorable encounter, he moved us into a fine four-room apartment that had gaslight and running water. My brothers were employed in the hat factory and my sisters were put to work in a tobacconist's shop close to the factory. There, with the aid of a little machine, they inserted tobacco into previously manufactured little paper casings. The younger children were sent to school. Every Sunday we dined en masse at Mr. Harris's sumptuous apartment on the fifth and top story of a vast building. It was great fun to rush up the iron stairways and wait on the top landing for the rest of the family, especially for my parents, who climbed slowly and paused for breath at each landing. Mr. Harris made my father and mother take the head and foot of the table, and behaved like a guest in his own home. We were waited on by an oldish woman in a flowered apron, who carried the dishes around to each of us in turn. We were expected to help ourselves with a large spoon and fork placed in the dishes for that purpose.

Our family prospered rapidly. Every payday those of us who were gainfully employed brought their pay envelopes unopened to my mother, and the kitchen table would be piled high with shillings and pence. New denominations, like florins and crowns, began to appear, and sometimes a paper bank-note. Mr. Harris was solely responsible for all this, and perhaps for much more that I knew nothing about.

All this time my father kept up his correspondence with his New Jersey relative. The more prosperous and settled we became, the more importunate grew the letters from America. My mother and the children would have been content to re-main permanently in London. For myself, I soon spoke Eng-lish of a sort and I acquired numerous playmates, with whom I roamed the Whitechapel district and even on one occasion penetrated the dazzlingly spotless West End and walked on London Bridge. Fortunately, I did not then realize that the bridge was the subject of a nursery rhyme I had recently learned, which began: "Land-the-britches falling down," or

I should have thought twice before trusting myself to so precarious a structure. My English, though progressing, was inadequate for the elucidation of the many phrases and songs I learned on the streets. These I spoke and sang glibly, but it was many years before I discovered their meaning. Thus, the ballad that I sang beginning with "As I walked along the base below with the undipendent-te," I had no trouble in identifying many years after as the opening line of "The Man Who Broke the Bank at Monte Carlo." But I never succeeded in deciphering or identifying another one of my favorites which went:

> *Down the street,*
> *A leeza can a quoia,*
> *Five-and-twenty batsa gata there,*

and its lilting refrain:

> *Faw me—faw me,*
> *iddy—veidy—backoo—see,*
> *Lefty, righdy,*
> *Backee, seiddy,*
> *Me-me-me-me-Me!*

One time my sister and I followed a monster parade for many hours. There were brass bands and magnificently costumed men on horseback, and the streets for miles were lined with people who applauded the pageant and especially an open carriage in which sat a plump old lady. Could she have been Victoria, the event the celebration of her Golden Jubilee?

My father's growing disposition to regard London as a way-station to America was, toward the end of the year's residence, fortified by the deleterious effect of the recurrent fogs on his health. In the light of modern psychiatry, the neuralgia that he suffered could have been brought on by his impatience to continue his interrupted journey. At any rate, my mother grew alarmed at his frequent indispositions.

Mr. Harris was duly consulted, and regretfully acquiesced in our contemplated departure, voicing a readiness to facilitate it. Our move, in fact, depended on his co-operation. From the first, my father had managed to impress on my mother the necessity of saving a good part of the family's earnings, which he entrusted each week to Mr. Harris for safe keeping. But the amount, while sizable, was not sufficient to defray the cost of the journey to New York. Without waiting to be asked, Mr. Harris offered a loan to make up the difference and to tide us over the first few months in America. To avoid a possible recurrence of the chicanery that had set us down in London, our benefactor himself purchased the steamship tickets, assuring us the while that such double-dealing was foreign to the nature of the English.

A little over a year after we left Russia, we sailed from Liverpool on the S.S. *St. Paul*, a vessel imposing enough to negotiate the "great waters" my grandfather had poetically feared. Mr. Harris accompanied us on the train from London, saw to our baggage, and gave us as a parting gift a large basket of fruit with colored silk ribbons. We all stood at the steerage deck rail as the steamer pulled away. My mother's eyes were full of tears as she waved her handkerchief. My father, my brothers, and I waved our toppers as Mr. Harris and London faded in the distance.

CHAPTER THREE

✒ Life on Stanton Street

THE *St. Paul* made a record run of less than seven days from Liverpool to New York. The trip was smooth and pleasant, though our quarters, which we shared with about two dozen other passengers, were somewhat cramped. This room, in which we could do little but sleep, was designed like a large egg crate, with three tiers of cubicles for bunks and with just enough room in the center to move about before climbing in and out of our beds. The ship featured a kosher kitchen for the orthodox Jewish passengers, but my father had doubts about its authenticity, and both he and my mother subsisted on oranges and the *kuchlech* my mother had baked in preparation for the journey. As a result of earnest representations by my mother, the children were permitted by paternal dispensation to eat the ship's food if they chose. But the dining-saloon was stuffy and airless, and the only food we

could keep down comfortably was raw herring and bread.
Besides, our parents' show of super-orthodoxy gave us, notwithstanding their sanction, an uncomfortable feeling of
guilt, and we debated among ourselves the possibility of being
overtaken by divine retribution on the Day of Atonement.
Although it was a good ten weeks to Yom Kippur, it was not
to be supposed that God would fail to remember our semi-
transgression on the day when He decides the fate of every
living soul.

The voyage introduced us to an olfactory phenomenon
known to all transatlantic travelers of those days as the smell
of "ship." This pervasive, insidious odor, a distillation of
bilge and a number of less identifiable putrescences, settled on
one's person, clothes, and luggage and stayed there forever,
impervious to changes of habitat, clothing, and the cleansing
agents available to the poor. It was many years before I
realized that only steerage passengers smelled of "ship."
Until then I assumed that all persons, rich or poor, traveling
on ships became, as a matter of course, victims of this affliction. And, like all afflictions that are protracted, it lost its
terrors through familiarity. One *expected* arrivals from Europe
to smell of "ship." So much so that on visits to the homes of
neighbors, one could tell at once by the pervading smell of
"ship" that they were entertaining guests from abroad.

Smells, in general, played an important part in our lives.
Not an unpleasant part, I recall, but one that in its way made
life a little easier, serving for identification of persons, their
habits and social position, perhaps as clues to character and
occupation. Everything and everybody had a smell. Some
smells were generic and impersonal, others particular, like
the leitmotivs in the music dramas of Richard Wagner. And
just as the introduction of a leitmotiv warns the listener that
the personage it represents is about to appear, so the insinuation of a smell in a room usually heralded the approach of
the person who had become identified with it. Immigrants,

however, could not so be identified individually for at least a year or two after their arrival, as their own odors were over-powered by and absorbed into the more exigent smell of "ship."

Old people had, in general, an acrid smell, and old men invariably smelled of snuff. Young people and children merely smelled unwashed. We knew that we too would smell of snuff when we grew old. That was in the nature of things. Life was stern and realistic, and the conditions it imposed were not subject to question or criticism. After taking snuff it was quite proper for people to blow their noses without the interposition of a handkerchief. In rooms not graced with spittoons, what was more natural than to spit on the floor! It was natural, though not desirable, for children to have lice in their hair and for grown-ups to harbor them in the seams of their clothing and underwear. Beds and bedding and all over-stuffed furniture were infested with bedbugs. The pests were periodically hunted and exterminated; but their presence was not considered a disgrace, and they shared with poverty and disease the status of divine visitation. "What brand of bedbug powder do you use?" was a natural query when housewives met on the street or entertained one another with tea and *kuchlech*. Presumably the question was also asked by house-wives on the *West* Side. The world was most probably the same for everybody. We knew that rich people had more rooms, better food and clothing, and easier lives than the poor; but we had no reason to believe that their lot was otherwise different, or that they were exempt from what we believed to be universal afflictions. On the visible world, half of which we knew first-hand, and the other half of which we could only imagine, there were, for us, certain unchangeable phenomena: children were dirty and were obliged to scratch their heads; mothers were unkempt and slatternly; every-body, old and young, had teeth pulled regularly, so that middle-aged and old people had few if any teeth; a great many children died young; everybody slept in underwear; parents always quarreled; mothers were generally indulgent to their children, but fathers either kept aloof or were brutal to them. And, of course, everyone over fourteen years of age was employed in gainful labor. Not before the age of fourteen could one obtain one's working papers. It took a considerable amount of experience in the realm of what is now called "the underprivileged" before I could collate these observations, draw my conclusions, and, by extension, relate the picture thus built up to that part of the world which lay outside my knowledge and beyond my reach.

When the *St. Paul* reached New York, we were met by my father's second cousin, the junk-dealer. This kinsman's name was Gold. It had been Goldstein, but on his arrival in America he had thus shortened it at the friendly suggestion of an immigration officer who was passing on the fitness of arriving aliens to enter the United States. Now, on the pier, our cousin urged my father to perform a similar operation on our own "useless" family name, as he termed it, suggesting "Chot" as a desirable abbreviation. My father rejected the idea on the ground that he failed to see the need for any alteration of any name. In an effort to convince him, Mr. Gold recalled how he, too, had resisted at first, but had been unable to deny the appositeness of the immigration officer's question: "What good is Stein to you?" He now demanded to be told what possible good the last two syllables of our name could be to us in a country so dynamic and so impatient of nonessentials as America. "For here," Mr. Gold said triumphantly—and we heard enunciated for the first time the then celebrated and popular slogan—"Time is money." My father, however, remained unconvinced, and, much to Mr. Gold's displeasure, we retained what he always regarded an impossible, noncommercial name. Many years later my three brothers arrived independently at the junk-dealer's philosophy of nomenclature. Indeed, they went farther than Mr. Gold by discarding altogether our family name, each one adopting a terse, one-syllable, indigenous, respectable, and consequently absolutely commercial surname. Louis, the youngest of the three, chose White; Solomon, the next in age, adopted Chase; and Albert, the eldest, who all his life meticulously observed the entire ritual of Jewish orthodoxy, selected the name of Church.

Although Passaic fell short of being the Eden that Mr. Gold had promised in his letters to my father, it proved to be a lively town, with horse-cars, interesting shops, and sidewalks paved with tar, which had a pleasant smell, and became so soft on very hot days that one's heels sank into it. Our cousin lived on the outskirts of the city in an area inhabited only by Jews. He occupied one floor of a two-story frame house. On the second floor there were two vacant rooms, which, with one room in Mr. Gold's apartment, were assigned to us. I do not recall in what manner the ten of us were disposed in this arrangement, but not many days elapsed before Mrs. Gold's exuberant show of hospitality was replaced by an impatience with our presence which could not be lost on any of us. On the other hand, there was no visible alteration in Mr. Gold's interest in us and in his solicitude for our future, though it soon was evident that he was unable to fulfill his promises of work for my brothers and sisters and a teaching position in a cheder for my father. To the end of our stay he kept reiterating his faith in the commercial possibilities of "Birdie Kahndie," his exotic mispronunciation of Bergen County. His pride in this region was immense, and he would prophesy that in ten years' time "Birdie Kahndie" would outstrip in population and wealth any territory of its size in the United States.

He seemed oblivious of the rancid smells of the long stretches of milky swampland in the vicinity of his home, and impervious to the bite of the large mosquitoes that filled the air the moment the sun went down. But I was not. And soon after we settled in "Birdie Kahndie" I developed malaria and walked about weakly, feeling queasy and running slight but uncomfortable temperatures. Mr. Gold took me to a dispensary in Passaic, where a doctor prescribed quinine and a change of climate. As there was nothing now to keep us in Passaic except Mr. Gold's unconvincing prognostications of a speedy change for the better in our fortunes, my health became a consideration of importance. And in a council held by the heads of both families it was decided—with Mr. Gold dissenting—that we should try the climate of New York as an antidote to my malaria, at the same time testing the reputation of the metropolis as a place of great opportunity for the enterprising alien.

Enthusiastically shepherded by Mrs. Gold, my mother journeyed to New York and rented a suitable apartment in Stanton Street, on the lower East Side, one block from the Bowery. Into this we moved one very hot morning in late August. Right in front of our house a large black horse lay dead in the gutter. He must have been there for some time, for the stench was dreadful, and flies, large and small, covered every inch of the carcass and hovered in swarms over it. Later in the day I looked out the window and saw several small boys astride the animal, engaged in skinning it with their pocket knives. Their sport was presently interrupted, however, by the arrival of a large van for the removal of the horse. This complicated operation attracted all the children in the neighborhood, who watched the departure of the beast with regret.

My health improved slowly in Stanton Street. Once a week I walked to a dispensary at Second Avenue and Fourteenth Street and received, gratis, a dose of quinine. My mother accompanied me there, for she, too, was unwell, frequently announcing in a dramatic tone of voice that her heart had stopped beating. I was not unduly alarmed, for I was at the time unaware of the crucial function of this organ. Nor did the doctor at the dispensary regard my mother's condition with the seriousness she thought it demanded. He would laugh at her extravagant claims and prescribe Hoffmann's drops. A few drops of this magic liquid on a lump of sugar had the effect of instantly reviving my mother's dormant heart.

The public schools opened in September. I was to enter the second grade of the school nearest my home, a large red-brick building on Houston Street. Preparations for the fall term could be observed everywhere. The shops on Stanton Street were displaying every necessity for the resumption of learning. All manner of boys' clothing, including ravishing sailor suits with whistle attached and smart brown knee-length gabardine overcoats, were on view behind the plate-glass windows. The candy stores had the most interesting display of articles used in the classroom. The number and variety of pencil boxes alone took one's breath away. There seemed to be no limit to the complexity of pencil boxes. Beginning with the simple oblong box, plain or lacquered, they evolved into two- and three-storied structures with secret compartments. Prices ranged from seven cents to the fantastic sum of a dollar. The pencil box was, admittedly, a necessity; but a box costing more than ten cents became a symbol of social superiority. The very few who could afford dollar boxes became the acknowledged leaders of their classes. A highly prized peek into the lavish interiors of their pencil boxes was vouchsafed only as a reward for services promised or performed.

It was out of the question for me to begin school without a pencil box and some other less important "supplies" that beckoned through the window of the candy store on our block. Those others ranged from plain and colored blotters to school bags in the shape of knapsacks. Though I pleaded hard for a two-storied pencil box costing a quarter, my mother bought me a plain, oblong casket with a sliding top for ten cents. When our shopping was done, my supplies consisted of the pencil box, four writing pads at a penny each, and a set of colored blotters costing a nickel, the last wrung from my reluctant parent after I had conjured up a classroom crisis in which the teacher would call for a show of blotters and I would be the only pupil unable to produce any. My mother had a horror of nonconformity, a failing I early spotted and often exploited.

On the first Monday in September my mother took me and my scanty supplies to school, where I was enrolled and given a desk and a seat in a large classroom. The teacher, a gray-haired, middle-aged lady, told us to call her Miss Murphy. I wondered if she meant to imply that this was to be her name in class and that at home she was called something else. The name sounded alien and therefore forbidding, and might have been chosen to emphasize the natural barrier between teacher and pupil. She was obviously a pagan—a *Chreestch*—our name for any non-Jew. Miss Murphy read out our last names from a long paper in front of her, and we raised our hands to signify our presence. She was severely distant, and her impersonal attitude, added to the formality of being called by our last names, cast a chill on the classroom. Soon one began to long for the sound of one's first name as for an endearment that would, at a stroke, establish a human relationship between oneself and Miss Murphy. But it was not to be. By the following morning Miss Murphy, having already memorized the surnames of her entire class, called the roll without once referring to her paper.

She then went to the blackboard and in beautiful script wrote *"Catt"* and, looking over the sea of heads in front of her, said: "Something is wrong with the spelling of this word. Katzenelenbogen, stand up and tell me what is wrong." A small, skinny boy rose in the back of the room and said something in an indistinct voice. "Speak up, Katzenelenbogen!" Miss Murphy sharply commanded. My heart went out to Katzenelenbogen in his ordeal. I was conscious of the disparity between the long and important-sounding name and the frailty and insignificance of its possessor. Miss Murphy, however, could not be blamed for adhering to a long-established practice in all public schools. Even in kindergarten, I learned, four- and five-year-olds were called by their last names. The practice was inevitably adopted by the children among themselves in their out-of-school hours, of course with suitable abbreviations of the longer names, and often with prefatory, highly descriptive adjectives.

Notwithstanding Miss Murphy's frigidity, she soon commanded our interest and respect, and we made good progress in reading and spelling. For some mysterious reason, we were more interested in spelling outside the classroom than in it. In the classroom we were content to plod along with the elementary vocabulary of *McGuffey's Eclectic Second Reader*. But at recess time in the yard, and on the street on our way home, we challenged one another to spell long and complicated words whose meaning we didn't know and never dreamt to inquire. Words such as "combustible" and "Mississippi" were somehow in the air. How the craze got started I never knew. But walking home one afternoon, I accidentally collided with a boy I didn't know. Instead of the usual, belligerent "Hey! Can't you look where you're going?" I was peremptorily commanded to spell "combustible." I couldn't, never having heard the word before; whereupon the boy rattled off "co-mb-us-ti-bl-e" with incredible speed and triumphantly went on his way. It was not long before I, too, learned to spell the fascinating word and others equally difficult and provocative. Soon I could rattle off "M-i-double-ess-i-double-ess-i-double-p-i" as rapidly as any child in the neighborhood.

The words in *McGuffey's*, though simpler, lacked the lovely sibilance and long, musical line of those we challenged one another with on the streets. In consequence, they were more difficult to learn to spell. But they did have the advantage of intelligibility, and as strung together in *McGuffey's Reader* they told connected, highly interesting stories. *McGuffey's* took the reader into town and country, but I was delighted to discover that, like myself, it had a strong bias for the latter. I was much taken with a story in the reader called "The Town Mouse and the Country Mouse," which presented a dialogue between two rodents residing respectively in a metropolis and on a farm. The city dweller, who spoke first, advanced apparently incontrovertible arguments on behalf of urban life, stressing especially the prevalence of food left carelessly lying around by humans and the plenitude of holes and crevices and other avenues of escape from cats and destructive agents in general. But when he confidently rested his case, the country mouse, a timid and gentle creature, spoke up, painting an idyllic picture of life in the open, gently emphasizing the delicious leftovers in the country kitchen, the sweet smell of hay in the barn, the coziness of attics in the winter, the feeling of space and freedom, and, above all, the security offered by fields and forests. The issue was settled after the country mouse had returned home, when the town mouse, overconfident of urban security, fell a prey to the machinations of a cat, who devoured him with the sophisticated relish peculiar to city felines. Miss Murphy, who read aloud to us, appeared neither interested in nor moved by the *McGuffey* stories. She read without nuances and exhibited no emotion. Completely indifferent to the music of poetry, she would recite a line like the exquisite. "How would I like to go up in a Swing, Up in the air so blue!" in a cold, earthbound voice, look up from her book, and say: "Plotkin, spell 'swing.'" Yet she was an excellent disciplinarian, and our class speedily gained a reputation for good spelling.

She also conceived and put into effect a new system for the handling of hats and overcoats which saved time and enabled us to begin our studies in the mornings a few minutes after nine and to be out on the street soon after the bell rang at three. The system was simplicity itself. As each boy entered the class, he deposited his hat and coat on a designated spot on the floor on either side of the blackboard. At nine o'clock, at noon, at one, and at three, two boys selected for their strength and stamina would station themselves in front of the class to right and left of the room. Each of the two would pick up a hat and coat from the heap in front of him, hold it aloft for recognition. The owner would then announce his name and open wide his arms to receive the garments flung in his direction. For a few minutes the air would be filled with hurtling coats, scarves, hats, and, on rainy or snowy days, rubbers and rubber boots. But it offered the pleasures of a humorous game, what with the uncertain aim of the throwers and the possibility of being knocked over by a too speedily propelled overcoat. For this innovation and her general efficiency Miss Murphy was soon liked and even admired.

Miss Murphy lived in Brooklyn, an hour's journey by the Grand Street horse-car to the East River, the ferry to cross it, and another horse-car on the other side. She therefore always brought her lunch with her. This consisted, much to our surprise, of one sandwich of jam, the bread remarkably white and of the texture of cotton, and one thin slice of sponge cake, each wrapped in tissue paper, and both done up in brown wrapping paper and tied with cord. It seemed to all of us rather meager nourishment for a strong-minded, powerful woman. But I had heard it said that Christians in general ate sparingly, the women especially showing a marked distaste for food. The men, on the other hand, were partial to drink, as could be verified by visiting the Bowery around the corner from the street I lived on. When she dismissed her class at noon, Miss Murphy would ask one of her pupils to run out and buy her a bottle of milk, and we soon began to regard this errand as a privilege and a special mark of favor. Yet she was careful to rotate us, and by the end of the term every boy in the class had bought her a bottle of milk. She had a way of saying: "Would you hand me my *puhss*?" which we thought elegant. When the pocketbook was handed to her, she would extract a coin from it delicately with her thumb and forefinger, the little finger stretched out as if she was about to bring forth something precious or highly dangerous. She ate her lunch privately, seated at her desk. Even with no one to see her, one could be sure that she ate her jam sandwich with the decorum of Chaucer's "Nonne, a Prioresse," and "let no morsel from her lippes falle." Incidentally, the sandwich was responsible for my first demerit in class, the morning when Miss Murphy taught us to sing "Columbia, the jam of the ocean." I thought of Miss Murphy's sandwich and could not repress a giggle when we sang the opening line with its stress on the word "jam." Sometimes Miss Murphy would bring a bunch of violets, which she would place in a glass of water on her desk. She looked stylish at all times, her hair in a pompadour, a gold watch pinned on her blouse, a large, black patent-leather belt around her waist. She was immaculate. At least twice each day she would remove the flowers, dip the tips of her fingers in the glass of water, and wipe them with her handkerchief. So conscious did the class become of Miss Murphy's fastidiousness that for Christmas most of her pupils gave her a cake of soap.

Stanton Street was an exciting place in which to live. It was the shopping center of the neighborhood, and in men's clothing it rivaled Hester Street. Perhaps in volume of sales Hester Street stood supreme; but its garments were in the main second-hand, while Stanton Street's were quite new. Furthermore, samples of the clothes on Stanton Street could be seen in all their chic and splendor on marvelous, lifelike dummies in the shop windows. One window that held me spellbound displayed a father with an elaborate mustache, surrounded by his five sons, ranging in size from an infant to a young man almost as tall as his parent. Each child wore the clothes suited to his age. I yearned for the blue sailor suit with whistle attached on the fourth son, a child of about my own age. It occupied my thoughts and even dreams for years.

Stanton Street had other attractions besides shop windows. Organ-grinders with monkeys would appear at all hours and play a varied assortment of music. Through them I learned many popular songs, but the only one I can now recall is *Sweet Rosie O'Grady*. I found it a sweet ballad and a tender declaration of love, notwithstanding its waltz-like rhythm. The organ-grinders played other tunes of a more serious character, which, through repetition, I learned to sing, though it was years before I discovered their identity. Among them were the *"Miserere"* from *Il Trovatore* and *"Addio del passato"* from *La Traviata*, both of which brought tears to my eyes. Often I would follow an organ-grinder through many streets and so hear the *"Miserere"* perhaps a dozen times over, never failing to respond to the somber, inexpressibly sad minor chords at the beginning and the noble but equally doleful melody in major which comes soon after. I have since wondered at Verdi's predilection for the major mode to convey sadness, and his success in doing the opposite of what all other composers before and after him did.

Stanton Street ended at the Bowery, a block away from the house in which I lived. The Bowery was in bad odor with all the parents of the neighborhood for a great many reasons, all of them concerned with the welfare of the children. The street was the habitat of drunks and criminals, the latter so bold and vicious that they were often more than a match for the policemen who attempted to restrain them. Nevertheless, the temptation to explore for oneself so infamous a street was too strong to resist. In company with a playmate or two for protection in case of assault, I frequently roamed the Bowery as far north as Eighth Street and south to Chatham Square. It is true that nothing noteworthy ever happened, but the din of the elevated trains passing overhead, their engines belching smoke and sending showers of sparks and cinders down on the wagons and pedestrians below, the noise coming through the swinging doors of the many saloons, the spectacle of drunkards swaying and teetering and talking loudly to themselves, combined to give us a delicious feeling of daring and fear. Sometimes the Bowery invaded Stanton Street in the persons of derelict women we called "Mary Sugar Bums." The poor, dirty, ragged creatures would come reeling into our block, cursing and swearing, and we would run after them, calling out "Mary Sugar Bum! Mary Sugar Bum!" and they would threaten us grotesquely with their fists and lunge at us futilely when we came too close.

There was always excitement on Stanton Street from the time school let out until supper time, and for an hour or two between that meal and bedtime. Something was always happening, and our attention was continually being shifted from one excitement to another. "What's-a-matter?" was a perpetual query as we were attracted by a sudden frantic exodus from a tenement, the clang of an ambulance as it drew up in front of a house, a person desperately running, pursued by a crowd, a runaway horse and wagon, a policeman forcibly propelling a drunk and twisting his arm until the wretch screamed with pain, an altercation through open windows between next-door neighbors. Occasionally there was the excitement of a Western Union messenger trying to deliver a telegram and asking the children playing on the street on what floor its recipient might live, for there were no bells or letter boxes in the entrance corridors of the tenements on Stanton Street. The mailman blew a whistle in the downstairs hall and called out names in a voice loud enough to be heard even on the fifth floor, and people would come running downstairs to get their letters.

The arrival of a telegram was a most serious occurrence. Everybody knew that telegrams were dispatched only to announce the death of a relative or friend or, at the very least, a serious illness; and the appearance of the fateful, gray-clad messenger was sure to draw a crowd. On hearing the name of the addressee, the people would speculate aloud on the identity of the deceased, and some neighbor might offer to precede the messenger and tactfully and mercifully prepare the bereaved for the tidings to follow. "Something *terrible* has happened—Mrs. Cohen just got a telegram!"

Every day after supper I would beg to be allowed to play for a while in front of the house, where I could be seen from our windows and, at the proper time, summoned to bed. Between sundown and evening, on fair days, Stanton Street had an enchantment of its own. The dying sun benevolently lacquered the garish red-brick buildings, softly highlighting a window, a cornice, or a doorway. We would play on the sidewalks and in the gutter until the air grew dark and we could barely tell who was who. Then the lamplighter would emerge from the Bowery, carrying his lighted stick in one hand and a small ladder in the other. In the light of the gas lamps we played leapfrog over the empty milk cans in front of the grocery store. Each of us would vault over a single can and then, if successful, augment the hazard by adding a can for the next leap. Some of us learned to vault over as many as seven cans! Or we would play hide-and-go-seek in the dim vestibules of the tenement houses. We very rarely left off our play to return home voluntarily. Those of us who were sought out and induced to go home by mothers or sisters were fortunate, for the appearance of one's father on the scene carried with it the certainty of punishment. Fathers, with few exceptions, were insensitive, brutal, and quick to resort to force in obtaining obedience.

Mothers, too, frequently resorted to force, but only after they had exhausted all peaceful means. I would sometimes try my mother's patience to a degree that drove her to the retaliatory use of what sounded like curse words. I suspected they were not actual words, though, spoken passionately, they sounded authentic enough. They must have been inventions that would have the force but not the connotation of

curses one could properly call down on persons one didn't love
or wasn't related to, for no one else ever used them and I
never discovered their meaning. "You can go tar-tar-ar-ee!"
my mother would shout wildly at me, as if she were consigning me to the devil. The effect, for the moment, was the same.
For the most part, however, my mother found relief in
rhetorical queries addressed to the heavens, like "What does
he want of me? Does he wish to shorten my life?" Or she
would hurl an epithet and cannily negate it in the same breath,
like "The cholera should seize him—not!" My father wasted
no time with me when by chance he came into the room at
such critical moments. "Let *me* handle him," he would say
grimly as he placed himself between us. "Skinning *alive*, that's
what he needs," and he would undo his belt preparatory to
carrying out what he thought I needed. My mother would
then interfere and make excuses for me and the half-with-
drawn belt would be reluctantly returned to its place. But on
one occasion the two acted in concert against me, thus bringing about the first great disillusionment of my life.

I had disobeyed strict orders not to go outdoors barefoot
on a cold rainy afternoon. I returned several hours later with
every expectation of being scolded by my mother or punished
by my father if he happened to be home. I found both of
them at home, but my apprehensions vanished when I saw
no anger or resentment in their faces. On the contrary, my
father asked me in a pleasant way if I had had a good time,
the while he busied himself undoing the knots in a clothesline.
I said I had and went to the window to signal my friends on
the street that everything was all right, when suddenly I was
seized from behind and felt my mother's arms hard around
me. A second later my father had bound my legs and hands
with the clothesline and dragged me with—shame to tell!—
my mother's help into the kitchen, where he tied me fast to
a leg of the sink. My father's deceptive behavior did not
surprise me; I could expect it of him. But my mother's perfidy

shattered in one instant my previously unquestioned trust in her love for me. My refuge and security were gone. My world had toppled around me. If such things could be, my only wish was to die. An hour later I was released, but my freedom, while physically gratifying, could not restore the faith I had lost. It was weeks before I would permit my mother to touch me.

We lived in Stanton Street for about a year. My father, not having the capital to open a cheder of his own, taught Hebrew to a few boys in their homes. This brought in very little money. Besides, the inattention of the pupils, who could not keep their eyes on the Bible, but kept staring out of the window, brought on my father's old headaches. Furthermore, he came up against a newfangled idea among parents that teachers were not to administer corporal punishment. It had not been so in the old country. And my father would rather give up a pupil than relinquish so necessary and important a prerogative. My mother reminded him that beggars could not be choosers, but he insisted that they *could;* they could choose starvation! At any rate, *he* required nothing, or very little, for himself. All he needed, he said, was a piece of bread and herring and a roof over his head.

Nevertheless, he usually ate what we all did. Friday nights he would expect and plainly relish a full ceremonial dinner of several courses, beginning with a stuffed fish, the head of which was reserved for him, and of which he ate all but the eyes and the more resistant bones. There would then follow sweet and sour meat roasted to a point of delicious disintegration and flanked by roast potatoes saturated in gravy, and limp, candied carrots. Soup would come last, and my father would help himself to two brimful plates from the large bowl placed in the center of the table. He was inordinately fond of calf's-foot jelly, which my mother would cook on Fridays and put out on the fire escape to cool. On Saturday after *Minche* (late afternoon prayers) it would be served, preceded by a little whisky, as a delicate collation for him and a fellow worshipper he generally brought home with him. All in all, he ate so very well that it was difficult to believe his declarations of austerity.

My oldest brother, Albert, had married and had gone to live in Waterbury, Connecticut, where he practiced carpentry and undertook small repair jobs. He had talked my brother Solomon, next to him in age, into going with him, with a view to their forming a partnership as builders and contractors. My brother Louis, aged fourteen, got himself a job as a presser's assistant in a tailor shop in the vicinity of Stanton Street. My three older sisters found work in a cigarette factory. My younger sister hadn't yet reached the kindergarten age. She played around the house and got in my mother's way, and when sent to play in the street, frequently fell down the stairs. Neighbors would pick her up and carry her upstairs, and my mother would have to drop her work and apply poultices and bandages and still her cries, thus defeating the purpose for which she had been relegated to the streets. After school hours I would help out my mother for an hour or so by "minding" the unstable child.

Though most of our family were employed, their aggregate earnings provided the barest subsistence for us. It is true that on Friday nights we invariably had a feast, but that repast was made possible only by economy and deprivation during the rest of the week. I was generally hungry, and I always invested the penny I infrequently got from my mother in "broken cake" at the grocery store. Sweet biscuits in that era were sold, on the East Side at any rate, from large barrels, and "broken cake" was the name for the bits and splinters of biscuits remaining in the bottom when all of the unfractured dainties had been removed. We longed, of course, for the biscuits in their original unharmed condition. Yet "broken cake" had a flavor of its own, owing to the very circumstance that caused its degradation. Lying crushed and chipped under the weight of its unharmed fellows above, it assimilated a variety of aromas, so that the flavor of a piece of "broken cake" offered a concentration of all the flavors of *all* the biscuits in the barrel. I preferred "broken cake" to candy at "Cheap Charlie's," where one could buy ten chocolate-coated walnuts for a penny.

Every street had a "Cheap Charlie." I used to wonder at the singularity of the candy-store business being exclusively in the hands of men of the same name. These candy stores had an extraordinary attraction for children because of the personal attitude of Charlie to his young customers. This was an even more potent lure than the advertised cheapness of Charlie's wares, which we accepted on faith without inquiry or comparison. Charlie was human and understanding, and was not above entering into the problems of his patrons. Thus it was possible, when one did not happen to have a penny at the moment, to confide in Charlie and, on a promise to pay up at the first opportunity, to leave the store with the chocolate-covered walnuts in a paper bag. The groceryman was less understanding. I suspected that my mother was responsible for his insistence on prompt payment for "broken cake." Nor did I have the heart to blame her. Her own relations with the man were often delicate. I myself had witnessed humiliating scenes in which he categorically refused to give her further credit. But my mother always managed to persuade him to change his mind, alleging an imminent favorable turn of events for us which would promptly take care of all our financial indebtedness.

In school the time for promotion drew near and a great uneasiness swept the class. The fear of being "left back" gripped all but a very few boys who were obviously so brilliant that it was early conceded by the rest of us, as well as by themselves, that there would be no question about *their* promotion. Being "left back" was definitely a dishonor. But not because it was a reflection on one's scholarship. Scholarship was, in fact, suspect, and the "smart" boys who got A's or "stars" became the objects of ribbing and were likely to suffer ostracism. Being "left back" doomed one to loneliness, the sudden disruption of friendships, and a separation from the intrigues, scandals, pleasantries, and feeling of solidarity of a long-established class. Long before the dreaded day arrived we could see Miss Murphy working on the "promotion list" during our study periods. We tried hard to guess at the names she so carefully wrote out by watching the movements of her pen. The crossing of a "t" or the dotting of an "i" could be a clue in that it ruled out a great many names that did not contain those letters. The boys who occupied desks in the first row were sometimes able to catch a name she was writing: a boy would raise his hand for permission to "leave the room," as our trips to the water closets were politely called, and in making for the door would sidle near Miss Murphy's desk and attempt a swift look at the promotion list. But Miss Murphy was aware of these stratagems and did what she could to defeat them. When she left the room, even for a moment, she would lock the list in her desk.

On promotion day the class arrived all scrubbed and neat, with hair combed and definitely parted, the labor of mothers who cherished a wild hope that in case of doubt an extra bit of cleanliness might tip the scales. Miss Murphy gave no indication that she was aware of anything unusual in our appearance. Neither by word nor by look did she indicate that she had sealed the fate of fifty boys in the document that now reposed in her desk. Tense, nervous, and dispirited, we went through our usual morning routine. At ten o'clock the monitors left their seats and opened the windows halfway with long poles while the class rose and exercised their arms and heads with Miss Murphy leading and commanding "Inspire!—Expire!" the class noisily breathing in and out in response. At a quarter to twelve the room suddenly became unaccountably still. Miss Murphy seated herself by her desk, opened it, and drew out the promotion list. I could see the red line down the middle of the page, looking like a thin blood barrier, which separated the names on either side. Miss Murphy, before addressing herself to the list, was exasperatingly deliberate in tidying the top of her desk, arranging her pencils in a row, and moving the water glass with its little bouquet of flowers to one side. At last she was ready.

"I shall now read the promotion list," she announced. "As your name is called, rise and stand in the aisle. Those whose names are not called will remain seated." This seemed to foreshadow doom for many. Classes were known to have been promoted en masse. Clearly ours would not be one of these. The class held its breath as Miss Murphy again gave her attention to the list. "Abramowitz," Miss Murphy intoned, and Abramowitz got to his feet precipitately and stood in the aisle. "Abrams, Abramson, Askenasy." The B's seemed endless, but at last Miss Murphy said: "Chasmanovitch." There was a pause. "Chisel" followed "Chasmanovitch" in the daily roll call. What about Chisel? Chisel's fate did not concern me. Ordinarily I would have wished him well. But if Chisel was not on the list my name should come next. Why did Miss Murphy pause? What could the hesitation portend for me? I waited for the blow. Should Miss Murphy now pronounce the name of Cohen, then both Chisel and I had been "left back." My eyes isolated Miss Murphy's lips as they began to form a name. "Chisel!" Miss Murphy pronounced, and the wretch (his desk was in front of mine), who had slumped down in his seat in despair, now looked about him incredulously, like a criminal who had received a last-minute reprieve. Slowly he got up and shifted over into the aisle. I continued to stare at Miss Murphy's lips. There was another pause, and then I heard my name, clear and loud. I stepped into the aisle in a daze and stood there for a long time, experiencing no sensation of any kind. It was like the suspension of consciousness. Then all at once I was aware of

many boys standing in the aisles and Miss Murphy was calling
out "Rabinowitz, Redin, Rickin, Sokolov, Spingold, Stein-
berg, Teitelbaum, Ulansky, Wissotzky, Yarmolovsky,
Zeitlin." It was all over. Three wretched boys still sat:
Katzenelenbogen, Gershowitz, and Vlacheck. Katzenelenbogen had covered his face with his hands and was crying
softly. Gershowitz, his face white, stared straight in front of
him. Vlacheck alone showed no signs of defeat. He had been
"left back" twice before, and he smiled and leered as if he
had expected nothing else and rather gloried in continuing to
belong to a minority.

We promoted boys, at a command from Miss Murphy,
closed ranks and were marched into an adjacent classroom,
where we found four dejected boys, the leftovers of our new
grade. Miss Murphy made us a formal farewell address and
turned us over to Miss Applebaum, our new teacher. Then
the bell rang and we marched into the street and scattered
quickly to our homes, for once not loitering to talk and plan,
in our eagerness to carry the good news to our families.

I was now a third-grader. My promotion had given me a
new confidence in myself, and I looked forward to an interesting term with my old schoolmates under the tutelage of
Miss Applebaum. But before a week had passed, my parents
decided, most unaccountably, I thought, to leave Stanton
Street and move to distant East Broadway, a neighborhood I
had never even seen. In consequence, I obtained a transfer to
P.S. No. 2 on Henry, between Rutgers and Market streets.
Except for the fact that I was assigned to the third grade in
the new school, I was in all other respects in the position of a
Katzenelenbogen, Gershowitz, or Vlacheck, for my classmates were all new to me and I had to set about making new
friends.

East Broadway was a wide thoroughfare. Our apartment
on the third floor of a house on the corner of Rutgers Street
overlooked a large square, or rather oblong, adorned by a large

black marble fountain, rising in several tiers. I could sense the possibilities of the neighborhood. For, besides the fountain, all the buildings on the west side of East Broadway, extending from Essex to Jefferson streets, had been razed for the eventual construction of a park, and the debris offered the very terrain for possible war games, with rival armies marching and counter-marching and striving to gain certain desirable heights. It would be at least a year before the place could be cleared and the park begun, and I foresaw many late afternoons and evenings, not to speak of Sundays, devoted to maneuvers, with myself in some kind of leading role, perhaps as captain of a powerful striking force. The potentialities of the place were innumerable. Looking up Rutgers Street toward the east, there was the river in the distance, with boats of every description plying up and down. Huge warehouses near the water's edge were forever discharging crates and barrels with mysterious contents, and at night one could sit on the large empty trucks parked on the wharves and watch the river and the lights from Brooklyn across it.

Within walking distance were splendors like Brooklyn Bridge, the City Hall, and the Post Office. The mysterious alleys of Chinatown were no more than half a mile away. Certainly East Broadway, at its meeting with Rutgers Square, was the center of the universe, and I looked forward to an exciting and fruitful existence on it. But the prospect of a strange school, a new teacher, and new schoolmates was unpleasant, and I would gladly have relinquished the future delights of East Broadway for the old routine and associations of Stanton Street.

CHAPTER FOUR

🖋 The Fountain

THE windows of our three-room railroad flat looked down on the big fountain in Rutgers Square, a huge plaza into which flowed four important thoroughfares: East Broadway, Canal Street, Rutgers Street, and Essex Street. The fountain was a tapering, eye-filling, circular structure surrounded by two semicircular stone benches. It had a broad basin four or five feet above the base, and two graduated smaller basins in tiers above it. The stone benches were always occupied. In the morning they held mothers and babies and women shoppers tired out from bargain-hunting, the pursuit of which necessitated visiting distant markets, sometimes a mile from their homes. In the late afternoon, schoolchildren took over the fountain, sailing paper boats in the lowest basin and playing tag around the benches. In the evening, after a hot day, old people sat around to catch what tenuous breezes might hover over the square. The old people seldom stayed long, and they were succeeded by young couples who had been walking hand-in-hand in the square, waiting for a chance to sit down in the proximity promised by the crowded benches around the fountain.

Presumably the small tenements could not accommodate the old people and the young at the same time. Privacy in the home was practically unknown. The average apartment consisted of three rooms: a kitchen, a parlor, and a doorless and windowless bedroom between. The parlor became a sleeping-room at night. So did the kitchen when families were unusually large. Perhaps because of the accessibility of the light refreshment that it was customary to offer guests, the kitchen rather than the parlor became the living-room until bedtime, and all social life centered in it. Made comparatively presentable after a long day of cooking, eating, and the washing of dishes and laundry, it was the scene of formal calls at our house and of the visits of friends and prospective suitors. However, the etiquette of courting was strict. A transplantation from the old country, it had well-defined prohibitions known to everyone. Chaperonage was an acknowledged institution, and the chaperon could even be, if necessary, a child. When a gentleman offered to call on one of my sisters on a night when I was to be the only other member of the family at home, my mother, before leaving the house, would openly caution me to remain in the kitchen until the visitor had taken his leave. On the other hand, it was considered proper for young people to go walking together, attend concerts and balls and the theater. But in such cases the parents were to be apprised beforehand of the extent and duration of the walk or the nature of the entertainment. It therefore turned out, ironically enough, that privacy could be had only in public. The streets in the evening were thick with promenading couples, and the benches around the fountain and in Jackson Street Park, and the empty trucks lined up at the

river front, were filled with lovers who had no other place to
meet. Boys of my age were required to be at home around
ten at night. Those of us who were still in the streets at that
hour might decide perversely to hang around the fountain
with the intent of embarrassing the lovers on the benches.
We would sneak up on them from behind and imitate the
amorous confidences we *imagined* they exchanged. "Darling!"
we would whisper, "I love you more than the world. Will you
marry me?" And one of us would answer mincingly: "Yes,
dear, I *will* marry you—and we will have *many* children,"
the daring afterthought being intended to convey the abnor-
mally advanced state of our sophistication.

The conversation of lovers I did overhear was on the more
serious plane of politics, religion, literature, and the theater.
The majority of these young people were immigrants, and
their language was still Yiddish, with an admixture of Russian, Polish, Romanian, German, and English words and
phrases. They worked in dark, fetid sweatshops, in airless
attics and cellars. They attended night schools and read
liberal, socialist, or anarchist newspapers and magazines.
Politically and ideologically they were at odds with their
parents and grandparents, who leaned through habit and
tradition toward conservatism and paternalism. In the minds of
the older people, unionism or criticism of constituted authority and resistance to it invariably led to atheism, or at
least to a slackness in the observance of the laws and tradi-
tions of religious orthodoxy. Yet, though their expressed
opinions were iconoclastic, the actual behavior of the young
people was strictly, though unconsciously, in the tradition of
their elders.

One of the topics in the air in that period was the double
standard of morality. The Russian author Chernishevsky
had written a novel on the subject, and the book, though not
new, was enjoying a vogue on the East Side. *What is to be
Done?* was its provocative title. It posed for its heroine and,

by extension, to all women, the question of acceptance or rejection of the hitherto unchallenged promiscuity of males. The author himself took the most serious view of the license enjoyed by men, and pleaded through the mouth of his heroine for a single standard for both sexes. As a final gesture of protest the heroine committed suicide, but I don't remember what effect this act of desperation had on the question involved. I do remember that *What is to be Done?* was earnestly debated in my own house, on the sidewalks, and on the benches by the Rutgers Square fountain, and that sympathy was generally on the side of the heroine and the author. The male arguments against a single standard appeared to lack force, and almost always capitulated to the sterner moral and spiritual convictions of the opposition. Perhaps the lack of privacy contributed to the high moral tone of the East Side intellectuals. *What is to be Done?* may have helped to sublimate this deprivation, as did the moralistic Russian and Yiddish literature that formed the chief intellectual fare of those days. "The wages of sin is death," Tolstoy had inscribed under the title of *Anna Karenina*, and no one ever questioned the stern judgment of the author on his beautiful and erring heroine. Infidelity, promiscuity, and all other sexual aberrations were held to be incompatible with the life of the spirit and the intellect in a serious world where young men and women labored ten and twelve hours a day merely to keep body and soul together. In these circles love was held to be primarily intellectual. Young people met in classrooms, in night schools, at lectures on politics, economics, and literature, at plays and at concerts, and seemed to be drawn to one another by a community of interests rather than by chemical affinity. The ignorant, the idlers, and loafers of both sexes managed to achieve vulgar and sordid relations, and there were frequent betrayals and sex scandals. But those attachments which had an intellectual basis generally led to marriage. A cousin of ours who worked in a sweatshop and studied dentistry at night was introduced to a girl at a concert and ball in Pythagoras Hall on East Broadway. While dancing with him the girl confessed to a passion for Dostoievsky's *Crime and Punishment*, the very book he admired most in the world. They fell in love, and on his receiving his dentist's diploma two years later, they married. Love was, indeed, a serious and lofty matter among the young men and women in Rutgers Square.

In summer the fountain in Rutgers Square played all day, and in the late afternoon and on Sundays the more adventurous boys of the neighborhood would strip and dive into the lowest basin. This was prohibited by law, and a warning to that effect was painted on the basin's rim. One of us would be delegated to stand guard over the heap of discarded pants, shirts, underwear, shoes, and stockings and to keep an eye open for policemen. Espying one, the lookout would let out a piercing "Cheese it—the cops!" grab a handful of garments, and make for a certain prearranged meeting-place. The swimmers would scramble out of the basin and scatter in all directions. This was also prearranged to confuse our pursuer, who, not being quick enough in deciding which direction to take, would generally stand helpless for the time it took the boys to make good their escape. A few minutes later we would all have made our way, dripping but elated, to some dark tenement vestibule, or have descended to the cellar workshop and living-quarters of some friendly ragpicker or shoemaker, whither our sentry had preceded us with our clothes. And sometime later we would emerge, singly, of course, to allay suspicion, and saunter nonchalantly back to the fountain, perhaps under the puzzled scrutiny of the very cop who had caused our flight.

Better swimming was to be had in the river a few blocks east of the fountain. There it was perfectly legal to dive off the docks provided one wore one's underwear. On really hot days we repaired to the waterfront, but we preferred the fountain because of its risks.

The law also frowned on gangs. For that reason it behooved one to belong to a gang. I applied for admission to the East Broadwayers soon after we moved into the neighborhood, and after submitting to a series of physical tortures to test my powers of endurance, I was accepted and solemnly installed as a member. The East Broadwayers was a loose association of young residents of a well-defined area. Their professed aim was to detest all outlying gangs whose forces were numerically comparable to their own, and to dedicate themselves practically to the harassment and, ideally, to the complete destruction of the others. Rival gangs of approximately equal man-power delivered ultimatums to one another and met openly in battle on their home grounds or on the enemy's terrain, the choice of battlefield being the acknowledged prerogative of the challenger. With sticks and stones and whatever else was at hand for weapons, the battle would often last from after school to past supper time, when the armies would disintegrate upon the advent of worried relations, who would collar and bear off large contingents of fighters, including, perhaps, the intrepid leaders themselves.

Every street had its gang, but the exigencies of geography necessitated alliances among gangs of contiguous streets. The East Broadwayers joined up with the Jefferson and Madison Streeters and the Rutgers Streeters and operated as a solid block against associated gangs residing in more distant neighborhoods. Our chief enemies were the combined forces of the Cherry, Pike, and Montgomery Streeters, though sometimes powerful gangs from the remote purlieus of Brooklyn Bridge or the Grand Street waterfront conducted swift raids on the East Broadwayers and retreated hastily before we could summon the aid of our allies. In these lightning skirmishes some of us were so conspicuously mauled that we feared additional punishment at home and consequently remained in the streets long after bedtime, laving our wounds in the dirty waters of the fountain and inventing plausible excuses to account for our injuries. When our wounds looked as if they might become serious, we repaired, escorted by an honor guard, to the Gouverneur Street Hospital, where we were bandaged neatly and sometimes outfitted with impressive arm-slings. We then made our way home, conscious of our importance, followed at a respectful distance by admiring comrades.

Gang laws prohibited members of rival gangs from passing through each other's territory. Strange faces aroused suspicion, and it was mandatory for an East Broadwayer to accost any boy he did not know and put the question: "What Streeter?" To incur punishment, the stranger did not even have to belong to a rival gang. It was enough if he lived on an enemy street. This was so well known that boys would take to their heels without answering the fateful query, and so frequently make their escape. To avoid unpleasantness, boys whose shortest way to school lay through forbidden territory were obliged to make lengthy detours.

Aside from the hazard of gang warfare, there was also the hazard of racial and nationalistic enmity. Cherry Street was completely Irish and Catholic, while the neighborhood of East Broadway and Rutgers Square was predominantly Jewish. Being numerically superior, we felt no antagonism for the non-Jewish in our midst, rather looking upon them with the friendly contempt one normally felt for goyim. An Irish family lived in a rear apartment on our floor. They were an unusually dirty group, the parents much given to drunkenness and quarreling. Yet our relations were cordial, and my mother and her Christian neighbor would exchange lengthy visits, though neither understood a word of the other's language.

I, however, longed to see for myself the forbidden, solidly

Christian territory of Cherry Street, and one Saturday morning I entered the street and walked, nervous and apprehensive, for several blocks without molestation. At the corner of Montgomery Street two boys leaning against a lamppost looked closely at me as I passed them. Trying hard to repress any signs of fear, I walked on. They left their lamppost and walked behind me. Suddenly they spurted ahead and barred my way. I said: "Wha's a matter?" and one of them countered with "What Streeter?" "Grand Streeter," I lied. The Grand and the Cherry Streeters, I knew, had recently concluded a mutual-assistance pact. This seemed to satisfy my questioner. But his friend now took another tack. "Hey!" he said, looking me over carefully. "Are you a sheeny?" "Me?" I said, summoning a wretched smile. "No! I'm a Chreestch." I had now silenced my second tormentor. "Well, I gotta go," I hazarded breezily, and started to walk. "Wait a minute," the first one said, grabbing me by the arm. "Let's *see* if you're a Chreestch." I knew what he meant. I broke loose from his hold and started running as fast as I could, the two after me. Fear gave me the speed to outdistance them, and presently my feet were on friendly territory and my pursuers dared go no farther. The story of my adventure and escape, embellished with some highly imaginative details, was speedily incorporated into the oral collection of the heroic exploits of the East Broadwayers.

The days in summer and winter were crowded with incidents, amusing, soul-satisfying, perilous, or adventurous (at the very least, one could find satisfaction in just being an onlooker). There were gang wars to be fought, policemen to annoy and outwit, and sentimental couples to be teased and ridiculed. Standing unobserved at one's window, one could focus a burning-glass on the face of a person resting on the stone bench of the fountain and relish his annoyance and anger as he tried helplessly to locate his tormentor. From the same vantage point, one could let down a weight attached to a long string, conk the head of a passer-by, and draw up the missile before the victim could look around for the offender; or, with the aid of an accomplice stationed on the curb, stretch a string head-high across the sidewalk, which, unseen by some unsuspecting pedestrian, would lift his straw hat or derby from his head and send it rolling down the street. There were the great games of leave-e-o, prisoner's base, and one-o'-cat to be played, the last limitlessly peripatetic, so that one might start to play on East Broadway and wind up, hours later, on the Bowery. There were ambulances to be run after and horse-cars to hang on to—unobserved by the conductor. If one was on intimate terms with a currier in a livery stable, one could sit bareback astride a horse and ride through the streets. Something was constantly happening which one had to repair to the spot to see at first hand. People were being knocked down by horse-cars. There were altercations on every street, often ending in blows. The changing of street-car horses at certain termini was a spectacle well worth a walk of a mile. One could run after an ambulance with a view to being in a position to give an eyewitness account of an accident to one's comrades. There were parades to be followed, also organ-grinders, bums, and itinerant sellers of cure-alls, who would assemble a crowd in a moment, deliver a stream of seemingly sensible, yet strangely incomprehensible, oratory, quickly dispose of some wares, and suddenly move on. There was Chinatown to be explored. Familiarity could not dispel the delicious fear of a walk through Mott and Pell streets or curb one's speculation on what went on behind the bamboo curtains in the dark interiors of dimly lit shops, or, for that matter, in the inscrutable heads of the pigtailed Chinamen who shuffled along on the narrow sidewalks or sat in doorways, smoking pipes and cigarettes. No young boy in his senses would face Chinatown alone. We always went in twos or larger groups. And when we entered a shop to purchase lichee nuts, one of us always remained outside to raise an alarm in the not improbable event of an Oriental attempt to kidnap us and mark us out either for lustful murder or for something less immediate but more dreadful, known to us vaguely as "the white-slave trade."

On election nights, there were bonfires to watch and perhaps assist in making. Fires broke out constantly in all seasons, and the air was seldom free from the clang of the fire engines, the shrieks of the siren, and the clatter of the horses on the cobblestones. Following the fire engines could conceivably occupy all one's leisure time. I found the water-front fires in winter the most gratifying, for the warehouses were large and their contents inflammable, and an entire block of buildings could be counted on to go up in smoke before the firemen gained control. An æsthetic by-product not to be underestimated was the lovely spectacle provided by the freezing of the water from the fire-hoses the moment it touched the buildings. Not infrequently the fire engines led directly to one's own house. These fires, whose origin even children suspected, were generally less interesting, containing no element of suspense, as all the tenants, acting as if through some common impulse, had left their homes and were on the sidewalks by the time the engines drew up. But they were fires none the less, and necessitated the dragging of miles of hose into the building and the wielding of hatchets and axes by the firemen. Often one arrived breathless at a fire only to find that it had been a *"fourjoulahm"* (a false alarm). *"Fourjoulahms"* were held to be the work of criminal-minded youngsters, who, we were told, were certain to end up in the electric chair. But if they were criminal-minded, they were always uncommonly clever in eluding detection. I sometimes thought they were actuated by nothing more evil than a desire (which I shared) to witness a full turnout of fire engines. On quiet days I should myself have loved to spread a *"fourjoulahm."* Fortunately for me, quiet days were very rare. Besides, there appeared to be no lack of these criminal-minded youngsters on the lower East Side. I really was not needed, for hardly a day passed without the excitement of a "*fourjoulahm.*"

Diversions were also available closer to home. One could spend a profitable afternoon in one's own back yard. The poles for clotheslines soared five stories in the air. To shinny up a pole was a feat in itself, and the exhilaration felt on reaching the top had a quality of its own. Also there was the sense of danger, not actually felt, but induced by the fears of the women who watched the ascension from their back windows and yelled: "Get down, you bum, you loafer! Do you want to get killed?" A restaurant in the adjoining house kept its milk cans in our yard. These served for games of leapfrog and also offered a means of revenge on the proprietor of the restaurant, a man insensitive to the need of children to play and make noise. Every time he chased us out of the yard, we would return at night, pry open his milk cans, and drop sand and pebbles in them. He (and his clientele as well) must have also been insensitive to the quality of the milk he was imbibing and dispensing, for our unsanitary peccadillo was either never discovered or else ignored.

Tenement roofs offered a series of connected playgrounds. The element of danger in playing tag on roofs was considerable enough to heighten the ordinary excitement of the game. Cornices were only knee-high. They could hardly be a barrier to destruction should one, in running to escape the tagger, fail to have the presence of mind to veer quickly to right or left. Some buildings were taller than others, thus necessitating a thrilling drop of ten or twelve feet, and on returning, an equally exciting scrambling up skylights and chimneys. A breath-taking hazard was the open air shafts that separated houses otherwise contiguous. To miss, even by an inch, a jump over an air shaft meant death, but death did not really matter. For death was only an academic concept, a word

without reality, at worst something that could happen only to
others.

Every variety of adventure was to be had in Rutgers Square
and its environs. Excitement lay in wait at the turn of a street
corner, in the somber hallways, in the windows of shops, in
manure-fragrant stables, in the rubble of demolished buildings,
in the ruins of fire-swept lofts, in open manholes (one could
climb down into them at noon when the men working there
knocked off for lunch). In the oppressive heat of summer, one
could revel in the deliciously painful sensation of running
barefoot over melting asphalt or stand bravely in the path of a
huge hose the street-cleaners trained on the garbage-strewn,
burning streets. Threatening skies, thunder and lightning,
cloudbursts, sheets of slanting rain that one watched from the
protective vantage of doorways and from behind windows or
boldly went out to meet in the hope that one would be observed and admired—all these manifestations of mysterious
power one enjoyed with uneasy delight. Walking barefoot
along the gutters in the rain, with the water gurgling over
one's toes, as it washed over the pebbles in the illustration of a
country scene in a story in *McGuffey's Reader*, the delicious
feel of wet garments, one's face upturned to the pelting skies
and one's mouth open to catch refreshing drops of rain—
these offered untroubled delights. In the late fall, one could
look forward to the week of Succoth, when my father would
construct a shelter close to the row of toilets in the back yard
and cover it with pine branches. Here we would have all our
meals, even on cold days or when it rained. This was decidedly
life in the open! Sitting at supper in the rustic hut, with the
rain leaking through the prickly foliage, gave one a sense of
communion with nature and the elements and, indeed, of
being a member of some close-knit, savage tribe. To pass
from the thatched structure in the yard into Rutgers Square
was an instant transition from barbarism to civilization.

In winter the rim of the big basin of the fountain was coated with ice, and I could walk on it gingerly, balancing myself with my hands like a man on a tightrope, to the admiration of my little sister, who watched me from our window across the street. One day I slipped in the act. She saw me fall and raised an alarm, and my mother rushed out and carried me into the house. The accident left a scar on my eyelid which for some years I could point to as a proof of my recklessness and daring. A few of the well-to-do boys (the sons of doctors) owned sleds, which they agreed to share with us on pain of being expelled from the East Broadwayers. The first snowfall always arrived on Thanksgiving Day (or so it seems now), and the time not spent in school was taken up in snowball fights and in making snowmen and building fortifications, enormous in size and elaborately constructed for defense. After successfully withstanding an attack that lasted till supper time, it was pleasant to be at home at night, lie on the warm floor face down near the stove in the kitchen, and give oneself up to the delights of *McGuffey's Reader*. Soon the sweet, fetid, airless, autointoxicating atmosphere of the overheated room would take possession of the senses and one would slide into a profound sleep, from which even violent shaking by one's mother and the command to "wake up and go to sleep" could not pry one loose.

CHAPTER FIVE

The Theater

WHEN I joined my comrades in taunting the lovers on the benches by the Rutgers Square fountain, I was also aware, through hearsay, that the world of the theater on Grand Street and the Bowery was, morally, quite untrammeled. Rumors came to my ears of fascinating irregularities in the lives of the chief personages of the Yiddish stage. The relish with which these rumors were heard by all but very old and very orthodox people, who shunned the theater on principle, proved that the stage was a world apart, one not subject to the moral code of the world around me. If what one heard could be believed, actors led as fabulous an existence in real life as in the theater. For one thing, they took their marriages lightly. It was said that the rival male stars of Grand Street and the Bowery negotiated among themselves an exchange of wives for a limited period, after which interlude

the lawfully wedded couples returned to their former mates.
In this way, over a period of time, the chief protagonists of the
Jewish drama got to know each other very well. For this
reason I determined to be a great actor when I grew up. All
my playmates did too.

On my excursions from Stanton Street to the Bowery I had
often passed the Windsor and Thalia theaters and had been
fascinated by the posters and photographs that adorned their
façades and lobbies. And now, in our house on East Broadway
and from the benches of the fountain, I heard talk of these
theaters and the new one on Grand Street, of the plays performed there and the leading players in them. I longed to
know more about people who each night, and on Saturday and
Sunday afternoons, assumed the guise of a variety of personalities, none of them resembling their own in the least. I learned
to know their faces from their photographs in the Jewish
daily, *Der Tog*, which my parents read, and from further
examination of the exterior and lobbies of the East Side play-
houses. Long before I saw them in the flesh, I was familiar
with the faces and figures of Bessie Thomashefsky, her even
more famous spouse, Boris, Jacob Adler and his ravishing
wife and fellow Thespian, Sarah, the tragedienne Mrs. K.
Lipzin, the great Kessler, who generally played opposite her,
and the lovely and gentle Bertha Kalich, with whose picture
on a window card I fell in love at first sight.

Among comedians there was the inimitable Mogilewsky,
whose very look as Kooneylemul on a poster would send me
into fits of laughter. Kooneylemul was a lovable character
whose incredible imbecility and side-splitting simplicity and
innocence could not conceal the most generous of natures and a
pathetic belief in the essential goodness of the crass world in
which he lived. The comedy was called *The Two Kooneylemuls*, but at this distance I can recall the presence of only
one Kooneylemul. I presume the other Kooneylemul was a
pretender (like the false Dimitri in *Boris Godunov*), who was

probably unmasked, at the denouement, by the genuine Kooneylemul. At any rate, Mogilewsky became wholly identified with the grotesque, lovable Kooneylemul, and, along with the stars I have enumerated, became the object of my veneration.

By chance *Hamlet* was the very first play I was taken to see. My two elder sisters had obtained passes for a Sunday matinee performance at the Grand Street Theater. People went to the theater only on passes because no one, apparently, could afford to purchase tickets. At least, I never knew anyone who bought one. Passes were obtained in several ways. The most common was to induce a shopkeeper on Grand Street, Canal Street, or Hester Street to relinquish his allotment by offering to make an immediate purchase of something in his shop or promising to make one on the very next payday. The passes were given out to shopkeepers in exchange for permission to display window cards advertising the week's attractions at the theaters. By patronizing and cajoling certain shopkeepers, my sisters became frequent patrons of the drama.

On this particular Sunday I experienced a craving to implement my theoretical knowledge of the stage and its players. Accordingly, I begged to be taken along, and when I was denied, on the absurd pretext of my extreme youth, I wept and screamed and barred the door to all egress. My mother interceding for me, and the time growing late, my oldest sister relinquished her pass in my favor, and my other sister and I ran at top speed to the Grand Street Theater. Our passes called for places in the gallery near the ceiling, and presently we were seated. For the first time in my life I beheld the inside of a theater. I sat and gazed in wonder at the vast interior, rich in ornament, at the dark-red curtain painted to look like the two halves of a lush, heavy drapery slightly parted at the bottom, with golden fringes outlining each half, the whole embraced by a heavy golden rope looped at the ends. The audience was still arriving, and there appeared to

be some confusion in the seating, for we had no sooner been
been shown to our places than other claimants for our seats
turned up, and on our being asked to show our stubs it was
found that ours and those of the newcomers called for the
same seats. As the less aggressive of the disputants, we
relinquished our seats at the suggestion of the usher and were
led to an unreserved section of the gallery, even closer to the
ceiling.

I could see that similar disturbances were taking place in
every section of the theater. Some people were being pulled
bodily out of their seats. The clamor of the opposing forces
intermittently filled the air or was lost in the even louder
shouts of the candy-, fruit-, and beer-vendors, who did not
hesitate to climb over people in efforts to dispose of their
wares. The noise was at its height when it was suddenly
pierced by the sound of music issuing from the direction of the
stage. I stood up in my seat and, looking down into the abyss
beneath me, saw—as if through the wrong end of a telescope—
a group of little figures huddled below the stage, playing
instruments of various sorts under the direction of a man
facing them. It was my first encounter with orchestral music,
my first acquaintance with the "Overture." I was to hear this
overture innumerable times during my theatergoing days, for
the pit orchestras were loath to exert themselves unduly, and
their repertoire was, in consequence, a limited one. The
Overture to *Zampa* or *Light Cavalry*, I was to discover,
served to ring up the curtain in all theaters and on all plays.
It was *Zampa* that now struggled to rise above the general din,
and at last succeeded in making itself heard. At its conclusion
there was deafening applause, in which I enthusiastically
joined, for what I heard was lovely indeed. The conductor
bowed to us innumerable times, quite oblivious of the noise of
stamping feet which now began to be heard from every part
of the house. This expression of impatience on the part of the
audience had its effect. The lights suddenly went out, the

curtain alone remaining illuminated by some curious agency.
Cries of "Sh—! Shut up!" and "Sit down!" were exchanged on
all sides. The vendors of fruits and liquids reluctantly retreated toward the rear and the house gradually subsided into
comparative silence. The play was about to begin, and I was
overcome with emotion. The leader of the orchestra rapped
for a still greater silence. He signaled his men to begin. A
brassy fanfare rose plangent on the hushed air, and with it the
curtain ascended. But when it was halfway up, it stopped and,
to my distress, would go no farther. But in a moment I had
forgotten the curtain and was lost in the wonders its partial
ascent revealed.

Semidarkness lay like a pall on a structure whose like I had
never before seen. Dim personages in capes brandished swords
and spoke oratorically in words I could not quite understand.
Yet I felt certain that momentous events were about to take
place, and I braced myself for the shock of a revelation that
could not long be withheld. And then the event that I both
dreaded and longed to see suddenly took shape as a faint,
sickly yellow light pierced the surrounding gloom and disclosed an eerie figure clad in diaphanous armor. I knew only
too well that I was looking at a ghost—strangely attired, but
beyond a certainty a ghost. "Gamlet," it said distinctly, in
Yiddish, "I am your father's ghost." And with Hamlet I
listened, with mounting horror, to the piteous tale of fratri-
cide. But how incredibly brave of Hamlet to confront alone a
ghost, no matter how closely related, bathed in unnatural
light, at dead of night! I now began to surmise the intention
of the plot, and could hardly wait for the scene that would put
everything to rights. But the author seemed most reluctant to
bring to a head the conflict he had set in motion at the beginning of the play. I was mystified and annoyed by solilo-
quies that brought matters no nearer to a solution. What *was*
wrong with Hamlet? Why did he put off, scene after scene,
the execution of the revenge he had at the outset resolved to

take? Why was he so cruel to Miss Kalich, his sweetheart, whose lovely air of innocent bewilderment broke my heart, and why, after a show of explosive anger, was he so lenient with his mother? I should certainly, under similar provocation, have behaved differently.

A change of scene now disclosed a cemetery and two men digging a grave. I had never before seen a cemetery or a grave, but I knew what they were, and they were as horrifying to behold as a ghost. And now, at last, Hamlet assumed again the boldness he had shown at his first encounter with the ghost. He fondled and apostrophized a horrible skull. And when he heard the shocking news—shocking to me, too—that the grave was being dug for the corpse of Miss Kalich, he leaped into the pit with no signs of fear at all. From that point on, the author, abandoning his former delaying tactics, moved swiftly to the denouement, and in the final scene of revenge and universal carnage he more than atoned for the inexplicable hesitations that had marred the greater portion of the play.

That night I could hardly sleep, for when I shut my eyes, the ghost stood before me and beckoned me to follow him; and to rid myself of his presence I quickly opened my eyes on the reassuring, dim outlines of the kitchen where I slept. In the daytime I could dwell on the ghost without fear, but on coming home from play at night I would run up the three flights of stairs with a beating heart and burst into the house like one pursued by a fiend, as indeed I was. A tiny gas-jet burned on the wall of each landing, and the faint yellow light it feebly spread was the *same* that had enveloped the ghost of Hamlet's father!

I do not recall seeing any other play by Shakespeare in my playgoing childhood on the East Side. But adaptations of some of the more celebrated tragedies were frequently given, and enjoyed great popularity. In their new guise the plays dealt with contemporary Jewish life in Russia or America. No one suspected their source, for the authors gave no hint of their indebtedness. The exception was *Der Yiddisher Koenig Lear* (*The Jewish King Lear*), one of Mr. Adler's great vehicles. While carefully omitting the name of the creator of the non-Jewish King Lear, the author of *The Jewish King Lear* hinted, if only to the cognoscenti, at his obligation to his fellow playwright. *Der Yeshiva Bocher* (*The Talmudic Student*), another favorite with East Side playgoers, contained no reference of any kind to Shakespeare, yet it seemed to me very like *Hamlet*. For the Talmudic student, on coming home from his religious studies afar, found that his beloved father had died, and that his mother was now married to his late father's brother. The story pursued its Shakespearean course, greatly to my astonishment. And when the play was over, I was obliged to concede that irresolution and inaction were more consistent with the character of the gentle, retiring student of the Talmud than with that of the Prince of Denmark. Even so, *Der Yeshiva Bocher* was a plain case of plagiarism, and I wondered whether the author was troubled about his deception.

Perhaps I enjoyed *Der Yiddisher Koenig Lear* more than I did *Der Yeshiva Bocher* because of its author's implied acknowledgment of his source; and never having seen the English *King Lear*, I had nothing to compare it with. This gave the advantage to the Yiddish version. The Jewish King Lear was, strangely enough, no king at all, but a wealthy old man who foolishly (to the disgust of his body-servant, a joking individual who, nevertheless, was devoted to his master) parceled out all his worldly goods among his three daughters and subsequently met the same fate as the legendary Briton.

I can remember one powerful scene that brought down the curtain and the house. The old man, now quite disillusioned, had suffered every indignity that the wicked ingenuity of his two elder daughters and their husbands could contrive. They had even deprived him of his facetious but devoted retainer Shamai, who was confined to the kitchen and given degrading chores. The climax of the play was now due. I cannot recall the nature of the final indignity. Could the patriarch have pleaded for a drink of water and been denied? Whatever it was, the old man suddenly drew himself up to his full height and, in a voice of thunder, commanded the housekeeper to deliver up the keys. This the astonished steward reluctantly did. And now the old man turned his fury on his daughters and sons-in-law and a large number of guests who came into the room.

"Out of my house!" he roared. "Out! Out!" Everyone fled in astonishment and dismay. He then called for his old retainer, who, dirty and in rags, came running toward him, weeping for joy. "Shamai," the old man cried, and he, too, wept as he spoke, "good, faithful Shamai, you will serve me again as of old. Yes, Shamai, I was a fool. I should have heeded your advice, but I didn't. I trusted in the goodness of my elder daughters, but I was blind to the goodness of Goldele, my youngest. But I have now returned to my senses. I have taken everything back. Yes, Shamai, we shall live again like men. We shall be happy again, Shamai." And the old man put his arms around Shamai and they clung to each other and wept loudly and hysterically as the curtain descended. The audience, too, abandoned all restraint, and people all over the house cried without shame.

In the last act the Yiddisher Koenig Lear was united with the gentle Goldele, impersonated by my adored Miss Kalich. I had now seen Miss Kalich in a number of roles, all of which exploited her charm, her innocence, and her unearthly beauty. I thought wildly of becoming an actor so that I might always be near her and perhaps in time marry her.

Aside from Miss Kalich, the actors I liked best were Mrs. K. Lipzin, David Kessler, and Jacob P. Adler. Both Kessler and Adler had the grand manner. They played at will on people's heartstrings, and audiences wept audibly in their big moments. Perhaps Kessler was more protean than Adler.

Like Adler, he could rise to a great climax, but he was also effective in quieter moments. Yet Adler's climaxes exceeded Kessler's in power and virtuosity. His gradual crescendo of invective and passion in the big scene from *Der Yiddisher Koenig Lear* was a shattering experience for an audience. Kessler, it is true, rose to great heights in the excommunication scene in *Uriel Acosta*, when he defied his rabbinical persecutors with passionate scorn. But he lacked the unabashed grandeur that Adler could summon in heroic roles.

Then, too, Adler was highly effective in seriocomic roles, in those comedy dramas which portrayed the difficulties of emigrants from the Old World in becoming adjusted to the American scene. These plays, known to us as *lebensbilder* (portraits from life), offered an equal proportion of laughter and tears, and were perhaps the most popular type of drama on the East Side. And, indeed, they were true to life in the sense that many such adjustments to a new environment were set in motion with the arrival of every steamer from Europe. In these plays the pious older people shrank from the unorthodox, materialistic, feverish, competitive life in the New World and insisted on clinging to the religious practices and the moral code of the world they had left. The young people, on the other hand, succumbed easily to the blandishments of their new environment. The inevitable conflict between old and new, age and youth, orthodoxy and heterodoxy and even, perhaps, theism, unfolding on the stage, had for the audience the excitement of recognition, as did also the familiar realistic touches of incident and character the authors astutely added.

"The baby is crying," Mr. Adler, playing the husband, remarked to Mrs. Adler, playing the wife in a scene from a *lebensbild* whose name I've forgotten. "Well," Mrs. Adler, busy with recognizable household chores, replied, with a show of scorn for male ineptitude familiar to every husband in the audience, "he probably wants to *pee!* Pick him up." The author had captured a bit of naturalism familiar to everyone.

And Mrs. Adler's tart admonition to her husband, who now held the baby awkwardly in his arms—"Run, or it will be *too late*"—set the entire house rocking with laughter and people commenting: "How true!" or "A real *lebensbild*, a slice of life!"

This play dealt with the familiar theme, with Mr. and Mrs. Adler attempting to hold the balance between Jewish orthodoxy, in the person of a pious old grandfather, and rebellion and Americanization, as represented by their teen-age son and daughter. In scene after scene the young people scoffed at religion, at parental and grandparental authority, and at old-fashioned decorum, proclaiming the advantages of nonconformity and insisting on the individual's unobstructed pursuit of happiness as guaranteed by the Declaration of Independence. A favorite device of the playwrights of the period was the frequent repetition of a phrase until it became identified with the personage whose line it had become. Such phrases were especially designed to be remembered by audiences, who would murmur them to themselves after the play, much as patrons of musical shows, on leaving the theater, hum snatches of tunes they have been hearing. So the young daughter would always wind up her defiance of the Old World and her defense of the New with the memorable words: "This is the *United States of America, that's all*." Her brother, sporting a wing collar, a fancy vest, and a straw hat with a string attached, interspersed American expressions in his speech, which were familiar even to the latest arrivals in New York harbor. "Don'tcha know" concluded every sentence. And "Go chase yourself," "Business is business," and "Time is money" were given out with delightful frequency. Of course, we knew that the young people would get into trouble, the girl romantically, the youth through his association with godless, thoroughly Americanized "bums and loafers," as his grandfather called them. The climax arrived at the moment of their contrition, and here the author revealed his knowledge of the psychology of the human heart. For in that moment of sincerity the young blade eschewed all his glib American expressions and spoke exclusively in *"Mamma Loschen"* (his native tongue, Yiddish). And his sister, weeping and calling for understanding and help from the relations she had so often mocked and derided, now made no reference to the United States of America or to the unhindered Pursuit of Happiness guaranteed by the Declaration of Independence.

Although Miss Kalich reigned supreme in my heart, I was able to recognize genius and even merit in her rivals. Mrs. K. Lipzin, appearing without fanfare one day in a tragic work called *Die Schechitte* (*The Butchery*), quite overwhelmed me with a display of emotional tension and an outburst of passion such as I had never before witnessed. Mrs. Lipzin was neither so young nor so lovely as Miss Kalich, but her sharp personality easily surmounted these handicaps. The play seemed especially designed to exploit her peculiar powers of both understatement and savage fury. In the first act her father bade her become affianced to an aging, cruel, and insensitive shochet (rabbinical butcher). Mrs. Lipzin moved across the stage as in a trance. She spoke only sparingly, but every word she uttered was heavy with portent. "Will you have a glass of tea?" she said in a low voice to one of the characters. It was obvious that she was not thinking of tea at all at the moment, but of something vastly more significant. She seemed a quiet and obedient daughter. She voiced no objections to her elderly suitor, but her self-possession, she made us feel, was only a triumph of art, for she could not possibly love the shochet. Thus far the act had been quietly expository. It was time for the curtain to fall, but nothing of a dramatic nature had occurred. Mrs. K. Lipzin stood facing a cupboard, her back to us, a plate in her hand. She was about to set the table for supper. In a room off-stage her father and the shochet were completing the business details of the match.

That done, the pair came on stage, unseen by Mrs. Lipzin. "*Mazeltov!* (Congratulations!)" the father called out. At the word, Mrs. Lipzin, still with her back to us, stiffened, the plate dropped from her hand and crashed to the floor, and she emitted a single, bloodcurdling shriek, then remained silent and frozen—as the curtain fell and rose a dozen times. We all wildly acclaimed a great new star and a new and powerful dramatist, whoever he was.

The second act found Mrs. Lipzin married to the shochet, and once again she underplayed at first, reserving her strength for what the second curtain might hold in store for her. Her restraint would have us believe that she had adjusted herself to a loveless marriage to a lecherous despot. It was made clear that her husband took a sadistic rather than a professional interest in ritual butchery. At one point he sharpened a long, gleaming butcher's knife with an expression of savage anticipation. He then left the stage on some pretext, but we knew it was to leave Mrs. Lipzin alone on the stage for her big moment. It was not long in coming. Mrs. Lipzin, artfully simulating unconcern, took up the knife and ran a finger along the edge to test its sharpness. Then, of a sudden, her body became rigid. The knife dropped from her hands and she let out an even more terrifying shriek than at the end of the first act. And again she stood paralyzed, staring into vacancy, while the audience cheered.

The third-act curtain, with Mrs. Lipzin again alone on the stage, was even more powerful, though I do not remember what exactly motivated that shriek. But the fourth-act curtain is indelibly printed on my memory. During a great part of the act the shochet had been unusually irascible, showing his displeasure with cruel and taunting remarks to his wife. At length, it having grown late, he retired for the night, slamming the door after him. Mrs. Lipzin, again left alone, opened her husband's case of knives, extracted the longest she could find, ran her finger up and down its edge, and walked rigidly into the bedchamber. There ensued a breathless silence. Mrs. Lipzin emerged from the bedchamber, the knife—now blood-stained—still in her hand. She walked calmly to the center of the stage and stood there, looking into space. Then she screamed. Of the four screams of that matinee, it was the most harrowing. Yet the real climax was to follow. Mrs. Lipzin now pointed the dripping blade toward heaven. *"Die schechitte! Die schechitte!"* she cried hoarsely, and broke into maniacal laughter. The curtain came down. Never had the Jewish theater witnessed such a triumph.

Playgoing had its lighter side in the musical comedies that alternated with the tragedies and comedy dramas of the *lebensbild* type. It must not be supposed, however, that the musicals were all sunshine and laughter. They, too, were founded on the universal theme of the Yiddish stage, the Russian Jewish immigrant and his difficulties in America. And while there was plenty of music and dancing and a humor unblushingly extravagant, pathos was always in the offing, and a person might have as good a cry at a comedy with music as at an out-and-out tragedy.

The musicals generally opened with a scene laid in Russia. A religious festival was being celebrated in ritual song and dance by devout persons with long earlocks and dressed in fur-trimmed caps and long satin robes. In due course, the hosts of the party, an aged rabbi and his wife, were prevailed on to dance a *pas de deux*, which they executed with a hearty agility that belied their years. At one point the dance took a romantic turn, with the rabbi offering to embrace his wife, who provokingly eluded his grasp, feigning distaste and anger. The rabbi, thus repulsed, danced dejectedly alone for a while. Whereupon the rabbi's wife relented and coquettishly threw her bandanna handkerchief at him as a sign of renewed favor. Nothing pleased audiences at musical plays more than the love-making of old people.

By the second act, the entire cast had been transported to

New York, their garments, but not their characters, changed. Now they recalled nostalgically, in song and dance, the delights of the simple, pious life they had left behind them. Yet the new surroundings failed to dampen the rabbi's amorousness or his wife's flirtatiousness. Younger romance was now provided by the attraction for each other of a brash, thoroughly Americanized young woman and a timid young student of the Talmud, freshly arrived and still clinging to his earlocks and gabardine. As for comedy, one laughed incessantly at the attempts of the older characters to learn English and their ludicrous inability to cope with New World marvels like illuminating gas, which they tried to shut off by *blowing* at it.

Mr. and Mrs. Thomashefsky were the most noted exponents of these musical plays. Their fame as singing comedians was comparable to the renown enjoyed by the handful of straight dramatic stars. Mr. Thomashefsky had, in fact, become the romantic idol of the East Side. Young men strove to look like him by growing their hair long and combing it into a pompadour. I thought he was a bit too plump for a romantic idol, but I had to admit that his voice was "made of silk," as the papers said. About Mrs. Thomashefsky I had no reservations whatsoever, though she too was plump. She was particularly enchanting in a musical play in which she disguised herself as a young bootblack. Barefoot and in tatters, a shoeshine box slung over her shoulder, she slouched around the stage with charming insolence, calling out in English, "Shine! Shine! A nickel a shine!" It did not take long for Mr. Thomashefsky, as a rich and pampered young man about town, to suspect her true sex. At their first meeting, as she shined his shoes, they sang a duet in which she confessed her admiration for him, and he wished, with all the pathos of his silken voice, that she were a *girl*. Copies of this song, with oval pictures of the celebrated pair on the cover, were on display in the window of Katz's music store on East Broadway, a few doors from where I lived.

My appetite for the theater was insatiable, and I stopped at nothing, even theft, to obtain the coveted passes. Several times I extracted my sister's pass from her pocketbook when she was out of the room, and by the time the loss was discovered I was well on my way to Grand Street or the Bowery. I had no preferences and reveled in every variety of play. I even yearned to attend a performance at Miner's Theater, an English-speaking playhouse on the Bowery, near the Windsor and the Thalia. The posters at Miner's advertised an entertainment called Burlesque, and featured plump ladies in disturbing garments, and funny-looking clowns. As no Yiddish was spoken at Miner's, its patrons, I assumed, were necessarily Christians. At any rate, Miner's had no window cards in the shops, and passes were therefore not available.

At home I indulged in play-acting myself when no one was around. By the time I had witnessed three performances of *Hamlet* with Mr. Kessler as the hero and had become familiar with the text, I was obliged to revise my original estimate of Shakespeare as only an intermittently inspired playwright. I had memorized, "*Sein, oder nit Sein?—dos is die Kashe!*" ("To be, or not to be: that is the question"), which I now prized for its music, the sense still eluding me; and, pretending that my long underwear approximated Mr. Kessler's tights, I would walk thoughtfully up and down the room reciting the soliloquy and imitating every gesture and intonation I could recall. I even pronounced the Yiddish words grandiloquently so that it sounded like German, a practice adopted by the great actors and actresses when they appeared in such poetic classics as *Hamlet*, *Medea*, and *The Robbers of Schiller* (it was long before I found out that *The Robbers of Schiller* was not merely the title of the play, but included the name of the author). Thus, instead of saying "*es is ah liegen* (it is a lie),"

Mr. Kessler would orate ostentatiously, in what we assumed
to be German: *"Es ist ein Leege!"* I should also have liked
to do a bit from *Medea*, but I never saw that tragedy, my
courage having failed me when I heard that that passionate
woman, made desperate by the defection of her peripatetic
lover, proceeded to tear her (and his) children limb from
limb in full view of the audience! I did, however, act out
choice bits of *The Two Kooneylemuls* in appropriate garb, and
I borrowed an old dress of my mother's and a bread knife
to do Mrs. Lipzin's great murder scene in *Die Schechitte*.
And slinging a cardboard box over my shoulder, I slouched
around barefoot, and in a feminine falsetto cried: "Shine!
Shine! A nickel a shine!"

CHAPTER SIX

Euterpe on Henry Street

O<small>N MY</small> way to and from Public School No. 2, I often stopped to listen to the sound of a piano issuing from the basement of a brownstone house on Henry Street near where I lived. I was ten years old. I had no knowledge of music beyond the ability to read the treble clef in the simple part-songs we were taught at No. 2 and sang on certain occasions in assembly. But I was able to identify the music issuing from the basement, either as technical exercises or "pieces." One or two of my playmates had pianos in their homes, and I got to know by sight and sound two books of finger exercises called, respectively, "Beyer" and "Hanon." One could begin the study of the piano only with Beyer's Book. It was when one reached a certain page in it, somewhere I think near the halfway mark, that Hanon's became mandatory as an adjunct to it.

The "pieces" I heard were, too, for the most part familiar
to me. I knew by name about a half-dozen, the sounds of which
reached me as I played in the streets in spring and summer.
They were for me not only marvels of melodic grace but,
more important, musical embodiments of familiar ideas and
images. There was, for example, *Lilly*, one of my favorites.
Did the composer have in mind a girl or a flower? At first I
inclined toward the flower. But when I got to know a girl of
that name, I was certain that he had in mind a Lilly as fragile
and tender as the one I knew. Actually, the "piece" could
easily be a celebration of either, or to go a step farther, as I
often did in those days, of all girls and all flowers. I felt that
music of the caliber of *Lilly* and *A Mother's Prayer* had a
special dimension that placed it above all other forms of art.
It was a dimension I found impossible to define but I was
conscious of its presence each time I heard *A Mother's
Prayer*. In this extraordinary composition the composer had
undertaken to reveal, by the use of a simple melody and its
transformation first in arpeggios, then in octaves, and finally
in repeated octaves, a mother's heart with all its hopes and
fears. It offered unlimited scope to the imagination of the
listener. After all, no two mothers were alike, even though
their hopes and fears were fundamentally the same. Certainly
my mother was quite different from the mothers of the boys
and girls I knew. The wonder for me was that the composer
of *A Mother's Prayer* had caught, without having ever met her,
the very special quality of my mother's hopes and fears.

The Burning of Rome, another favorite, was of a different
order. Less emotionally disturbing than *A Mother's Prayer*, it
was a musical piece of realism which never failed to grip one.
The title page, with its picture in color of the ancient city
enveloped in lurid flames and the toga-clad and laurel-
crowned obese figure of Nero gleefully plucking a harp as he
stood on an apparently safe superstructure in the background,
offered an appropriate foretaste of the musical interpretation

of that sadistic concert. The composer, quite properly reluctant to trust the historical knowledge of the player and his audience, had scattered at various places in the composition verbal hints of what the music was about. They were meant to provide, in addition to historical information, suggestions to the executant for a realistic interpretation of the scene, and for this the printed words were ideal. For myself, I felt that the full impact of *The Burning of Rome* could only be experienced by standing behind the performer and reading these comments over his shoulder. I can see them vividly before me, as I did half a century ago. "Rome lies deep in slumber. . . . A sound of chariot wheels is heard in the distance. . . . What is that faint gleam in the distance? . . . The sky is now alight. . . . Fire? Fire!! . . . The flames sweep the Eternal City. . . . Rome, roused from its slumber, flees! . . . But who is that strange figure on the balcony? . . . It is the Emperor. . . . The tyrant Nero! . . ."

There were other tone poems of equal power, fully annotated and realistically illustrated. I knew *Ben Hur's Chariot Race* long before I heard about the book. Ben Hur, a handsome Roman with a ribbon around his brow, leaning forward in his two-wheeled chariot and urging his horses on to victory! There was *The Chicago Fire*, minutely documented from Mrs. Leary and her cow to the destruction that ensued; the *Sinking of the Battleship Maine*, and some other violently descriptive "pieces" that I can no longer recall. In time I was to become aware of the music of Bach and Beethoven, Chopin and Liszt; for the lower East Side of my era was a cultural center full of earnest students of all the arts as well as incipient gangsters. But in my tenth year I was drawn exclusively to programmatic music of the kind I have tried to describe.

If I spent a good deal of my spare time in the vicinity of the piano teacher's basement on Henry Street, playing hopscotch so as not to arouse the curiosity of my playmates and the people who always sat on stoops, I did not neglect East

tion was that of an intercepter. On the day of the week on which an installment fell due, I would be stationed on the street to watch for the approach of the collector. When he appeared, I would give him the quarter or plead for a postponement. I was on no account to let him enter the house.

No, this was certainly no time even to dream about owning one of Spector's shining pianos. As I turned away from the plate-glass window, I wondered if there ever would be a time. Money was not the only barrier. There was also my father, who regarded all secular music as noise and all instrumentalists as disturbers of the peace. If I were ever to learn to play the piano, it would have to be away from home and managed as secretly as my mother's installment buying.

Katz's music store, next in importance for me to Spector's piano store, was a smaller shop, but equally dream-provoking. Its window display featured copies of many of my favorite compositions, notably *Lilly* and *A Mother's Prayer*; also the piano methods of Beyer and Hanon. The store had a reputation as a hangout for musical notables, and the composer of *A Mother's Prayer* was a frequent caller. The celebrated baritone Beniamino Burgo would also drop in to examine the latest publications for his type of voice. Burgo, I learned, had had a fascinating and meteoric career. Only a year before, he had worked under his own name of Benjamin Ginzburg as a sign-painter in the neighborhood. Mr. Katz had heard him sing while at work, and had brought him to the attention of a famous Italian vocal teacher residing on East Broadway. After a year of intensive study with the Maestro, and with his name transformed, Beniamino Burgo had made his debut at a concert and ball at Pythagoras Hall, a few doors from Spector's. His success had been phenomenal, and now there was hardly a concert or ball that did not feature him as its main attraction. It was rumored that his popularity had gone to his head, and that he now avoided the company of his former friends and (in winter) affected a coat with a fur collar, a "soft" hat with a large brim, and a nickel-topped cane.

All the really important musical events took place in Pythagoras Hall, a vast room that also housed large-scale weddings and the better-class *bar mitzvahs*. The concerts were invariably followed by balls, and the two were considered as entities. A concert was a most generous entertainment that usually lasted from eight in the evening to midnight, after which the seats were removed in preparation for the ensuing ball. The participating artists were numerous, and as I watched them one night brush past the ticket-taker at the entrance, uttering the single word "Talent" by way of identification, the idea came to me that the word could be an "Open sesame" to me too. At the very next concert and ball I presented myself, armed with a bundle of wrapping paper that looked like a roll of music, at the gate of Pythagoras Hall, spoke the magic word, and was admitted without further inquiry. It was at that concert and ball that I had the good fortune to hear Beniamino Burgo sing and instantly repeat, by popular demand, the "Toreador Song" from *Carmen.*

If one's taste also ran to literary celebrities, and mine did, we could watch them enter or leave Malkin's bookstore, a few doors from Pythagoras Hall. The window of this shop was cluttered with volumes of the world's best literature from the earliest times to the present. One could spell out the authors and titles on the backs or fronts of cloth- and paper-bound books: Shakespeare, Shelley, Byron, Goethe, Heine, Tolstoy, Turgeniev. There were framed portraits of poets, painters, musicians, philosophers, and revolutionaries. The name of Michael Bakunin identified a portrait of a truly terrifying man, wild and disheveled, with blazing eyes. And next to him, a picture of the benign and affable Ivan Turgeniev, whose complete works dominated the window. Of all the great men on display there, I picked Turgeniev as my

looked forward to the weekly appearances of Miss Tinker, visiting music teacher at No. 2. Miss Tinker was a small, prim, quite unprepossessing woman with graying hair parted in the middle and tied in a knot at the back. She generated a melancholy that the mournful sound of the pitch-pipe on which she always sounded a preliminary C, and her own hollow falsetto as she repeated it, made more depressing. But she was a capable teacher and an expert in the intricacies of part-singing. Her repertoire of part-songs was extensive. Among other things, she taught us what I considered a poignant arrangement in two-part harmony of "The Lord Is My Shepherd." I was among the altos, and when we sang "I sha-ha-ha-hal nah-hot want" in florid counterpoint under the forthright, severe ascending melody of the sopranos, the effect, at least to me, was shattering.

Miss Tinker opened new vistas in music. But it was Mr. Strassmeir who, unconsciously, gave direction to my love for the art. The piano was to be my instrument because it was his. My mastery of it would, I hoped and believed, break down his indifference to me, compel him to recognize me as a true disciple and treat me with the courtesy, if not the affection, due a co-worker in the realms of art and humanitarianism. A definite picture of the great moment when I would stand thus revealed to Mr. Strassmeir had begun to take shape in my mind: the school would be on the point of marching into assembly, and Mr. Strassmeir would be about ready to strike the opening chords of the march, when he would be seen to falter. Mr. Denscher, standing at his lectern near by, prepared to read his daily passage from the Bible, would turn to the stricken teacher and help him into an adjoining room. He would come back a moment later to tell us that Mr. Strassmeir had suffered a slight attack of dizziness and to assure us he would soon be all right. In the meantime he would call on any student or teacher who could play the piano to step forward. I would then leave my place in the line and make my way to

pages addressed to "The Teacher," and opened it to a picture of a keyboard with the letters a, b, c, d, e, f, g, identifying the white keys. As I picked out the corresponding notes on the piano, I could not help reflecting for a moment on Miss Taffel's utter lack of curiosity about me. She had not asked me my name, my address, or what school I attended!

I learned the treble and bass clefs very quickly, and in no time arrived at the little exercises in finger technique disguised and made palatable to the beginner by provocative titles like "Little Polka," "The Running Brook," and "Little Dog Chasing His Tail." Miss Taffel never wasted a word. Her lesson lasted exactly one hour, not a minute more or less, as I could see by a kitchen clock that stood on the piano. Her efficiency was beyond question, but her impersonal attitude, toward both me and music, seemed increasingly strange in a disciple of an art that I considered the most emotional of all. Either she was unaware of the poetic flavor of the titles of the little pieces she taught me or she deliberately chose to consider only the technical problems they illuminated. When I essayed, on my own, a bit of poetic realism in the "Little Dog Chasing His Tail" by speeding up the tempo toward the end, Miss Taffel implied her disapproval by beginning to count four in a bar in very strict time, in her sharp, impersonal voice. When, during my practice period, alone in the room, I might yield to some poetic impulse and indulge in "interpretation," the old lady who had answered the doorbell the very first time I rang it would put her head through the door and say: "My daughter says you shouldn't."

Miss Taffel was out a good deal of the time giving piano lessons to pupils in their homes. She shared the dark basement with her mother and an older brother, whose querulous voice often reached me from some back room in the house. I gathered he did no work of any sort and was content to let the entire support of the household devolve on his sister. The two were in a perpetual state of war, and their recriminations in the back room sometimes grew so loud as to drown out the sound of the piano. At the height of these, Miss Taffel would command her brother to leave the premises and never return. But he scorned the suggestion as having no relation at all to the settlement of whatever it was they were quarreling about. Miss Taffel was soulless and mercenary, but less so than her brother. One winter afternoon, when the room grew so dark that I could not see the music before me, strain as I might, she came in and lit the gas-jet. I had hardly time to thank her when her brother rushed in, gave her a withering look, turned off the gas, and ran out. Miss Taffel followed him, and the noise of their quarrel seeped into the front room as I struggled in the gloom to decipher the new piece I was learning.

I finished Beyer's Book in what some of Miss Taffel's pupils assured me was record time, but there was never a word of praise from Miss Taffel herself. I went on to Burg-mueller's Book, a collection of twenty-four veritable tone poems, one to a page, excepting the last, which required two full pages for the complete exposition of its poetic idea. At the same time, I was given sheet music, some with haunting titles, but all of them embodying technical problems. *The Alpine Shepherd's Evening Song*, by a German composer whose name I cannot recall, was a poignantly evocative piece that I never grew tired of playing. Nor can I remember the technical problem it posed. The picture on the cover showed a mountainous landscape resembling that in the picture of *Napoleon Crossing the Alps* over the piano. Its mood, however, was beautifully idyllic. The shepherd, having presumably rounded up his flock, sat on the ground, playing his rustic pipe while the setting sun cast a beautiful sad glow over the landscape. The piece itself was built on a lovely melody expressive of the gentleness of the shepherd's immemorial occupation, and a series of bell-like echo effects evoked the rarefied atmosphere of the Alpine countryside in summer. So touching was this pastoral music idyl that I seldom got through the piece dry-eyed. How different from the somber effect of *Napoleon Crossing the Alps*! There was, it is true, something heroic about this picture, the indomitable will of the general, perhaps, as indicated in the stocky figure, muffled up to the neck and astride a white horse whose nostrils emitted icy streams of air, and urging on with an imperiously extended right hand some ragged soldiers desperately lugging pieces of cannon up the rocky terrain behind him. I was not aware at that time that Napoleon *had* succeeded in crossing the Alps. In the dim light of my practice hour the outcome of the brave expedition appeared to me highly uncertain. I would sometimes have nightmares in which I would see Napoleon no longer urging on his men, but lying dead, his soldiers and cannon, half-hidden by the snow, strewn around him, the only survivor the noble steed, his nostrils still emitting streams of icy air. I often wondered why the composer of *The Alpine Shepherd's Evening Song* had neglected to portray in music the other, the terrifying side of life in the Alps.

It was now almost a year since I had begun to study the piano. Mr. Katz had lived up to my mother's estimate of him, cheerfully keeping me supplied with whatever music Miss Taffel thought I required. For her part, my mother tried valiantly to observe her side of the bargain, but on several occasions she was obliged to make visits of a propitiatory nature to the music store. It was not long before Mr. Katz induced me to buy some of his publications, though he was well aware that Miss Taffel did not consider any of them pedagogical necessities. In time I added *The Mosquito Parade* to my rapidly expanding repertoire, with the possibility always in mind of the hoped-for dramatic turn of events at school, which would in one moment reveal me to everyone there, but especially to Mr. Strassmeir, as a musical prodigy. I devoted most of the time of Miss Taffel's absences to the perfection of the march until I felt I would be equal to the occasion, come when it would!

In the meantime, my mother and sisters were clamoring to hear me play so as to judge for themselves the extent of the progress I claimed to have made. I felt sure of making an impression on *them*, and it only remained for me to get permission to invite my family to Miss Taffel's front room during one of my practice hours. Miss Taffel, when I put the idea of a little recital to her, didn't seem to care one way or the other, stipulating that I was not to light the gas, because her brother had the strongest objection to unseasonal illumination. I was hoping that Miss Taffel would not be at home at the hour of my projected concert, and when my mother and sisters sat down on the Wiener chairs in the front room, I played a few bars of *A Mother's Prayer* to find out. The forbidden melody brought no reaction from the rear of the house, so I knew for certain Miss Taffel was out. This made it possible for me to include at least two proscribed pieces in my program. I began with *The Mosquito Parade* and, fearing that Miss Taffel might unexpectedly return, followed it quickly with *A Mother's Prayer*. I could see in their faces that my mother and sisters were quite unprepared for the facility I exhibited and the feeling I put into the music. My rendition of *A Mother's Prayer* had the expected effect, all the more so as it was the only familiar music on my program; but I reserved my best efforts for *The Alpine Shepherd's Evening Song*, the echo effects of which elicited murmurs of delight from my audience. Soon the room grew quite dark and the ominous shadows I knew so well began to play on *Napoleon Crossing the Alps*. Remembering Miss Taffel's injunction about the gas, I closed the piano lid and ushered my family out of the basement into the light of a late spring afternoon.

On the sidewalk, my mother kissed me extravagantly and cried, in full view of boys playing prisoner's base. My sisters were more circumspect, though I saw their eyes fill with tears. In their enthusiasm they promised to buy me a certain sailor suit with white trimmings and a white cord with a whistle at the end, which I had long coveted. I knew it would be some time before they could find the dollar and a quarter that was the asking price for the suit. But in the past year I had discovered that the most unlikely things could happen. It now seemed to me quite possible that I would be wearing the sailor suit and blowing the whistle at the end of the cord by the time another year came around.

CHAPTER SEVEN

🍃 Mr. Silver, Individualist

IT WAS nine o'clock on the morning of a new term in P.S. No. 2. The class was standing, each boy next to his desk, waiting for the new teacher. A monitor had placed us in alphabetical order, and my desk was in the first row immediately in front of the teacher's desk. Presently we heard the sound of footsteps in the hall, and a tall, thin man came hastily into the room. Without so much as a glance at the class, he strode to the blackboard, seized a piece of chalk, and quickly wrote in beautiful script: "*Mr. Silver.*" He put down the chalk, brushed one palm against the other with the elegance of a cymbal-player, and sat down at his desk. He took out a paper from a drawer and read out our names. "Raise your right hand when your name is called and sit down," he said. And as each boy raised his hand and sat down, Mr. Silver bestowed on him a sharp, fleeting look.

Mr. Silver's face was long, freckled, and delicately formed. His eyes were steely, yet curiously expressive of his mental reactions to what they revealed to him. A second after he looked at an object his eyes would, as it were, pronounce judgment. The roll call over, he leaned forward, put his elbows on the desk, intertwined the four fingers of each hand, and with his thumbs began stroking in opposite directions an imaginary mustache on his lip. As he stroked, he turned his concentrated gaze on each boy in turn. When he came to me, he stared longer and harder and worked his thumbs with calculated deliberation. I felt uncomfortable under this scrutiny. At the same time I was obliged to repress an impulse to laugh at the industrious workings of his thumbs on his lip. At length he spoke, still looking straight at me. "I'll have no nonsense here," he said sharply and, I thought, rather irrelevantly, since the class sat silent and serious, its eyes on him. "We're here to work and for nothing else. If anyone doesn't like it here," and he suddenly jerked his left thumb in the direction of the door, "he can go *elsewhere!*" As he snapped out the word "elsewhere," it conjured up a bleak, purposeless, sterile, trackless region as unprofitable as the moon. It seemed as if he meant to address the class through me, and I tried hard to look away and so retreat into the safe anonymity of the other boys. But his hypnotic eyes held me fast, and a silence ensued during which the thumbs resumed their work on his upper lip. I knew I should be unable to bear the sight much longer without laughing, and the inevitability of my breakdown and the punishment that must ensue filled me with terror. As far back as I could remember, I had been fighting a propensity to laugh. I would laugh at anything or at nothing at all. I would laugh when I felt sober and grave. I laughed at deformity and mishap when I would rather have cried. Sometimes I had to repress a perverse desire to laugh when a funeral passed by. Yet I had no impulse to laugh at Italian funerals, in which the mourners marched to the sad music of brass bands.

But now, as if at the command of some "Imp of the Perverse," I laughed straight into the face of the formidable teacher who stroked a mustache he didn't have. It was a loud, staccato laugh, and it left me frozen with horror. To my surprise, it came again a second later, ignoring the terror I felt. Mr. Silver left his desk, came close to me, and with his fist struck me repeatedly in the face. I did not mind the blows. Indeed, I was grateful for them, for they released my tears. I was beginning to feel a sense of relief, when Mr. Silver seized me by the scruff of my neck and hustled me out of the room. "You may come back when you've laughed yourself out!" he shouted after me as he closed the door.

It seemed to me that I had laughed myself out *forever*. As I paced the hall waiting for the passing of a decent interval before I re-entered the classroom, I was certain that nothing would ever again seem comical or ludicrous to me. But when I opened the door halfway and saw Mr. Silver at his desk, his thumbs again stroking his lip, I knew I must laugh or die, and I shut the door hastily and fled down the hall and into the basement, where I took refuge in one of the open toilets that stretched in a row the length of the building. My next attempt to enter the classroom proved successful. Mr. Silver was on his feet talking to the class, one hand in his trouser pocket, the other playing with his bunch of keys. I did not want to laugh.

Having established his authority so sensationally on the very first morning of the term, Mr. Silver could presumably afford to relax. And soon he disclosed a provocative and even engaging personality. When not angered and moved to take disciplinary measures, he was breezily efficient and coolly but interestingly informative, even on dry subjects like arithmetic. His approach to teaching was informal—deceptively so we were to discover, for at the first sign of camaraderie on the part of a boy he would instantly change into a tyrannical disciplinarian. He impressed us by doing the unexpected. For example, when explaining sums on the blackboard he eschewed the use of the traditional pointer, using instead a key selected from a ring of keys he carried in his pocket. This lent an air of intimacy to his demonstrations. We could not of course avoid speculating about the large number of keys he carried about. It was one boy's opinion that Mr. Silver could be another Bluebeard who kept a corresponding number of wives under lock and key. We had to admit that he was handsome enough to marry as many women as he desired. Of one thing we had no doubt. His ambition, his competence, and his authoritativeness were bound to carry him to the greatest pedagogical heights.

Mr. Birnbaum, the principal, might well be jealous of him. Mr. Birnbaum was not a man to be trifled with, notwithstanding the unctuousness of his reading of a paragraph from the Bible in assembly each morning. These paragraphs were baffling. They seemed to make no sense in English, and they lacked the musical appeal my father endowed them with when he intoned them in Hebrew. When they did begin to make sense, Mr. Birnbaum would perversely terminate his reading and leave the story in mid-air.

"And the Lord appeared unto him in the plains of Mamre: and he sat in the tent door in the heat of the day. And he lift up his eyes and looked, and, lo, three men stood by him: and when he saw them, he ran to meet them from the tent door, and bowed himself toward the ground, and said, 'My Lord, if now I have found favour in thy sight, pass not away, I pray thee, from thy servant: let a little water, I pray you, be fetched, and wash your feet, and rest yourselves under the tree: and I will fetch a morsel of bread, and comfort ye your hearts; after that ye shall pass on: for therefore are ye come to your servant." (Genesis, Chapter xviii.) Mr. Birnbaum spoke the final phrase as if he were asking a question, placed the embroidered marker on the page, and piously closed the tooled-leather tome, leaving us wondering just whom the Lord appeared to and what subsequently happened.

We even preferred Mr. Silver's quick temper to Mr. Birnbaum's studied reactions to the problems of a principal. Mr. Silver might flare up at a boy, and in his passion hit out at him; but he cooled off rapidly. And if the victim bore the onslaught stoically and showed no resentment, Mr. Silver rewarded him by electing to forget the incident and thenceforward treating the boy with the breezy condescension we thought so becoming to him. As for his attitude to Mr. Birnbaum, it was gratifyingly aloof. Mr. Birnbaum would make unexpected visits to classrooms, hoping, it was generally assumed, to catch his teachers off guard or, at the very least, to make them self-conscious and apologetic. "Please keep right on with what you are doing," he would command genially on entering a classroom. But we learned that most teachers found it quite difficult to carry out this injunction. They floundered about, showing plainly their want of self-possession. On the other hand, some of them, sensing an opportunity of making a favorable impression, pretended a severity that was alien to their natures. This threw the class into a confusion that was not lost on the principal. Mr. Silver, however, always took Mr. Birnbaum at his word and continued what he had been doing without any show of either bravado or fear.

One morning a messenger appeared and told Mr. Silver that Mr. Birnbaum desired to see him in his office without delay. Mr. Silver said: "Very well," breezily, as if he didn't care; but his face flushed and his eyes roamed over the class, seeking out the boy who had betrayed him. The class had reason to be apprehensive about the interview that would take place in Mr. Birnbaum's office. The day before, Mr. Silver had lost his temper and had struck a boy, who had thereafter sulked all the morning and afternoon. The boy had gained a reputation as a cry-baby and a sissy. For this we blamed his mother, who accompanied him to school and waited for him on the sidewalk when school was let out. We had little doubt that the boy had "snitched" on Mr. Silver and that his mother had lodged a complaint with the principal. The boy now gave himself away by crying softly. Mr. Silver returned as briskly as he had left. The flush on his cheeks glowed more brightly and his eyes looked steelier. "Rabinowitz!" he called out sharply. "Stand up!" The boy got to his feet. Mr. Silver regarded him contemptuously. "Rabinowitz," Mr. Silver resumed, "I am asked to apologize to you for striking you yesterday. I now do so. Sit down!" Rabinowitz took his seat. The tears were pouring down his cheeks. We could hardly blame *him*. It was all his mother's doing. It went to show what an evil unbridled parental affection was. We were sorry for Rabinowitz, but we gloried in Mr. Silver's display of withering scorn. And we were pretty sure that in his brief interview with Mr. Birnbaum Mr. Silver had given the principal little cause for satisfaction.

We discovered faint overtones of contempt in Mr. Silver's demeanor toward his colleagues. We couldn't tell whether he disliked the teachers or the subjects they taught, but we were prepared to adopt his opinions and prejudices if we could but know them. We did know that he was partial to realistic subjects, to studies that would be useful in commercial life. But he disdained to be specific and left us to guess at his opinions from his occasional impromptu remarks on politics and current events. These hinted at a philosophy that favored the survival of the fittest and leadership by the confident and strong. Poverty, Mr. Silver intimated, was merely the consequence of laziness, want of ambition, and a disbelief in the potentialities of the active man. He stressed the fact that "our forefathers" (most of the boys and their parents had been born in Europe) "could not have thrown off the British yoke and launched 'our' great and successful Republic had they not been proud, hard, and industrious individualists." And commenting on the reports of a sanguine clash between striking coal-miners in Pennsylvania and the armed forces dispatched to the area by

the Governor of the state, Mr. Silver reminded us that there
were no unions and no strikes at Concord, Valley Forge, and
Yorktown. No, sir! Only the frustrated and the cowardly
would favor unions and engage in strikes. It was the aim of the
Socialists to destroy initiative and take from the industrious
rich their well-earned possessions and hand them over to the
lazy, shiftless poor. And what would be the gain, Mr. Silver
inquired oratorically. Why, there would be no gain! he
answered himself. If the wealth of the country were to be divided equally, the rich would lose everything and the poor
would hardly gain anything!

Whatever the boys, the majority of whom were only too
well acquainted with poverty, may have thought of Mr. Silver's contempt for the poor, I could not, try as I did, quite
share it. Wishing earnestly to adopt Mr. Silver's opinions on
all matters, I examined the habits and behavior of the indigent
class of which my family was a part. I found, much against
my will, hardly any evidences of laziness.

Perhaps if Mr. Silver had stopped in Rutgers Square some
evening and listened to the speakers of the Socialist Labor
Party he would have revised his estimate of the poor. I would
often join the small crowd in front of one of these men and
listen to descriptions of soul-and-body-destroying sweatshops
and impassioned enumerations of the iniquities of the "bosses"
who owned them. I heard that fathers left for work while
their children were still asleep and returned home after they
had gone to bed. In consequence they saw their offspring so
seldom as to make a mockery of parenthood. I heard with
horror that the "bosses" were drinking the blood of their
workmen and women. And while I knew that to be only a
figure of speech (my mother often accused me of drinking
hers), the image it evoked gave me the measure of the soulless
cupidity of the possessing class. As the one remedy for all its
cruelties and abuses, and on his assurance that we had nothing
to lose but our chains, the speaker urged us to unite. The loss

of our chains was also a figure of speech which I was able to translate. But the speaker was vague about the exact change that would occur in our lives following that desirable eventuality. An outline of some program would have enabled me to oppose Mr. Silver's philosophy of competitive individualism. But it was not forthcoming; and the enthusiasm the speakers communicated to me in Rutgers Square was likely to evaporate in the classroom, where I could not withstand the force of Mr. Silver's opposition.

On the other hand, my elder sisters were ardent Socialists and believed strongly in the necessity of unionization. Their arguments were rather persuasive, the more so as they had great affection for me, frequently fondled and embraced me, and sometimes gave me pennies to buy chocolate-covered walnuts or candy-coated apples on a stick. Mr. Silver did not seem like a man who could dispense or even feel affection, though he could easily inspire it. Perhaps his aversion to the poor was really caused by this lack in him and by his confidence and pride in himself. I thought that if all people had his strength and ambition, there would be no need for unions. But my sisters said that Mr. Silver sounded like an unfeeling and despotic man, the kind that takes delight in grinding down the poor. I had to admit to myself that there was some truth in this estimate. Yet one had to see and know Mr. Silver to do him justice. True, he was a despot. But I, who had had occasion to experience his cruelty, could nevertheless appraise him as a benevolent one. At any rate, I was perpetually torn between Mr. Silver's dynamic conservatism and my own inclination toward the liberalism of my sisters and the orators in Rutgers Square.

From one of the speakers I learned one evening of the heroic efforts of the workers in the East Side bakeries to form a a union. The man exhorted us to aid these courageous souls by refusing to eat non-union loaves. "Even a child can help 'the Cause,' " he cried, espying me in the group around him.

"When you get home tonight, little boy, look for the union label," he said directly to me. I followed his injunction when I got home, and I discovered that neither the rye loaf nor the twist bread my mother had bought that day had the union label pasted on them. When I told my sisters of the bakers' plight, they agreed with me that we were honor bound to forgo eating the unhallowed loaves. My mother, however, took the position that as the bread was not returnable, our eating the loaves could not possibly harm the embattled bakers. Henceforward, she assured us, she would take care to buy only properly unionized bread. It seemed to me that more was involved in the situation than expediency, and I was for consigning the offending loaves to the garbage pail or, if that was sinful, for giving it to our Christian neighbors across the hall. Not being subject to scruples of any kind, Christians, it was commonly held, were prepared to eat everything. My mother would not hear of such a foolish disposition of what she said was perfectly good, non-returnable bread, and my sisters reluctantly agreed with her. I vowed that I would not touch the loaves. But at supper that night my mother remarked that as I had made my point, it was foolish to labor it by starving myself. She then cut and buttered for me a thick slice, which I ate with the melancholy satisfaction of a pragmatic martyr.

The following evening I found the same passionate defender of the revolutionary bakers addressing a meeting in Rutgers Square. He recognized me and inquired whether I had acted on his suggestion of the night before. When I told him I had, he invited me to mount the podium and tell the crowd about it. I climbed onto the box, but the unexpected invitation deprived me for a while of my powers of speech. The encouragement of my sponsor, however, and the friendliness of the crowd soon exercised a reassuring effect on me, and I began to speak, at first haltingly, then—carried away by my subject and the commanding position I had suddenly attained—volubly and with consideration for dramatic effect. I described with much detail my rushing home the night before and the discovery of the unlabeled loaves in our bread box. Then, assembling my entire family, I put before them with all the eloquence I could command the aims and ideals of the insurgent bakers. My family (I confessed to my audience) had always been reactionary in thought and feeling, and my pleas, therefore, fell on deaf ears. I adjured them not to touch the accursed loaves or, if need be, give them to the *Chreestchs*. But they were adamant, and at supper prepared to eat them. This I said I could not countenance, and before my mother could reach for a knife, I seized the loaves, ran out of the house, and dumped them in some near-by garbage can. I spent the night on a truck in Water Street, scorning to go home. And with the pathetic prophecy that punishment would certainly await me on my return, I finished and stepped down. Then it was that I first tasted the tremulous delight of applause. In that instant I knew what Jacob P. Adler, Mrs. K. Lipzin, and my own adored Bertha Kalich felt when the curtain descended on one of their bravura scenes. If through some unforeseen obstacle I was not to achieve my ambition to be a great actor, I would certainly devote my life to the cause of downtrodden labor and address crowds nightly in Rutgers Square and on the street corners of the East Side.

Although I had distorted the events of the night before, there was some truth in my assertion that my family held conservative views on political and economic subjects. At any rate, my father held them, while my mother adopted for diplomatic reasons a neutral attitude, though my sisters and I felt that her sympathies were secretly with us. She and my father read *Der Tog*, a conservative daily, while my sisters took *Der Forward*, the organ of the liberals and Socialists.

My sister Molly, who loved poetry and could mimic the declamatory style of the best tragic actresses on Grand Street and the Bowery, memorized some of the poems that were printed in *Der Forward*, which she recited to us when my

father was away from home. There was one poem I never
grew tired of hearing. It was a rather long poem, an epic of
suffering, hopelessness, and death which gave full scope to my
sister's histrionic talent. "In Grand Street, not far from
Suckerstein's store," she would begin in a deceptively conversational tone, but with due regard for its rhythm, proceed-
ing to describe a bent and seedy man who daily haunted that
busy spot and peddled matches to the indifferent and hurrying
passers-by. I cannot recall what transition the poet used to
bring this wretched man to the office of a prosperous but
conscientious doctor in the neighborhood. But, wild-eyed and
importunate, he broke into the doctor's study, and my sister's
voice reflected the agony and desperation of the intruder. "My
wife! You must hurry! There's no time to lose," my sister
intoned rhythmically in accents of anguished impatience. The
room became tense with the imminence of tragedy, though we
were all quite familiar with the story. At this the heart of the
sensitive physician melted. "The doctor snatched his hat and
coat," my sister said in an accelerated tempo, "And they
hurried on their way." When they arrived in the match-
vendor's dimly lit garret, the doctor took one look at the
wasted form on the bed and cried: "You murderer! What
have you done! Of undernourishment she's dead!" My sister's
supreme moment came with the final lines: "The husband
with a piercing shriek himself fell dead across the bed." The
tears were in her eyes, and she stood rigid, staring ahead, as
Mrs. K. Lipzin did in the theater at the end of each act. The
tableau my sister conjured up was as corporeal to me as if I
were seeing the tragic figures in the flesh. It seemed to me that
if Mr. Silver could hear my sister's dramatic reading of this
poem, his mind would be cleared of his misconceptions about
the poor and his heart would be softened toward them.

I used sometimes also to wonder whether my father's dogmatic conservatism would be able to withstand the assault on
the emotions of the poetry in *Der Forward*. There seemed to

be a good deal of poetry in the holy books he read or chanted. His voice, too, as he prayed had a decided musical quality, and he employed artfully a variety of tonal shades. The Lamentations of Jeremiah were strangely emotional and dramatic as he sang them, and he intoned the Song of Solomon and the Psalms of David so rapturously that they were moving to hear even if one could not grasp their meaning. There could be no question about the genuineness of his appreciation of the poetry and music of the Bible and other sacred books. What puzzled me was that this appreciation had no influence on his character, opinions, and behavior. They brought him no closer to a consideration of the misfortunes and problems of the poor. Though he was not so lucid as Mr. Silver, he managed to convey the same bias for capitalism the teacher could so brilliantly rationalize.

He seemed never to consider anyone but himself. His displeasure with what he called my mother's extravagance which was summed up in his oft-repeated "I need nothing, myself," could not be justified by the small contribution he made to the support of the household. It is true that my mother spoiled him, as she did me, and I was often jealous of the indulgence she showed him. I could not conceive of a mother loving anyone more than her children, especially more than an only son. Love for children, especially for an only son, I was certain, was rooted in nature. It was therefore immutable. Not so a wife's love for her husband, which was ordained by nature to be secondary. When a husband died, the wife after a suitable period of mourning and quietude found herself another husband. If she truly loved the first, how could she marry a second? It followed therefore that sexual love was an inferior, temporary emotion. On the other hand, when a mother lost a son, any replacement was unthinkable. I had heard of instances where mothers killed themselves rather than live on without their sons. My oldest sister had even read in a novel by a French author about a mother who sacrificed her life for her daughter. For a daughter I thought that that was going a little too far. In general I was certain that my mother loved me in that absolute fashion. And when she quarreled with my father, as happened frequently, I read in her bitter reproaches the proof I was always seeking, that she did not love him as much as she loved me or in the same way. For while she was often angry with me, and even went so far as to slap me, she was always remorseful immediately after and would kiss and hug me and weep and call me her treasure and joy.

But there were times when I thought she showed a solicitude for my father exceeding the demands of secondary affection. Significantly enough, such instances always occurred on a Friday. It was generally on Friday that my father chose to take umbrage at something or other, and it was not long before I discovered the reason.

He had struck up a friendship with a fellow member of his synagogue, a venerable man with a long beard who lived with his wife in a three-room tenement on Pike Street. Zalman Reich was his name, and my father held him to be the most fortunate of men. For Zalman Reich had been blessed with six sons, all of whom were married and prosperous, and generous to their father to a fault. Mr. and Mrs. Reich (their offspring had united in dropping the "e" out of their surname), my father repeatedly told us, lived in ease and luxury at the expense of their children, who took great pride in their parents' well-being and contentment. Because of the munificence of his sons, Zalman had unlimited leisure at his disposal, and he spent most of his time at the synagogue, where he was greatly respected for his readiness to bid high for the privilege of holding the Torah and to purchase the most expensive seat on Rosh Hashonah and Yom Kippur. My father never tired of expounding the virtues of his friend and calling attention to the never-ending generosity of the sons.

The latest proof of their solicitude for Zalman Reich made a

deep impression on my father, who came home from synagogue one day bursting with the news. He could hardly wait
to wash and dry his hands to tell us. "Some men have all the
luck," he said, looking accusingly at me. He then turned to
my mother. "What do you think those boys have done for
Zalman now? They have made him a present of an operation
on his left eye, the one that has the cataract. Zalman told the
whole congregation about it today. They've engaged the best
eye-doctor, and it will cost twenty dollars! That's what I call
children!" I looked abashed and ate in silence. The name of
Zalman Reich was always on my father's lips, and his visits
to the Reichs grew more and more frequent.

One Friday when I came home from school, I knew by the
unhappy expression of my mother's face and by my father's
calculated, punitive silence that there had been a quarrel. I
saw my father take his prayer shawl and phylacteries from a
bureau drawer, wrap them in an old newspaper, and tie the
bundle with a string. He then put on his hat and coat and, with
the bundle under his arm, stalked out of the house without a
word of explanation or farewell. At supper time he had not returned. My mother, unable to conceal her anxiety, sent me
to the synagogue to see if he had loitered there. I found no
one at the synagogue but the beadle, who told me that my
father had gone off with Zalman Reich. This information
mollified my mother, but she ate little at supper. When I went
to bed he had not yet come home. Early the next morning my
mother woke me. She appeared much agitated. "Get dressed,"
she commanded, "and run to Zalman Reich's. Tell your father
to come home. Tell him I'm sorry." At the Reichs' I found my
father alone in the kitchen wearing his prayer shawl and
phylacteries. When he paused for a moment in his prayers, I
delivered my message. He made no reply, and I ran home.
Toward evening my mother wrapped two pieces of gefilte fish
and half of a twist bread in a sheet of newspaper and bade me
go again to the Reichs' and deliver the package to my father.

Again I found him alone. He opened the bundle and saw what it contained. He showed no surprise, but sat down at the table and ate the fish with his usual relish.

On Sunday morning he returned home and was received by my mother with, to me, shocking manifestations of remorse and delight. For days after, I found myself neglected by her, her mind only on the problem of avoiding a repetition of his flight from home. I could not now deny to myself that she felt an unnatural love for him. I lay awake suffering agonies of jealousy and wondering how she could prefer him to me. For aside from my being her own flesh and blood, her only son, I knew myself to be kind and affectionate (except for a few inconsequential exhibitions of willfulness), and could feel pity for others; whereas my father was self-centered and unfeeling, and had, like Mr. Silver, no use for the poor. I had to admit he was handsome, but was that sufficient to make up for his outbursts of temper or his long, apparently premeditated silences, which were even harder to bear? Could it be that I had misread the character of my mother, that she had not really merited the love I had trustingly lavished on her? I determined to withdraw my love from her entirely and give it all to my older sister, Hannah. Hannah, I had no reason to doubt, loved me and no one else. She was lovely to look at, and had such a beautiful voice that I could not concentrate on my homework when she sang old Russian songs, and even the next-door neighbors refrained from rapping on the wall in protest. Once in a while a suitor would appear. But thus far she had shown no preference for anyone but me.

A few days after my father's memorable flight my mother became her old self again and I found myself once more the center of her life. I was now, as in pre-flight days, the "apple of her eye," her "Benjamin," her "staff," and her "rod." I decided I had mistaken a momentary aberration for a fundamental change in character, and I submitted at first warily and later unreservedly to her embraces. Only on Fridays I was aware of a certain faint aloofness and reserve in her attitude toward me, a preoccupation with something that I felt had no relation to me at all. But her indifference to me vanished the moment my father came home from synagogue. She met him at the door with a basin of water and a towel. And when he had silently washed and dried his hands and taken his place at the head of the table, preparatory to saying a prayer over the pair of twist breads in front of him, she hovered near him, poised to interpret his peremptory gestures and wordless sounds; for piety forbade the use of speech until the prayer was over and bread had been broken. In those suspended, critical moments my father, perhaps finding the salt missing, would point with his right forefinger dramatically at the loaves and make impatient sounds like "M-m. M-m." And my mother would try to guess what he meant and offer him one thing after another, while his voice rose in pitch more and more irately as she successively guessed wrong. At length the process of elimination would point to the saltcellar, and the ordeal would be over. My sisters and I always watched this performance with resentment. I wondered if Zalman Reich behaved so imperiously toward *his* wife. I determined that when I grew up I would *force* my mother to rebel against her husband's high-handedness, whether she loved him or not. There was, too, such a thing as divorce. Many couples we knew threatened to divorce each other, though none ever carried out the threat. At any rate, someday I would insist on a divorce. I would then find out once and for all which of us she really loved.

In the meantime I would dedicate myself to the important task of making the world a better place to live in for the people around me. With the end of the school term and my promotion to the next grade, the influence of Mr. Silver's jaunty conservatism began to wane, and in the summer vacation it disappeared altogether. Night after night I made impromptu speeches from crates or the back ends of wagons. And the more I spoke and the more I was applauded for my impassioned delivery, the more certain I was that the workers of the world must either unite or perish. There came a moment, however, when I wavered between socialism and anarchism. One night, what I thought was a Socialist meeting turned out to be an anarchist rally. I had heard vaguely about anarchism, a philosophy even more abhorrent to Mr. Silver and my father than socialism. But now, as the speaker explained it, it seemed to hold greater promise for a better world for the poor and suffering than socialism. Indeed, socialism could be considered only as a steppingstone to the ideal of human existence which anarchism promised. When, with my help, the workers of the world had united and lost their chains, I would then examine the philosophy of anarchism in greater detail. At the moment the possibilities for man appeared limitless.

CHAPTER EIGHT

🌿 *"Then We Were Eight"*

Our family was presently reduced to eight by the marriage of my sisters Gertie and Lea. To everybody's astonishment, Gertie married her uncle (and mine), my father's younger brother Sam, who had recently emigrated from Ula. Like ourselves, Sam had come to America at the suggestion of Mr. Gold. This time the amiable junk-dealer made good his promise of a job. He gave Sam the spare room in his house in Passaic, staked him to a second-hand utility wagon and an aging horse, and set him up as an itinerant peddler of household wares. Sam spent his Sundays in our house, and after supper Gertie would accompany him to the Madison Street car, the first of several conveyances, not counting the Duane Street ferry, which relayed him back to Passaic. One Sunday the two left the house as usual, but reappeared half an hour later and announced that they had decided to get married.

Much to my surprise, my father saw no objection in their close family relationship. To me it seemed ludicrous for two people who knew each other so intimately to marry. On the other hand, the marriage had the advantage of being unusual, and I hastened to spread the news among my playmates on the street. None of my friends could match so sensational an event. I could now boast that my oldest sister possessed a husband and uncle, and I an uncle and a brother-in-law, all in one person.

The marriage of my sister Lea was less sensational, though equally unexpected. Lea worked in a ladies' garment factory on Canal Street and, except for attendance at night school, generally spent her evenings at home. She was small and dumpy, had a mass of blond hair and a pug nose, and was shy and self-conscious with strangers. We were therefore surprised to hear that she had been seen walking on East Broadway with an unknown man several nights after supper. The rumor finally reached my father, who made a scene about it one morning at breakfast, demanding to be told what manner of man would go walking with a presumably respectable girl without first presenting himself to her family. What was even worse, his daughter and her unidentified beau had been observed sitting together on our stoop! Nice people, my father said witheringly, did not sit on stoops, where they became the subjects of the ribald speculation of the world as it sauntered by. Lea, weeping, confessed that she had been walking out with a man she had met some time ago at night school. They had also sat on the stoop once, but only by reason of fatigue. The man's name was Mannie—Mannie Kalb. He was a house-painter, and he lived at home with his father and mother. Pressed for further details, Lea confessed that he stammered slightly and had little hair. But against these unimportant defects she claimed for him the virtues of industry and good nature, and for his parents piety and respectability. She hadn't asked Mannie up because she was afraid his stammer would subject him to ridicule. My father, though alive to the necessity of marrying off Lea to the first respectable suitor (respectability and a job were all that he demanded), listened impassively and gave her an ultimatum. She must either produce Mannie Kalb for inspection forthwith or drop him altogether.

Two or three evenings later Mannie paid us a formal visit and was at once subjected to the closest scrutiny. His two deficiencies were decidedly more marked than Lea had indicated, both appearing to have reached completion. His stammer, now aggravated by nervousness, made conversation with him almost impossible and much embarrassed Lea, who valiantly and (for her) rather defiantly attempted repeatedly to help him out in his struggle with some particularly refractory word. Though I could hardly keep from laughing at his grotesque, frantic efforts to make himself understood, a simple pathos about his helplessness drew me toward him. All the same, my mother was obliged to make occult, threatening signs to me from behind the unfortunate suitor's chair to observe decorum. And somehow, by means of a variety of facial contortions and desperate gesticulation Mannie Kalb managed to project a naïve and kind personality that bore out my sister's opinion of him. No one laughed even during the critical moments when he seemed irrevocably sunk in unintelligibility. As she usually did in moments of crisis, my mother brought in tea and cakes. Mannie, grateful for the respite, drank glass after glass, and so did the rest of us, hardly knowing what else to do. Suddenly Mannie pushed his glass aside, rose, advanced to my father, and tried to speak. It was a long and painful attempt. He had reached a climax of incoherence when Lea, moved by shame and pity, hastily took over and interpreted the furious struggle for expression we had witnessed as Mannie's announcement of their engagement. At this intelligence, my father, wasting no time on Mannie, addressed himself to Lea and drew from her such details about the state of her

lover's finances and kindred matters as might determine our
family's attitude to the proposed alliance. Satisfied at last on
all points, he blessed his daughter, shook hands with the perspiring, happy Mannie and suggested a speedy meeting between himself and the senior Kalb for the discussion of arrangements for the wedding.

The elder Kalb, while a good man with an unsullied record
for piety, was, like his son, a house-painter and therefore at a
disadvantage as a *m'chutan* (in-law). One need not be ashamed
of a m'chutan who was in business for himself, one who, for
example, ran a butcher's shop, a shoe store (a cobbler, like a
tailor, was taboo, as in the old country; tailors, however, were
fortunately nonexistent in America, where everyone wore
ready-made clothes), a "men's furnishings" store, a kosher
delicatessen. But one could be proud of a m'chutan who was
engaged in "big" business, an employer of labor on a grand
scale, say a proprietor of a sweatshop with five or ten em-
ployees, or even a "boss" carpenter or painter with two or
three men under him. One could hardly boast in the synagogue
about a m'chutan who was only a day laborer, or bring him
around to meet the congregation. Yet (as my mother pointed
out to him) my father was in no position to talk about *kovod*
(honor). Lea had no dowry. She was, in fact, penniless. And
while dowries were less important in America than they were
"at home," a man could hardly be blamed for expecting
"something" to go with his bride. Granted that Mannie was
no longer young, and that his defects were serious enough to
decrease his value in the marriage market, nevertheless as a
man he was worth "something." And if he had had the sense
to place himself in the hands of a shadchen, he might have
fetched a decent sum, though perhaps not a fortune. My
mother recalled to my father the unfortunate case of her own
sister's daughter Beylke, in Russia. For two years now
Beylke's marriage had been held up for lack of a sufficient
dowry. My mother had a stack of letters from her sister in

Vitebsk relating to Beylke's still unsettled position. Beylke was in no sense an objectionable creature. Yet the only suitor the shadchen was able to scare up for her demanded a dowry of one hundred rubles. He had finally come down to ninety, and it was at that figure that both he and his mother took their rock-bottom stand. My aunt's frantic efforts to raise that sum had so far netted only fifty rubles (ten of which my mother had somehow obtained and contributed without, of course, the knowledge of my father). In her last letter, the distracted mother had written that she had made a supreme effort to effect a downward revision of the impossible sum. But the suitor's mother remained heartlessly, even godlessly ob- durate. "I'd rather see him *rot*," was her final crushing answer. And there the matter now stood.

My father took the hint and accepted the situation with what grace he could command. He did *not* invite the senior Kalb to his synagogue, but accepted his invitation to dinner, though not before assuring himself of the house-painter's strict observance of the dietary laws. The invitation included the rest of the family. Molly and I, who had a propensity to laugh at everything, were warned to behave. The dinner went off without a hitch. The senior Kalb offered my father the head of the table, which my father accepted as his due and as the symbol of the house-painter's understanding and ac- ceptance of a secondary role in his future relationship with our family. Mrs. Kalb had cooked a very large dinner, the climax of which was a great chunk of sweet-and-sour meat. It was my father's favorite dish next to gefilte fish, and he looked pleased, unaware that Lea had given her future mother-in-law the hint.

Mrs. Kalb, a large, fat woman, resplendent in a long black taffeta dress, and wearing a small gold watch attached to a gold chain long enough to encompass her ample neck twice, served the meal and, like all housewives, did not sit down at the table until the dessert, of stewed prunes and dried apricots, had tapered off the repast. My mother owned no jewelry except an imitation mother-of-pearl pin in the shape of a fish, with a tiny black bead for an eye, which she wore at her throat on ceremonious occasions. The scaly pink fish now appeared insignificant alongside Mrs. Kalb's watch and chain. And when Mrs. Kalb finally sat down at the table, my mother subtly established her own disdain of worldly possessions and her cultural superiority over her hostess by casual references to her eminent father, Reb Shnayer Tresskanov of Vitebsk, and the love of austerity he had inculcated in his children. Mr. Kalb called my father "Reb," and Mannie, more at ease in his own house, stammered less and succeeded in telling, albeit with a certain difficulty, a joke relating to the foibles of housepainters. When we were ready to take our leave, the elder Kalb produced a bottle of whisky and two long, thin silver goblets, gold-faced on the inside. The two machutonim had one drink apiece, my father saying: *Sholom aleichem*, and Mr. Kalb answering: "*Aleichem sholom*." This ceremonious exchange made the engagement of Lea and Mannie official.

I had hoped that at least one of my sisters would marry into a family rich enough to afford an elaborate wedding at Pythagoras Hall, with a string of hired carriages to take us there. It was true that Pythagoras Hall was only half a block from our house, but I knew that proximity to Pythagoras Hall did not deter affluent or ostentatious families residing close to it from conducting their weddings on a scale that imposed hired carriages. The Hirsch wedding was a case in point. Mr. Hirsch lived even closer to Pythagoras Hall than we did, but when he married off his eldest daughter, the wedding party went in five open carriages from the Hirsch residence on East Broadway through Rutgers Street, turned left at Henry Street, turned left again at Jefferson Street into East Broadway, and drew up, as if after a long journey, at Pythagoras Hall. It was a most impressive cortege, and crowds of pedestrians, myself among them, followed the slow-moving vehicles. People watched us from the sidewalks and from

windows, admiring the rented white satin dress of the bride
and the shiny stovepipe hats of the groom and the more important male relatives. Having cleverly melted into a party of
the children of invited guests, I slipped unnoticed into
Pythagoras Hall, which presented a vision of opulence. The
ceremony took place in a richly decorated room, I standing on
a chair to get a better view. Under an elaborately embroidered
chuppah (canopy) of red velvet, a stout, bearded rabbi in a
tight-fitting surtout with velvet lapels intoned the service in a
strong falsetto and with many coloratura embellishments of
his own. First the rabbi addressed himself to the bride and
groom in turn. But soon after, intoxicated with his own
virtuosity, he looked away and gazed at the ceiling as he sang,
like an artist at a recital glorying in his mastery of his art. At
the end of the rabbi's eloquent performance, the bride was rotated around the groom several times. The rabbi then lifted the
bridal veil, and the bride touched the rim of the wineglass that
he held out to her. The groom sipped next; then the ring was
placed on the bride's finger. The room was now hushed as the
rabbi, carefully wrapping the wineglass in a napkin and placing
it on the floor, crushed it loudly underfoot.

The crunching noise set off great shouts of "*Mazoltov!*
(Congratulations!)," the machutonim embraced, the violin,
cornet, drum, and piano, which had been waiting for this very
signal, broke into "*Choson, Kaloh, mazoltov!* (Groom, bride,
congratulations!)." The married pair sailed away in a dance
across the length of the room, between two long lines of
guests formed to provide a narrow lane for the exhibition.
These favored guests clapped their hands in rhythm with the
music, sang and laughed and called the bride and groom by
their first names. Having initiated the revels, the couple retired to throne-like chairs at one end of the room to watch
their guests cavort and to receive the personal felicitations of
those able to make their way to them through the great press
of celebrators. Strangely enough, the groom seemed to be the

more popular of the pair, especially with the male guests, who
flocked around him and whispered in his ear such things as
made him laugh and blush. When the general exuberance had
begun to subside, an impressive-looking master of ceremonies
stood up on a chair, motioned the drummer to execute a roll,
loud and long, and in the ensuing silence announced in a voice
of thunder that supper was ready in the great room downstairs
and ordered the gentlemen to escort their ladies below to the
strains of a grand march that the orchestra would immediately
strike up. Led by the bride and groom, with the machutonim
following behind, a procession of couples formed and marched
to the quick step of the grand march. But not for long; for
some of the guests, overeager to get to the banquet hall first,
broke ranks and ran ahead. In a moment the orderly march
had become a stampede, with the children (myself among
them) snaking their way to the forefront and rushing down the
wooden steps with a great clatter. Down in the dining-room
confusion reigned for a long time. People who had rushed to
seat themselves near the bride and groom had to be forcibly
dislodged by the master of ceremonies, who held a paper with
the seating arrangement and could not be swerved from his
determination to fill the long bridal table according to the
strictest protocol.

The supper was the most varied and lavish I had thus far
encountered either at home or at the house of relatives. For,
besides such common hors d'œuvres as herring (this herring, to
be sure, was "*schmaltz*" and therefore a cut above the tough,
salty variety we could afford at home), raw onions, *malinki*
(black olives), *helzel* (stuffed neck), new dill pickles, and
chopped liver, there was chicken fricassee as the main dish
and crown of the repast. I had known chicken exclusively in its
austere boiled state, garnished with whole, waterlogged
onions or accompanied by masses of noodles, the whole swimming in an overgenerous supply of broth. But chicken *fricassee*
was so special a form as to make it seem improbable that it

could ever be served in any home, however pretentious. It was
known by reputation to most of the children of the neighborhood, but only a few had ever come face to face with it. I
could now testify that it deserved its fame. A huge earthen-
ware casserole was placed on our table. Its cover being removed, a soft aromatic vapor rose from the interior and engaged our nostrils. And inside the vast dish lay who knows
how many golden chickens in ruins, in innumerable pieces,
large and small, like a scientific assemblage of the parts of pre-
historic creatures. Breasts, wings, legs, giblets, gizzards
languished in glistening, brownish gravy in inviting disorder!
The supper might well have come to an end with the fricassee.
But there followed a large variety of honeyed desserts and,
for a finish, piping-hot noodle soup. Wine was served only at
the bridal table, where toasts seemed never-ending, except
during the chicken-fricassee course, when a silence fell on the
room and only the sounds of chicken bones being crunched
and the smacking of lips could be heard.

At one point during the dessert the master of ceremonies
opened and read aloud a telegram that had just arrived. I was
astonished at the extravagance of the sender, for telegrams
were too costly for joyful occasions. The message was from a
near relation of the bride residing in faraway Baltimore. It was
both ingenious and witty. As all telegrams were restricted
(I believed) to ten words, I marveled at the sender's clever
choice of words. Indeed, the restriction had the positive effect
of challenging his ingenuity. It would have taken, ordinarily,
twice that number of words to express sentiments so various
and complex. "Hundred years happiness bride—groom may
troubles be little ones." Such was the message—which was
translated into Yiddish for the benefit of the elderly machutonim and guests—combining neatly the obvious with a
witty play on words that brought laughter and applause from
everyone there, even from the children.

This was the kind of wedding I had hoped for. And on

first beholding Mannie Kalb I felt that there might be a
chance that his deficiencies would be counterbalanced by a
corresponding affluence, and that he and Lea would be married
in Pythagoras Hall. But that hope was soon dispelled. For
Lea assured us that Mrs. Kalb's gold watch and chain represented the sum of the family's savings. Indeed, the economic
situation of the Kalbs was little better than our own. Perhaps
their *prospects* were better than ours, for they invested heavily
in lottery tickets, buying at regular intervals as many as three
at a time at fifty cents apiece. They had been buying lottery
tickets steadily for three years, and by the law of averages
they were due soon to win five hundred dollars. In the meantime they were in no position to stage an expensive and
fashionable wedding. So my sister's marriage took place one
Sunday morning in our house before a limited number of
relatives and friends. Though resigned to a small wedding at
home, Lea pleaded with my father for a white satin wedding
dress, veil and slippers to match, the rental of which would
cost seven and a half dollars. My mother could not but protest
at such extravagance in a man who eternally preached
economy. Nevertheless, my father yielded to Lea's plea, and
as he raised the money by himself, my mother's objection
had little force. I was glad not only for Lea's sake, but for my
own. For while I could not boast to my friends about a
wedding in Pythagoras Hall, I still could talk in a casual way
about my sister's wedding outfit. Certainly the dress was in
every way as fine as the one Miss Hirsch had worn. It may
even have been the very same, for it came from the most
patronized wedding outfitters on Essex Street. I had seen one
exactly like it on the life-size dummy bride which, holding on
to the arm of a life-size dummy groom, stood, smiling and
radiant, behind the huge plate-glass window of the shop.

On the pressing invitation of her parents-in-law Lea
moved into their tenement on Rivington Street. There she
resided for some time in "idleness," claiming that she was not

permitted to "touch a thing" except to do her own room and her own and Mannie's laundry. Such indulgence was unusual. But Mannie was an only child, and the elder Mrs. Kalb, when called upon to justify Lea's luxurious idleness, laughingly said that nothing had changed in her house except that she had acquired a boarder in the shape of a daughter-in-law. Mrs. Kalb's gain was also ours. We now had more room and the use of still another extra blanket when the weather grew cold. Also, the withdrawal of a member of my father's side of the family left the opposing factions less unbalanced than they had been heretofore. Tension still continued to be felt like a faint but ever-threatening undercurrent. But Lea's marriage and absence held in check for a time the deep enmities that divided our house.

CHAPTER NINE

Hannah

MORE and more I took my stand with my mother, Hannah, and Molly against my father and his children. The issues became increasingly clear-cut. My two sisters (and my mother, in an inactive way) represented culture, enlightenment, and pure affection. The rest of the family symbolized ignorance, conformity, and selfishness. At the time, I was only vaguely familiar with words like "culture" and "enlightenment," but I gathered from the reverent inflection my sisters gave to them that they were desirable things with which the "enemy" could have no connection. On my own I compared my sisters' sensitivity to nature and beauty with the "enemy's" bland indifference to everything not material. I could not recall that my father or any of his children had ever noticed the color of the sky (there were beautiful sunsets to be seen from our front window); but Hannah and Molly were quick to notice and call to my attention the changing beauty of the heavens and the streets.

There was the clock tower of R. Hoe & Co., Inc., the printing-press factory, visible from our window, though half a mile away, close to the East River. One early summer evening Hannah, leaning out of the window, called to me to come and see R. Hoe & Co., Inc., floating in the sky, and when I looked I saw she had spoken the truth; for there indeed was R. Hoe & Co., Inc., or at any rate the clock tower, hanging unattached in the sky in the far distance. Nothing of the building was to be seen except the tower—a faultless blue sky above it, with a single limpid star, and below it creeping darkness that obliterated the familiar sky line. Seen in the light of Hannah's description, it was a breath-taking sight. Never again would I look at R. Hoe's merely to tell the time. I began to *feel* the gradations of light and shade in the air and on objects that in themselves I had used to think prosaic.

One late afternoon I ran into the house from play to get a piece of bread and butter. My father sat at the kitchen table absorbed in a volume of Hebrew commentaries. I had seen him in the same position often enough, but this time I was struck by the *picture* he made in the twilit room, his face and beard in shadow, the page of the book before him alone reflecting the sad, attenuated light that suffused the soot-covered kitchen window. I felt an ache in the region of my heart as I looked. My father was beautiful for the moment, and the shadowy outline of his brooding form and hazy features seemed the plastic symbol of noble melancholy.

Molly, while not so delicately responsive to beauty as Hannah, appreciated its more obvious manifestations. Her reactions were passionate where Hannah's were diffidently poetic. She took me on an *excursion* one summer morning, to show me and share with me the beauties of the countryside. To embark on an excursion was a difficult undertaking, requiring untold patience and fortitude. The excursion was run

free for the benefit (I believe) of the East Side poor by a
patriarchal Tammany Hall city administration. Once a
fortnight during the summer a dilapidated ferryboat filled
with as many persons as it would hold left the foot of Montgomery Street and plodded heavily, uneasily, and sagging to
one side with its overload of people, up the East River, into
Long Island Sound, and after three or four hours pulled up at
some rural wharf. There the passengers were disembarked and
let loose in the adjoining fields for an hour, after which
several long blasts of the ship's whistle brought them back
and the boat began its homeward journey.

So many people, especially children and their mothers,
desired to go on an excursion that by five in the morning a
queue many blocks long had already formed at the wharf.
Molly and I were among them. We stood, holding our lunch
of bread and butter and pickles in a paper bag, from sunrise to
ten o'clock, the hour of the ferryboat's departure. The sun,
at first dispassionately spreading light, soon warmed to its
primary task of heating the cobblestones under our feet,
luridly spotlighting the warehouses behind us and scorching
our heads and faces. Before sailing-time many elderly people
collapsed and were helped by the younger and tougher-
fibered excursionists to shady stoops and alleyways, their
places in the queue having first been guaranteed them. At ten
the gates of the pier were opened and in a few minutes the
boat was tightly packed with noisy children, screaming
babies, distracted mothers, and feeble, bewildered grandparents. The excursionists outnumbered the seating capacity
of the boat to so large an extent that for every seated person,
at least five stood up. We marveled that the boat did not
overturn (it was to overturn one fateful morning, with a
great loss of life!). Nevertheless it *was* an *excursion*, and we
enjoyed, tightly wedged as we were, the sea air, the passing
steamers and sailboats, and the prospect of spending an hour
in the country. When we landed, Molly bade me run with her

ahead of the crowd toward a distant copse where we might be alone. There we rolled on the grass, lay flat on our backs, and watched the lazy, cottony clouds melt into one another. I could see that Molly was determined to make the most of the hour allotted us, and her enthusiasm was contagious. She danced around, did handsprings, and for a few minutes stood still with her face turned to the sky and her arms outstretched, inhaling and exhaling noisily and challengingly. I did the same. Then we ate our lunch in great contentment. Four hours later we were back in Montgomery Street, tired and perspiring from standing up during the entire trip back. But we had been on an *excursion*, and the hour we spent on the shores of Long Island (or was it Connecticut?) became an enchanting memory for us both.

The "other" side of the family knew no such physical and æsthetic raptures. Its members, with the exception of Albert and Gertie, were content with the briefest of educations. Writing and reading elementary English were their acknowledged goal. Gertie's espousal had automatically placed her beyond any need to try even for this limited objective. Albert was forging ahead so rapidly in his business of carpentering and building that his ignorance of the English alphabet could hardly be regarded as a hindrance to success. His faith in his dynamism was so complete that on discovering that a cross constituted a legal signature, he abandoned a previous determination to learn to sign his name. And it was only when he was made to realize the anomaly of a devout Jew like himself adopting the very symbol of Christianity as his signature that he undertook the, to him, distasteful labor of mastering the spelling of his name.

For Hannah and Molly night-school courses in English constituted the gateway to English literature. They had read much in Russian in the old country, and they continued reading Russian books in the new. On the third floor of the Educational Alliance, on the corner of East Broadway and Jefferson

Street, was the Aguilar Public Library, where books in all
languages might be borrowed for two weeks at no cost. One
could not, alas, browse in the Aguilar Free Library. A floor to
ceiling partition kept the borrowers from all access to the
books that crowded the numberless shelves behind it. Two
small openings punctured this solid wall, and two ladies in
white shirtwaists and starched collars stood behind these
apertures. To one of them one handed a slip of paper on which
was written the title of the book one wished to borrow and a
half-dozen alternates should the desired volume be out.

Once a fortnight I was my sisters' messenger to the Aguilar
Library, bearing their choice of books on a folded sheet
of paper. At home I would ask my sisters to tell me the
stories of the books I brought them. In the window of
Malkin's bookstore I had seen the same books in English
translations, and now I learned that in Dostoievsky's *Crime
and Punishment* the hero, Raskolnikov, was a good man
driven by poverty to murder his landlady. Tolstoy's *War and
Peace* and *Anna Karenina* resisted all my sisters' attempts to
extract a story that might intrigue me, and I lost interest in
Goncharov's *Oblomov* when I heard that this so-called hero
was simply a lazy man to whom nothing whatever happened,
who was content to lie on his bed or on a couch all day long.
But one day I brought home from the library Victor Hugo's
Les Misérables in English translation. On my way I had opened
the book to look for illustrations, and the only one in it
represented a terrifyingly uncouth man on a park bench glaring
at a small boy who stood near by in a supplicating attitude.
Not as yet having read the book, Molly, for whom I brought
it, could not identify for me this pictured encounter.

A few nights later I was awakened from sleep by the angry
shouts of my father. He had himself been awakened by a
sound of sobbing. Rising and going into the kitchen, he had
discovered Molly with a book in her hand reading by the light
of a low-burning gas-jet and crying to herself. She was reading

Les Misérables and had become so absorbed in the story of Fantine (she told me the next day) that she could not bear to put the book down and go to bed. At the point where the wretched Fantine sells her beautiful blond hair to pay for the board and lodging of her little daughter, Cosette, Molly could not repress her sobs. And now my father raged at her extravagant, unauthorized use of expensive illuminating gas, and in turn roused the entire household. His anger at length subsiding, he left the kitchen vowing that he would see to it that no "foolish" books would ever again enter "his" house. Nevertheless I continued my fortnightly visits to the Aguilar Library. My sisters read the books I brought back at times when my father was away from home. And they concealed them in the only safe place in the house, under his own bed, where my father never looked.

I liked to think that my two sisters and I were a kind of secret society like those existing in Chinatown, but bound together by æsthetic and poetic perceptions that the "other" side of the family both envied and decried. My mother's role was that of an ignorant but sympathetic adherent of "our" side, whose duty it was to alert us to the plans of the enemy and to side with us openly in the event of hostilities. Yet this very close alliance was not without its own frictions. Indeed, at times it seemed that the association itself would not bear the strain of the bickerings of its members and would eventually atrophy as a fighting force. In her impatience with my numerous peccadilloes, my mother would often say things that would incite me to retaliation. I guessed shrewdly that the most effective form of revenge was to remain out of doors long after my accustomed bedtime. And many nights I had the satisfaction (not unmixed with regret) of watching her, from my place of concealment behind an ash can, roam the street in search of me.

My sisters, too, sometimes fought with each other and with me. Hannah's disposition, except in moments of wrath, was angelic. Yet I found a perverse pleasure in teasing her and causing her discomfort and even pain. On Sunday mornings Hannah worked at home manufacturing "cases," the paper containers for the insertion of tobacco later.

As I stood behind her chair one Sunday morning watching the cases pile up in a heap, I took it into my head to tease her about Mr. Chaikin, a gentleman who had recently taken to calling on her. I pretended I was talking to myself. "She might just as well marry Mr. Chaikin," I began *sotto voce*, "for everybody knows she's sweet on him." I waited for some reaction, but Hannah went on producing cases quickly and silently. I tried again with a statement about Mr. Chaikin's perfervid attentions to her. This time I drew a response of a kind calculated to infuriate me. Hannah began humming a snatch of a song in Yiddish the words of which I knew were aimed at me. "A dog," she sang, without retarding the speed of her work, "may bay at the moon . . . but he remains a *dog!*" As she sang the final word, I took a long breath and suddenly shot it out at the large, foamy pile of cases. The feathery things floated from the table in all directions, some to the ceiling, to which they clung effortlessly, but most to the floor. At the same time I made for the door and flew down the stairs two at a time, with Hannah in enraged pursuit behind me. But by the time she reached the street, I had already disappeared from view.

When I felt myself safe, remorse gripped me, as it always did after an "incident" with any of the three persons I loved most in the world, and soon I was back home, resolved to make what amends I could. Hannah was on all fours on the floor attempting to reassemble the elusive cases. I got down beside her and helped restore the pile to the table. Then, overcome with shame, I flung my arms around her and said I was sorry and implored her never to sing that hateful song again in my presence. She held me close and promised to abandon the song forever. "Don't you know," she murmured,

"I love you more than anyone in the world!" All the same, sometime later—probably after some grave provocation on my part—Hannah forgot her promise and began to sing the dreadful phrase again. This time I did not think of revenge. Instead I began to cry and Hannah stopped short before the offensive word and begged forgiveness, which I, through my tears, magnanimously granted.

Except for these infrequent distressing episodes, my relations with Hannah were on a lofty plane. Young as I was, I could not help being aware of the difference between her nature and that of any other person I knew, not excepting Molly and my mother. Her features were disarmingly open, yet delicately troubled with some hidden concern. She was long-suffering and kind, where Molly was impatient and openly resentful. She responded almost automatically to all appeals, and as something was always happening to the people we knew, Hannah was continually on the go. The most unfortunate among these was my mother's third cousin, Chaie Rive Flayshig. Chaie Rive lived with her husband, Nochum, and her little twin sons in a distant section of Brooklyn, where rents were cheaper than on the East Side. The Flayshigs were so desperately poor that by comparison we were rich. At least the Flayshigs regarded us as rich. Nochum was a short, skinny man who had no particular trade and only infrequently found anything to do. He referred to himself as a printer, though it was never discovered on what grounds. His wife, who knew better, chose not to challenge this statement, at least in public. He was very garrulous and, I thought, altogether convincing when he expatiated on the vicissitudes of the printing trade. The trade, it appeared, was riddled with intrigue and suicidally bent on keeping the best-qualified men out. I wondered that my mother thought him lazy and shiftless. But Chaie Rive, although perpetually on the brink of starvation, defended him passionately against all attacks, blaming the inequalities of the American economic system for her misfortunes. And, indeed, no outsider listening to Nochum would have any suspicion of the Flayshigs' economic plight.

Nochum had a passion for telling jokes and anecdotes of a humorous nature, even at inopportune moments. He would show up at our house looking seedy and unshaven, but genial and breezy in manner, and ask if we were familiar with the latest story about McKinley. We weren't, of course, and he would proceed to tell it slowly, like a well-to-do householder relaxing on a Sunday morning with congenial friends or relatives. I found his sallies amusing and his manner rather charming. But with the exception of Fannie the rest of our family tolerated him with impatience and abused him behind his back as a heartless, moronic husband and father. To be sure, Nochum never came out openly with the real reason for his visits; but we learned to know that his appearance at our house invariably presaged some misfortune at home, some illness or accident, or the imminence of starvation or eviction.

The colloquy that would eventually disclose his troubles would be devious and would consume precious time. My mother, by way of a beginning, might suggest a glass of tea. Nochum would give her a winning smile and say: "Why not? A glass of tea never hurt anyone, as the would-be choson [groom] said to the would-be kaloh [bride] when she plied him with tea. I suppose you know that story—after the young man had consumed eighteen glasses of tea without declaring himself—" My mother interposed to inquire about Chaie Rive and the children. Not at all discomposed at having to abandon the anecdote, Nochum, still smiling, cried: "Now, *that's* a good question. At this very moment I don't know how they are. How should I? I'm here, not in Brooklyn, heh! A man hasn't got eyes in the back of his head, has he?" He chuckled as if he had scored a point in a jolly game. Then after a sip of tea: "But when I left home an hour ago, Chaie Rivke wasn't too well. No. She wasn't well at all. In fact," and he beamed, "she was quite sick. I don't mind saying it. Why should I?

She was very sick." Nochum's face was radiant, but his eyes became shifty and looked rather frightened. It was the signal for Hannah to put on her things and leave with him.

Hannah would sometimes visit the Flayshigs out of sheer friendliness and bring them back with her for a hot supper. The twins, aged five, were always neatly, even stylishly dressed, their dark hair done up in long, tubular curls looking like inflated sausage skins. Chaie Rive was proud of these curls, whose perfection must have cost her many hours of labor with her forefinger, for she owned no curling-irons or curling-pins. To prevent any disturbance of the shape and symmetry of their curls, the twins were forbidden to participate in any game that could not be played standing still or sitting quietly on chairs. Like her husband, Chaie Rive never in public so much as hinted at the poverty that embittered her existence. But when she spent the night at the Flayshigs', Hannah would overhear Chaie Rive reproaching her husband for his shiftlessness and indifference to the bare needs of his family—outbursts that Hannah said were like an angry sea thundering against an indifferent and impregnable coast. When visiting us, Chaie Rive always spoke warmly of Nochum. She would tell us in confidence that he was at that very moment snarled up in negotiations for a lucrative printing job, holding out, if the truth must be told, for more money. There could be little doubt that his demands would eventually be met. Nochum was not a man who would suffer himself to be taken advantage of.

These confidences Chaie Rive peppered with aphorisms. Her aphorisms *sounded* like the concentrated distillations of experience which are current in all lands, but on examination they seemed either quite unrelated to experience or else too obvious to be worth mentioning. "When one sits in a streetcar," she would say, "one does not know what is happening on its roof!" There certainly was no gainsaying that, and Chaie Rive would assume a look of triumph. Chaie Rive's maxims

were impressive because they were all so remarkably *true!*
"A man in prison is not *free*," "You can't expect the sun to
shine when it rains!" "Schools are for learning!" "During a
storm it is safer to be indoors!" I often wondered why Chaie
Rive did not apply her store of wisdom to the solution of her
daily worries. Perhaps she tried, but neither her philosophy of
life nor Nochum's jaunty indifference to reality ever had the
slightest effect on their disastrous fortunes. Nor could their
friends and relations achieve more than temporary ameliora-
tion of their economic troubles. I see, throughout my childhood and boyhood, the figures of Nochum and Chaie Rive
frozen in their respective attitudes, like the pair sculptured on
the Grecian Urn in Keats's ode—he forever amusedly (yet not
without a hint of terror in his eyes) pursuing an intangible and
ever-receding job, and she forever affirming propositions of a
self-evident nature, the while she curls her children's locks
with a determined forefinger.

There were others besides the Flayshigs whom Hannah
befriended at the cost of her leisure. The one I remember best
was Sarah Schwartz, a widow who sat next to Hannah in the
cigarette factory. Mrs. Schwartz was in poor health most of
the time and was often obliged to knock off work early in the
afternoon and go home. On those occasions Hannah worked
overtime and gave the widow her extra earnings. Mrs.
Schwartz had a daughter of my age, and the two lived in a
small hall bedroom on Henry Street. The little girl was
blonde and plump, with a round face like her mother's. Her
name was Lily, to my great joy, and when Hannah went to
visit the ailing Mrs. Schwartz, I begged to go along and play
with Lily. While Hannah ministered to the patient, Lily and I
played jacks on the floor. During one of our visits Mrs.
Schwartz, sitting up in bed and feeling better, called my
sister's attention to the happy young couple on the floor and
said out loud what a fine thing it would be if they married
each other when they grew up. Though I expected to marry

someday, I had never given the subject much thought. But the widow's suggestion, while it made me blush, placed Lily in a new light. Since I had to marry someone, why shouldn't it be Lily, who was cheerful and pretty and looked like her mother, who was herself handsome in a mature way, especially when she wore her pince-nez with its attached silver chain looped over her ear? One of my wedding gifts to Lily would be pince-nez, and I would also get a pair for myself. I could picture us walking arm in arm on East Broadway of a Sunday wearing our pince-nez, which we would often take off and wipe with our pocket handkerchiefs, at the same time revealing to passers-by the raw dents on either side of our noses made by the tight-fitting convex metal clasps.

Presently Hannah sent us to play in the street while she tidied up the room. And in the street Lily told me that she loved me and asked me to swear that I would marry her. This I did, but with some misgiving, for I knew that an oath was a solemn thing registered in heaven, and could not be broken without the gravest consequences to the swearer. I was also somewhat taken aback by Lily's boldness in declaring her love, for I had been led to believe by the poems and stories we had read in school, as well as by the synopsis of some of the books my sisters read, that it was the man's role to be the pursuer. However, we were declared sweethearts for some weeks, until the advent of summer, when Lily went to spend her vacation with a relation in Stamford, Connecticut, who kept a candy store on the Main Street and lived in an apartment above it. When we parted, I promised Lily halfheartedly to visit her in the country. But I knew that such a trip was beyond my means. And when, on her return from Stamford early in September, we met again, both of us were unaccountably seized with shyness. Our interview grew strangely impersonal and awkward, as if we were strangers meeting for the first time. From then on we met rarely. I was surprised by the instability of my affections, and, looking around to find some explanation for it, decided that true love, abiding and unchanging, could be felt only for one's mother and sisters.

It seemed to me that so beautiful, kind, and unselfish a girl as Hannah would attract to herself most of the eligible men of the East Side. Yet, notwithstanding her great desirability, the number of her suitors was negligible. I cannot have looked forward complacently to the time when Hannah would marry and leave me. At the same time, I wanted her to be besieged by suitors, none of whom she would consider seriously because of her great attachment to me. At the moment, I had little cause for worry. She showed no unusual interest in either of the two men who were her steady callers. Though I teased her about Mr. Chaikin, I felt no serious danger in that quarter. Mr. Chaikin made no attempt to conceal his intentions. He was always at the house, and often stayed so late that my mother was obliged to apprise him of the hour by roundabout hints. As every room became a bedchamber at night, none of us could go to bed while a stranger was in the house.

I did not fear Mr. Chaikin, because he lacked the romantic flavor that I believed a man must possess to interest a woman. Yet he had every other attribute of a desirable suitor. He was handsome in a florid way, tall, slightly plump, and soft of body, his hair curly and parted on the side. He resembled, in fact, Boris Thomashefsky, but he missed, somehow, that celebrated singing actor's charm. In keeping with this resemblance to that idol, Mr. Chaikin was a devotee of music and drama, with a flair of his own for acting and singing. With his numerous anecdotes of life on the stage and in the opera house, he brought the world of art right into our house. In his pleasant baritone he sang entire operas for us. In this he was often joined by the true, sweet soprano of Hannah, to whom he had taught the feminine portions of his repertoire.

To cap these musical delights, Mr. Chaikin brought, one unforgettable day, a most startling contrivance, which, on being wound up, reproduced the actual voices of artists singing celebrated arias and even duets and trios. These wonderful sounds emerged from an enormous horn attached to the machine. Hollow, cylindrical wax molds, carefully protected by cotton casings when not in use, imprisoned the voices and the music. How Mr. Chaikin could afford so elaborate and obviously expensive a machine remained a mystery to us all, for he could not with any semblance of truth be called a rich man. Mr. Chaikin spoke of himself as an artist, and more definitely as a "Fresco-painter." My father professed to find little difference between the art of Mr. Chaikin and the unglamorous labors of Ida's husband. "A painter," he would say with cold finality, "is a painter." But while Mr. Chaikin had often impressed on us the difference between a "Fresco"-painter like himself and a house-painter like my brother-in-law, he was reticent about which of them was paid better. We suspected that art was not as lucrative as it deserved to be; for Mr. Chaikin inhabited a tiny, dimly lighted top-floor bedroom in a decaying tenement on Allen Street, the window of which was level with the tracks of the elevated railroad. Mr. Chaikin claimed he had chosen the room for its north light, the one indispensable condition for "Fresco"-painting. But if the light was north, there was, because of the presence of the elevated tracks and the station shed, very little of it.

For my part I enjoyed visiting Mr. Chaikin and sitting by his window while he painted in water-color small pictures of fat cupids to serve as models for his "Fresco" paintings on the walls and ceilings of houses he hoped to be engaged to decorate. It seemed to me I could spend a lifetime at his window enjoying the long crescendo of sound of approaching trains and the brief but vivid glimpses of the passengers inside the cars and on their crowded platforms. When he finished a water-color, Mr. Chaikin would show it to me, ask what I thought of it, and beg me to bear in mind that what I saw was only a small counterfeit, deficient in scope and brilliance, of the real thing as it would look in a "Fresco painting." There was a house uptown he knew about which was scheduled for renovation, and this very water color would be submitted to the proprietor as a sample of Mr. Chaikin's skill in art decoration. It occurred to me that Mr. Chaikin might have borrowed the money for the purchase of the phonograph on the strength of such prospects. At that he was making a good living out of it—one sufficient to *marry* on. The fact that he appeared to enjoy a good deal of leisure meant, Mr. Chaikin assured me, nothing. One or two jobs of "Fresco-painting" brought him enough to live on for a year. There were plenty of prospects "uptown," that vague, affluent region far to the north of us, half an hour by horse-car. There rich people with a craving for beauty were waiting to be convinced that their satin-covered walls and plain ceilings were outmoded and inartistic, and that "Fresco-painting" was the desirable decoration of the future. Because he had no access to these would-be clients, he had put himself in the hands of a friend who, as the proprietor of a paint store in a neighborhood adjacent to "uptown," was in a position to recommend him to householders wishing to redecorate their houses.

From a worldly point of view Mr. Beylinson, Hannah's other constant caller, would be a better match. For one thing, Mr. Beylinson was the manager of an ice-cream plant on Madison Street. For another, he was a man about whom everything was known. He had been one of the earliest of my father's pupils in Vitebsk, and he would good-humoredly recall several beatings he had taken on the occasion of formal visits made by his parents to the cheder. He had come to America long before us, and had from the smallest beginnings risen to his present eminence in the commercial world. He was tall and slim, and his cropped hair stood straight up, with no part. He had an earnest, intelligent, rather serious face, and when he laughed, his teeth were white, a rarity among the men we knew. Strangely enough, he had a sentimental attachment for his old rabbi. Indeed, we suspected that Mr. Beylinson supplied my father with the mysterious funds that made possible such extravagances as Lea's wedding dress. But his kindness was not confined to my father alone. He was always willing to alleviate misfortune. In that he resembled Hannah, and his appreciation of her humane propensities may have drawn him to her. He was perhaps the only friend acceptable to both sides of the family.

He would sometimes take Hannah to a concert and ball at Pythagoras Hall, and once when I begged hard he took me along. That evening Hannah looked radiant in a pink silk shirtwaist and long black satin skirt, and Mr. Beylinson looked quite handsome in a dark suit and a tall, upstanding starched collar with a large bow tie. I could not figure out how Hannah obtained her beautiful outfit. There never seemed to be an extra quarter around the house. Yet Hannah and Molly always managed to look smart when they went out. There was a needlewoman in the neighborhood who made clothes for the girls for what my mother told my father was practically "nothing." Yet the material was of the fashionable kind and must have cost something. But if the pink silk shirtwaist was an extravagance, Hannah took measures to preserve its freshness. She had tied a large white handkerchief around her waist, so arranged that it would protect the back of her shirtwaist from the perspiring right palms of her dance partners. Mr. Beylinson was always careful to place his right hand squarely on the handkerchief. Not so one or two other men who asked my sister for a dance. To these Hannah said politely: "Lower, please," and, the hand being adjusted, the two would solemnly waltz away. Mr. Beylinson's manner to my sister was indulgent and at the same time condescending, or perhaps I should say, impersonal. He certainly did not behave like a suitor, nor did Hannah show any preference for him over Mr. Chaikin.

Molly was too young to think of marriage, but old enough to have beaux. So far there was no question of *her* being in love, and I could look forward to many years of intimate companionship with her. She was not nearly so kind and good-natured as Hannah, and her personality had no spiritual overtones like Hannah's. On the coarser plane of life in a crowded ghetto Molly and I enjoyed a community of sympathy and interest such as I could never share with Hannah. Her vitality was unusual. Like me, she never grew tired. She was impulsive, savagely intolerant of injustice, embarrassingly outspoken, and, like me, prone to laughter. We were both just as prone to tears. In fact, almost everything we saw or heard made us laugh or cry. The people who came to our house either engaged our affections or excited our scorn. We knew no moderate emotions. My mother would scold us for "looking at each other," as, indeed, we did look at each other in the presence of those who fell short of our inflexible standards of looks and behavior. And very often we would rush out of the house to avoid outbursts of derisive laughter we felt we could not check.

On hot summer nights Molly and I would seek relief from the heat in Jackson Street Park. The park, innocent of grass and trees, was a large asphalted area close to the East River, with many lanes of benches for the convenience of visitors and a stone pavilion like a Greek temple, where a small brass band played occasionally and milk was dispensed at a penny a glass. The park was always crowded. The men were in their undershirts. The women, more fully dressed, carried newspapers for fans. Hordes of barefoot children played games, weaving in and out of the always thick mass of promenaders. It was on these walks in Jackson Street Park that Molly revealed her more serious side. She talked about the perpetual schism in our family, about our depressing poverty and my mother's indulgent attitude toward my father's tyrannical behavior. Once she hinted that she and Hannah

were at the breaking-point, especially Hannah, the chief target
of my father's displeasure. Except for their reluctance to leave
their mother and me, they were prepared to leave the house
and set up for themselves.

It was in Jackson Street Park that Molly imparted a disturbing piece of news. Hannah, she told me, was in love! I
braced myself to hear the name of the stranger whose appearance I was uneasily expecting. But no stranger had
appeared. Hannah was in love with Mr. Beylinson! I could
hardly believe it. Hannah had given no intimation. Molly
laughed and said that I was only a child. There had been many
intimations. I was probably the only member of the family
who hadn't guessed. At any rate, Molly had asked her sister
point-blank whether she loved Mr. Beylinson, and Hannah,
caught unaware, had been unable to deny it.

Molly had no doubt that Mr. Beylinson was fond of Hannah
and that a little encouragement from her would bring him to
the point of a direct proposal. What she feared was my
father's influence over him. My father was certain to oppose
the marriage for two reasons. First, he would regard such a
brilliant match as a victory for the "enemy," and, second,
Mr. Beylinson married to Hannah might easily lose his sentimental attachment for his old rabbi and withdraw the benefits
that had gone with it. Molly professed to have noticed ominous signs of opposition on my father's part, and who could
tell what he was saying to his former pupil in private?

Burdened with this intelligence, I began to watch my father
for those evidences of opposition Molly had remarked. My
father was seldom direct in undermining what he wished to
oppose. He was clever at devising secondary annoyances to
disguise his real objective. If, for example, his aim was to
punish my mother, he would talk disarmingly about Mrs.
Reich's devotion to her husband, Zalman, or he would set
himself against my going to a matinee that cost nothing, and
would force me to stay home and read the Bible with him. I

now observed that when Mr. Beylinson was present, my father missed no occasion to animadvert, in half-serious fashion, on my mother's propensity for extravagance and on Molly's idleness on Sundays and holidays. The latter accusation would bring Hannah to her sister's defense. And this in turn would offer him the opportunity of hinting that Hannah herself was not beyond reproach, that the apple does not fall far from the tree, and that angelic dispositions often have a secret layer of all too human imperfections. And when, of an evening, the rest of the family would discreetly retire to the front room, leaving Mr. Beylinson and Hannah by themselves in the kitchen, my father would make no move to leave, but would pretend to be absorbed in one of his religious books. In short, it became clear to me that my father had set himself against the romance and was doing everything he could to prevent its consummation.

This unavowed campaign against my sister's happiness came to a dramatic head one Saturday. It was Hannah's chore to set the table for the midday dinner and to place the two chalehs (twist breads) in front of my father's place. My father had just come from schul (synagogue) and had washed his hands and sat down at the table, ready to remove the napkin from the chalehs and bless them. But the chalehs were not in their accustomed place! What all-absorbing preoccupation had caused Hannah to forget the chalehs that fateful Saturday I never learned. My father rose from his place, his face white with rage. As he had not yet broken his fast, he was forbidden by rabbinical injunction to vent his anger in speech. Silently, his eyes ablaze, he seized Hannah, dragged her to the door, opened it with one hand, shoved her onto the landing, and sent her flying pell-mell down the flight of stairs to the ground, where she lay dazed, in a heap. My mother, hearing the clatter, came running from the kitchen, and Molly and I rushed down the stairs and helped Hannah to her feet. In a furtive council the four of us held at the bottom of the stairs, it was decided that Hannah could not return to the house, but should go forthwith to Chaie Rive's in Brooklyn. I was to accompany her there. Molly went upstairs and fetched Hannah's hat, veil, jacket, and pocketbook.

On our way to Grand Street a resolution was forming in my head, and when we were seated in the streetcar I confided it to Hannah. I told her I had made up my mind to kill my father. I had been harboring thoughts of revenge for a long time, but they had been amorphous until that morning. Now I saw clearly, for the first time, what had to be done. A man who was so inhuman to a person as blameless as Hannah must not be permitted to live. Nor could I foresee any consequences to me as a result of his assassination. I would explain the nature of the man to the judge and jury, who would then have no alternative but to set me free. They might even extol the parricide as an act of divine justice and hold it up as a warning to all unfeeling parents. Hannah's reaction to my resolve was disappointing. She heard me out gravely; but when I finished she smiled and drew me closer to her and said I was foolish to have such ideas, that after all he *was* my father, and that I must at least wait until I grew up before I could pass judgment on him. I replied with some warmth that I saw no virtue in the accident of relationship, else I should love my father's children as much as I loved my mother's, which she well knew I couldn't. Her disapproval had no effect on my resolve, and soon I found an unexpected ally in Molly, who, when I outlined my plan, showed no surprise and intimated that she had independently arrived at the same solution to our troubles.

On the following morning my mother appeared unexpectedly at Chaie Rive's. She had come to persuade Hannah to return home. She told us that my father had calmed down as suddenly as he had flared up the day before. She declared that his assault on Hannah was inexcusable, yet she thought it could perhaps be explained by the fact that he hadn't had a morsel to eat since supper the night before, and on top of that the absence of the chaleh! . . . Unlike me, Hannah could never harbor a grievance for long. Perhaps she felt that she had no right to abandon the three of us to my father's uncertain temper. The upshot of my mother's visit was that we all returned home later in the day. Hannah assumed her old duties as if nothing had happened. On Saturday the chalehs were in their place on the table, facing my father's chair. My father, too, appeared to have quite forgotten the dreadful episode of the previous Sabbath. After he had blessed the bread and eaten a morsel, he chatted amiably about his friends at the synagogue and, as usual, singled out Zalman Reich as the most enviable member of the congregation.

But from then on, Mr. Beylinson's visits to the house grew less frequent. Molly was certain that through subtle innuendo and calculated misrepresentation my father had finally convinced Mr. Beylinson that Hannah was not the wife for him. Or Mr. Beylinson may have decided against marrying into a family so torn with internecine strife as ours. Hannah confided in no one, not even in Molly. But Molly could tell by certain signs she had learned to interpret that her sister was passing through a crisis. On the other hand, the tension at home lessened with Mr. Beylinson's increasing reluctance to visit us. My father assumed an air of placid aloofness, and from this radical change of behavior Molly surmised that Mr. Beylinson was now definitely lost to Hannah. As far as I could ascertain, Hannah showed no trace of any disappointment or of what Molly called a broken heart. Her solicitude for me even increased, and her kindness to those who enlisted her help never faltered.

Mr. Beylinson having finally betaken himself from the scene, I was not surprised to see Mr. Chaikin, who had for a short while succumbed to pessimism, double his visits and his efforts to interest Hannah and to charm the rest of the household. Molly kept me abreast of the progress he was making. Riding on a new wave of prosperity occasioned by the successful efforts of his friend the paint-store owner, who had obtained for him a big job of "Fresco-painting" in a house on the fashionable upper West Side, Mr. Chaikin suddenly made a formal application for my sister's hand. My mother, eager to see Hannah married before people could learn about Mr. Beylinson's defection, had no objections to Mr. Chaikin and referred him to Hannah, who, to my utter astonishment, accepted him. I could not understand how, loving Mr. Beylinson, she could marry Mr. Chaikin! But Molly said she understood very well, and she was sure that Hannah would forget Mr. Beylinson, once she was married. Furthermore, Molly would have approved of any marriage if only for the reason that it would liberate Hannah from the tyranny of her stepfather and the dissensions of the house. Upon consideration I was forced to agree with her. For one thing, her marriage would remove at a stroke the necessity for my father's assassination. In the placid and genial mood he had assumed, I could not slay him in cold blood. And I remembered Hamlet's inability to kill his stepfather for a reason not unlike mine. For another, Hannah's marriage assured the continuation of the flow of operatic art, if not in our house, then in my sister's future abode. And, finally, there was implicit in this marriage the assurance that I would not be supplanted in my sister's affections, something I could not have taken for granted had she married Mr. Beylinson.

The wedding took place a fortnight later. It was held in our front room. Hannah wore her monkey-jacket suit and a white shirtwaist. The only other guests besides the members of our family were Chaie Rive, her husband, and the twins, and Mr. Chaikin's elder brother Morris, whom we saw for the first time. Morris Chaikin lived in St. Louis, Missouri (he never mentioned the city without adding the state), where he was engaged in the mattress business. His presence in New York combined, he said, business and pleasure. Right after the refreshments, the couple departed for a week's honeymoon in a boarding-house in the Catskills owned by a relation of Mr. Chaikin's friend and agent, the paint-store proprietor. I could not say that I was jealous of Mr. Chaikin, yet I felt depressed and could not keep back my tears when I saw Molly and my mother crying. Nochum Flayshig began a humorous anecdote, but, finding that no one was listening, abandoned it in the middle and sat smiling to himself as if in pity for our lack of humor. Chaie Rive applied herself to straightening out the ringlets of the twins and reminded us that this was an occasion for merrymaking, not for sorrow, an opinion that she hastened to clinch with an aphorism to the effect that at birth one cannot possibly guess what the future will bring. This appeared irrefutable, and a silence descended on the room. When I could no longer bear the pervasive sadness, I ran out into the street to seek relief and forgetfulness in a game of "one-o'-cat."

CHAPTER TEN

Business Affairs

WHILE each marriage in our family left us with a roomier apartment and an extra blanket, it also resulted in a tighter economy. Hannah had been the chief support of the household (Molly stubbornly reserved a large percentage of her earnings for her own use), and her departure brought a financial crisis to the family. All my mother could now count on were Molly's modest contribution and my father's meager and erratic earnings. Sarah was not yet fourteen, and therefore could not be legally sent out to work.

To meet our new emergency, the first thing to do was to find a cheaper apartment. Many such were available, but they were "in the back," facing a great network of clotheslines and immodestly close to the windows of the rear apartments of the tenements opposite ours. My mother found a first-floor apartment "in the back" in a house on Rutgers Place which faced the livery stable I knew so well. I missed the view I had loved for some two years. I could no longer see from my window the meeting of four busy streets and the long stretch of East Broadway to its vanishing-point where it merged with Grand Street. Gone from view was R. Hoe, Inc., with its sky-piercing clock tower. Of course East Broadway was only a few blocks away from Rutgers Place, and for a few weeks after our removal I visited it daily and looked up longingly at our old front windows in number 157. But my appetite for this sentimental pilgrimage dwindled as I entered more and more into the life of Rutgers Place. I soon joined the Rutgers Streeters and espoused its enmities and alliances—happily the Rutgers Streeters and my old gang, the East Broadwayers, were on friendly terms, so that I was not obliged to make war on my former comrades.

Our next step toward improving our financial situation was a bold invasion of the realm of trade. My mother had noticed the increasing tendency of housewives to spare themselves the labor of cooking by patronizing the delicatessen store. Originally a German institution, the delicatessen store reached the East Side through the agency of the reassuring word "kosher." Kosher delicatessen stores soon appeared on every street, and kosher sausage factories sprang up to supply them and to encourage the creation of new stores by offering to provide store fixtures on a long-term installment arrangement and to extend credit on an equally generous scale. Children took to delicatessen for its spiciness, preferring it to the bland, boiled meats their mothers served at home. Elderly people still frowned on delicatessen and clung to their accustomed boiled and sweet-and-sour meats, but they were powerless to attack the pickled viands on religious grounds. Even my father, while himself eschewing delicatessen, had no doubts about the orthodoxy of the rabbinical supervision under which it was manufactured.

It occurred to my mother one day that the proprietorship of a delicatessen store was our best hope for financial security. Two obstacles immediately presented themselves: my father's opposition (an automatic first reaction to any suggestion put out by my mother) and our complete lack of money. My father stated categorically that there was no future in delicatessen and that what my mother saw as a trend was only a temporary deviation from normal Jewish eating habits. He also pointed out that the best restaurants (the one at 159 East Broadway was a good example) offered a "regular dinner" of no less than six courses for fifteen cents, which, while not cheap, was certainly for bulk and quality a better buy than fifteen cents' worth of delicatessen. My mother replied that only a housewife could have an authoritative opinion on the future of delicatessen. She also reminded him that his prognostications had in the past always proved wrong. He was, she said, by nature too conservative and pessimistic to understand the power of imagination when backed by persistence. Had she taken his advice, they never would have found Mr. Harris in London. And if they hadn't found him they would not now be in New York.

My father's objections were more easily disposed of than the chief obstacle, our lack of money. After exhaustive inquiries in delicatessen circles, my mother reported that the Mandlebaum Sausage Factory on Houston Street was prepared to contribute a part of the fixtures to the proposed store and to extend credit for merchandise for a period of three months. There were delicatessen stores for sale in the neighborhood, but the prices asked were far above anything my mother could contrive to borrow. It was cheaper to rent a store and start one's own business. Taking into account the fixtures proffered by Mandlebaum and the offer of a loan of a soda-water fountain by a manufacturer of carbonated water, my mother arrived at the sum of one hundred and fifty dollars as sufficient to launch the venture.

It was a staggering sum to raise, and my father wished to be informed how she proposed to raise it. "Mr. Beylinson," my mother said succinctly. We had not seen Mr. Beylinson at our house since some time before Hannah's marriage. But we suspected that my father saw him frequently at his ice-cream factory. After pooh-poohing the suggestion, my father wanted to know just what guarantee he could offer Mr. Bey-linson that the loan, if granted, would be repaid. "Give him," my mother promptly replied, "a receipt." That seemed to settle the matter. I knew that a receipt was a decisive docu-ment. Our landlord gave us one each month. My father, how-ever, received the suggestion without enthusiasm, though he agreed to speak to his pupil about a loan. My mother was so sure of my father's influence over Mr. Beylinson that she went at once to Mandlebaum's factory and made final arrangements with the manager for the extension of credit and the installa-tion of store fixtures. She rented a vacant store in the building we lived in. And days before Mr. Beylinson handed my father the one hundred and fifty dollars in (for some reason) one-dollar bills (and impressive they looked as my mother counted them out carefully with the aid of a continually wet thumb), the store had been swept and a vanload of fixtures and tables and chairs had cluttered up its length, waiting to be put in place.

Mannie Kalb came over on Sunday morning and lettered the plate-glass window in masterly fashion. The letters were huge, in black with strong white borders around them. Shaped like an arc, the first line read:

KOSHER DELICATESSEN

And underneath, in straight lines:

MANDLEBAUM'S MEAT SUPPLIES
SODA WATER, ALL KINDS SYRUPS
CIGARETTES
MOSHE BAER CHOTZINOFF, PROP.
REGULAR DINNER 15 CENTS

The final item was a concession to my father, who thought it might attract people accustomed to eating in restaurants. Secretly my mother had no faith in its drawing power, for she made no preparations for serving "regular" dinners. But she assured my father that she was capable of handling any customer who might require a "regular" meal. Nor was she boasting. On several occasions I saw her successfully steer a "regular dinner" customer away from his expectation of appetizer, soup, fish, boiled meat, dessert, and tea and cake to a plate of corned beef or pastrami and a schooner of raspberry soda to top it off!

The day finally arrived for the "Grand Opening." Grand openings on the East Side were conducted on a standardized pattern, and ours had the usual features. For all its familiarity it was, nevertheless, an exciting event. A week before, Mannie had painted on a large piece of cardboard: "GRAND OPENING JULY 5." The sign, resting on an improvised cardboard easel, was placed ostentatiously in the store window. On the morning of the great day a large wicker basket with artificial flowers arrived, the gift of Mr. Beylinson. We knew Mr. Beylinson had sent it, though the painted inscription on the silk ribbon tied in a bow on the handle said only: "Best Wishes From A Friend." Who else but Mr. Beylinson could afford such an expensive gift? My mother placed the basket in the center of the window and grouped around it many chunks of uncooked corned beef and pastrami. Viewed from the street it made an impressive picture, and along with the two dozen long, hard salamis hung by cords from the window ceiling, this grouping of flowers and food attracted the attention of passers-by from morning till night. In fact the window-shoppers were so numerous that the customers (disappointingly few) had difficulty in making their way through the crowds outside.

Inside, the store looked fetching indeed! The salami motif, so effective in the window, was also carried out in the counter display. Separated from customers by a low glass partition, the counter bristled with bisected salamis, hard and soft, and bolognas thick and thin. My mother, flanked by an experienced young man the Mandlebaum firm had obligingly delegated to assist at the grand opening, stood behind the counter, knife in hand, filling the orders rapidly, like a veteran delicatessen-store owner. Behind her on a ledge lay tall stacks of slices of rye bread, and next to them stood an enormous jar of soft, soup-like, bright golden mustard. My mother dispensed sandwiches, taking care to cut the corned beef, pastrami, or salami paper-thin, as she had been taught to do by the Mandlebaum young man, who himself concentrated on "plate" orders for the occupants of tables. Sometimes as she "closed" a sandwich with a top slice of bread a customer would protest against the meager ratio of meat to bread and my mother would reopen the sandwich and add a slice or two, and with a smile say that she was grateful for all suggestions. Also at the suggestion of the young man from Mandlebaum's, my mother had invited a dozen friends and relatives to sit as guests at the three tables that lined the wall of the store. She had cautioned them to behave in all respects like customers, to order what they wanted (within reason, of course), and to send substitutes when they themselves had business elsewhere, for the tables had to look at all times quite filled. My father—for reasons of pride (it was easy to justify his wife's venture into delicatessen, but a respected teacher of Hebrew who was preparing for the career of rabbi could hardly do more with propriety than lend his name to it)—kept himself aloof, walking up and down the opposite side of the street to note, unobserved, the success or failure of the grand opening.

When lunch time arrived at noon, business took a spurt. People who worked on our street came in for a sandwich, a pickle, and a glass of soda water, or bought a few cents' worth of meat and bread to take out. When a few customers, desiring a more elaborate meal, went toward the tables, some of the seated relatives exhibited embarrassment and looked to my mother for guidance, some even rising as if to leave. These my mother subdued with significant glances, and they sank back in their chairs. My mother was quite willing to take a loss on this day for the sake of a future gain, for the rumor would soon get around that the new delicatessen store was such a success that not a table was ever to be had.

The store hours were from seven a.m. to midnight. My father came in at closing-time by the back door and watched my mother count up the day's receipts. The gross was about fifteen dollars, and the net, after much figuring, came to six. My mother had reason to feel elated. A grand opening offered no financial yardstick; but she felt that if the business eased off to ten dollars gross per day, which meant a profit of four dollars, or twenty-four dollars a week, the sum would more than fill the financial loss occasioned by Hannah's marriage. Faced with the concrete proof of an actual day's profit, my father admitted that he might have been overpessimistic about the venture. At the same time he complained that he had had nothing to eat all day but a roll and a saucer of cream. My mother assured him that she would find time to prepare a hot meal for themselves every day. And if all went as well as she hoped, she might even hire someone to tend store mornings till noon. This would enable her to clean our apartment, cook and serve dinner, and wash up afterwards.

With a wealth of delicatessen available at all hours, I failed to understand my father's preference for home cooking. I abandoned myself without restraint to the food in our store. For lunch I alternated between "plates" of corned beef, pastrami, and large bologna. The large bologna, though a coarser meat, was especially good between draughts of sarsaparilla out of a schooner. When school let out at three o'clock, I made straight for our store and made myself a sandwich extravagantly bursting with many slices of quite unpenetrable salami buried under a thick coating of the yellowish mustard. Salami called for a schooner of raspberry soda. For supper I selected slices of several meats, which I heaped high on a plate and ate with a large pickle and several acid pickled tomatoes. I was permitted to wait on customers, and I frequently released my mother to her household chores upstairs. I learned to slice salami, tongue, and bologna paper-thin (when I served myself, the slices came out thicker), and I managed to eat a morsel at every sale I made.

In the rear of the store was a large, sunless room, with a long slit of a window, heavily barred. This was my mother's room of all work, where she cooked the corned beefs, tongues, and pastramis in a tin clothes-boiler over a three-burner gas stove. When she lifted the lid of the boiler, the fatty, bubbling water spilled over on the floor, and the delicious, aggressive aroma of superheated pickled beef would mingle with and soon overpower the prevailing insistent, native, musty, dank smell of perspiring, decaying paint and plaster. As clouds of steam burst from the boiler and rushed to the ceiling, my mother plunged a great iron fork into the submerged chunks of beef and, finding the flesh unresisting, she raised them one by one out of the caldron and carried them, steaming and dripping, quickly into the store. There she deposited them on the counter and with a large sharp knife proceeded to pare away as little of the surrounding fat as she could get away with, for most customers eschewed fat and resolutely demanded its excision, notwithstanding my mother's insistence that so extravagant paring would take all her profit out of the transaction. The sight and smell of the meat—by now the knife had exposed to view the rosy, corrugated, succulent fibers behind the protective gray coating of fat—generally proved too much for me. I might have only just finished my lunch or dinner or an afternoon snack, but I would plead for, and always get, a slice, which I dispatched clean, without the leavening intervention of a slice of bread. Such was my pleasant, exclusive diet for the nine months' life of our delicatessen store. Frequent intestinal discomfort, which kept me in bed for short periods, failed to curb my enthusiasm for delicatessen, pickles, pickled tomatoes, mustard, and soda water, and I always returned to the store with my appetite sharpened by deprivation.

The nine months were so packed with adventure that they passed quicker than other periods of the same duration before and after. Aside from the pleasures of eating and drinking, I loved to tend store, and I learned to be expert in handling the variety of knives on the counter and in guessing exactly how many slices of meat would register a quarter, a half, or a pound on the scales. The soda fountain was an unceasing fascination, and I never without a feeling of surprise and pleasure reversed the lever that released a sharp needle-like spray to agitate and bring to a foam the schooner of soda. I sold cigarettes too, mostly singly for a penny, and handing them over the counter gave me a sense of being grown up. I would keep my mother company until closing-time at midnight, often against her wishes. I hung around, not for any help I could be (customers were few between seven and twelve p.m.), but for the satisfaction of being in the store, inhaling the delicious confusion of smells, and watching in the large mirror behind the counter the reflection of the tables and chairs and the advertisements of Mandlebaum's products, and even of things the store did not carry, like Passover wine, matzoth, and Brown's Celery Tonic. I presume we did not dispense Brown's Celery Tonic, which was a favorite drink in the neighborhood, because it was bottled, and the margin of profit from it would be less than that of the syrup and carbonated water we sold at the soda fountain. (I was to revel in the celery taste and aroma of Brown's Tonic some years later.) The mirror also reflected a placard on the wall urging people to drink "Moxie," and showing a dapper young clerk in white, with sleek black hair parted mathematically in the middle, pointing a commanding forefinger and looking at one directly, and rather threateningly. We served, alas, no Moxie, which, as depicted on the card, looked deliciously dark and racy.

My mother always resorted to boiling water in our unceasing war on vermin. Neighbors argued the merits of popular bedbug and cockroach powders, but my mother, who had in her time tried everything, put her trust in a kettle of hot water. In the summer she would devote an entire evening to bedbugs. Every coil of her own bedspring and the iron folding bed would be penetrated by a spurt of boiling water and the vermin would fall to the floor, zigzag crazily for a moment, and suddenly stiffen into extinction. She would even pour water on the buttons of her mattress and cover it with the oilcloth from the table at bedtime. Nor was she content with half measures in dealing with lice. Most mothers of the neighborhood would sit of a summer evening on the steps of their stoops, patiently exploring the heads of their children and deftly extracting the vermin and crushing them between the nails of their thumbs. But my mother periodically subjected my head and my little sister's to whole kettles of water heated to a temperature we were barely able to endure. And where everybody else examined the seams of their underwear for lice nightly on going to bed, my mother adopted the (more) preventive measure of doing the family wash (in scalding water) as often as twice a week!

The delicatessen store was closed from sundown Friday to sundown Saturday. One Saturday afternoon there was a knock at the door of our apartment upstairs, and a tall man wearing a dark suit and a derby hat came in. In a mild voice he announced that the store had been robbed. The robbery, he said, must have occurred during the night. The lock of the back door had been broken, and the thieves had denuded the place of every edible thing. We hastily went down to the store with him and found that our informant had not exaggerated. Not a salami was left hanging in the windows, nor had the thieves left so much as a slice of large or small bologna.

Gone were the half-new jars of pickles and even the enormous jar of mustard.

The strange man showed us the extent of our losses like a cicerone leading a party through a point of historic interest. He then said that his name was Mac and that he was a private detective, and he offered to protect the premises for a fee of two dollars a week. I translated the proposition to my parents. Seeing my mother hesitate, Mac told me to tell her that he was well acquainted with the thieves of the district and was in a position to guarantee absolute protection. My mother, he said, was at liberty to take or leave his offer; but if she did not engage his services he was sure that robberies like the one that had just taken place would become a commonplace. Mac spoke suavely, in a low, engaging voice. My mother looked him over while I translated his words; then she abruptly told me to say that he was hired. On hearing this, Mac tipped his derby hat politely and told us that from that moment on, our worries were over.

The robbery, it was computed, set us back about fifty dollars. If it had taken place the following Monday, when we expected the delivery of a very large order from Mandlebaum's, the loss would have been nearly double that. There was nothing for it but to get another loan from Mr. Beylinson. The moment being critical, my father did not, for once, demur. And on Monday morning before the new order arrived, he called on his old pupil at the ice-cream factory and obtained the fifty dollars. The store was duly replenished that very day. My father even professed to see the hand of providence in the extraordinary coincidence of the appearance of the private detective on our street on the very morning of the robbery. He could also read an assurance of power in Mac's gentle, persuasive manner. And, indeed, Mac was as good as his word, for we did not have another robbery in the two or three months he protected the store. During that time he would visit us nearly every day around supper time, sometimes bring-

ing along a friend or two. They would all sit down at a table
and Mac would play host generously, ordering large platefuls
of corned beef, his favorite among all the meats. We never
charged him anything, for he assured us at the outset that he
enjoyed the full hospitality of those of his clients who owned
eating establishments, and he gently offered to have his meals
elsewhere if we preferred, as, of course, we didn't.

I found Mac and his friends very entertaining. They talked
a good deal about politics, especially in relation to local matters. One afternoon Mac arrived in a moving-van and craved
permission to store some things for a few days in the back
room. Before I could translate his request to my mother, two
men began carrying oblong crates into the store, with Mac
gently but confidently directing the operation. I recognized
the objects as ballot boxes of the sort I had seen in voting
places, and on my expressing interest Mac laughingly told
me he was playing a joke on a judge, an old friend of his; that
the boxes were, indeed, full of ballots as a result of an election
that had just been concluded, that he was playfully holding up
the count, and that he would return the boxes in a few days
and disclose to his friend the prank he had played on him. In
conclusion Mac hoped I would keep his secret, which, naturally, I did. Some days later the same van drew up and the
boxes were taken away. Mac reported that on hearing the
trick that had been played on him his friend the judge had
been vastly amused. But a week later Mac disappeared as
mysteriously as he had arrived. We never saw him again, and
all our inquiries around the neighborhood failed to throw any
light whatsoever on him or his whereabouts.

CHAPTER ELEVEN

✒ *The Freedom Method*

THE delicatessen store failed to realize our hopes. After the initial flurry of the opening day, it settled down to a disappointing net profit of about six dollars a week, with slight fluctuations on one side or the other. My father, too, was earning less than usual, for he now gave a good deal of his time to the rabbinical studies mandatory for future shochets and mohels. I was by now a big boy of ten, and what with my piano lessons, music books, clothing, and shoes I was—and I realized I was—a drain on the family economy. Because I spent most of my time on the streets in games and in the more belligerent activities of my gang, I was very hard on clothes and especially on shoes. Hardly a week went by without a visit to the cobbler. Even the iron guards he nailed on toes and heels wore to razor-thinness within a few days. I felt I had to do something both in the way of retrenchment and in that of earning some money. Retrenchment suddenly became possible through the fortuitous appearance of a lady who moved into the third-floor front of our tenement and pasted up a printed card in the entrance hall reading: "Madam Zamoshkin, Teacher of Piano and Voice."

The day she moved in I watched a beautiful upright piano being carried up the three flights by four men. This operation, which I aided in spirit from a position close behind the movers, caused me agonies of concern for the safety of the instrument, which, like some huge, timid creature resenting exposure, seemed bent on self-destruction. Later that day I went out on our landing and heard the piano being played upstairs in accompaniment to a loud and acid soprano voice. When the song was finished, I ran up the two flights and knocked at the Zamoshkins' door. Mrs. Zamoshkin herself opened it and asked me what I wanted; and when I told her I was a pianist and lived on the first floor, she invited me in. She was a big woman, with a heavy bosom that rebelled against the confining ribs of a corset showing through a fashionable-looking, transparent, dirty silk dressing-gown she had on. There were no buttons on the gown, nor any other visible mechanism to keep it from flying open, which it repeatedly did, revealing a dirty white petticoat edged at the bottom with coarse brown lace. When the flaps of the gown separated, Mrs. Zamoshkin said: *"Pardonne—verzeihe—*excuse, please," in a husky, languid voice, at the same time covering herself modestly. She asked me how long and with whom I had studied, and invited me to play a piece. I chose *The Alpine Shepherd's Evening Song*, which I played with the utmost expressiveness. Mrs. Zamoshkin had lit a cigarette (I had never before seen a woman smoke) and sat near me. When I finished she said, again setting to rights the unruly dressing-gown: *"Zamitchalnya"* ("Beautiful," in Russian), *"sehr gut!"* She got up and knocked at the door of an adjoining room. *"Chéri,"* she called in a soft, haunting, elegant tone of voice which made me experience a sensation I could not identify as ever having felt before, one that I found simultaneously disturbing and pleasant: "Darling —may I disturb you for a minute?" The door opened and a young man came into the room. He looked pale and not very well. He was tall, thin, and sandy-haired, and had a long, sharp nose. He was heavily dressed, though it was summer. A large muffler was wound twice around his throat. "*Sonza*" ("Sun," or "Pretty one"), she said, and she smiled deprecatingly as her gown separated again and she made haste to arrange it properly. "Did you hear this child? *Zamitchalnya—n'est-ce-pas?*" The young man echoed the Russian word in a weary voice. "This is Grisha—my husband," Mrs. Zamoshkin said with pride, and I rose from the piano stool and offered my hand. The young man, to my embarrassment, refused to take it. Instead he turned slowly around and without a word went into his room and closed the door behind him. "Cover your throat, angel," she called after him.

Mrs. Zamoshkin explained that her husband was a poet and didn't have much time to spare, being at that very moment engaged in the creation of a cycle of gypsy poems, which she was setting to music. She went to the piano and sang and played one of them, and I recognized the very one I had heard from my landing. The poem was in Russian, and Mrs. Zamoshkin obligingly translated a line for me. It was a wild, rhapsodical poem, the sense of which eluded me. But I appreciated the effectiveness of its insistent refrain, which came after every second line and addressed the gypsy directly. "Tara-ra-ra-ta-ra-ra-ra" was the meter of the Russian lines, and then the refrain: "Ho! Gypsy! Ha! Gypsy! Hey! Gypsy! Hi! Gypsy!" Mrs. Zamoshkin's voice was uncommonly strident, and at one point her husband put his head out of his door and said: "I thought you were finished with that one!" She threw him a warm smile and said: "Yes, I wanted *Dushinka*" ("Darling"—meaning me) "to hear it." The song cycle would comprise six numbers, she confided to me, each

one dealing with a different phase of gypsy life. She was looking around for a publisher. Whoever took the songs was bound
to make a fortune, for the passion of the verses would excite
the blood and imagination of the most sluggish purchaser. I
therefore recommended Mr. Katz of East Broadway, hoping
thus to show him my gratitude for his kindness to me in the
past year.

Mrs. Zamoshkin then went into my own situation. Her
opinion of my playing was most flattering, but she thought the
time had arrived for me to tackle a more ambitious repertoire
than the one I had studied. Her own piano method was a
revolutionary one, and under it her pupils had made brilliant
progress. She described this method in one word: "Freedom!"
she said, and the word rang out impressively violent. "My
method is liberty! A teacher should not be a jailer. He should
be a liberator. What difference can it make, *Dushinka?*"
(here her dressing-gown, agitated by a sweeping gesture of her
left arm toward the piano keys, opened wide and forced me to
look away for a moment). "What difference, I ask you
seriously"—she had retrieved the loosened flap of the garment—"whether you hold your hands high or low? Is that the
important thing? I ask you, and I want you to answer me
honestly and frankly—is that the important thing?" I shook
my head dubiously. It certainly could not be important. Had I
wasted a year in slavishly taking the fingers suggested by the
composers in their printed works, or by Miss Taffel? Mrs.
Zamoshkin saw me waver, and pressed her advantage. "Does a
bird take lessons in flying? Does someone tell her to use the
right and not the left wing? All she needs is freedom! Release
her from the cage and she will fly away, never mind how! It's
the same with people. They have been tied and bound with
laws, with institutions, like ropes. They have been tied from
head to foot by governments, presidents, tsars, priests, rabbis" (I blanched at the word "rabbis," for I had lately
wondered about them in respect to their insistence on im-

posing their beliefs on everybody, especially the young). Mrs. Zamoshkin continued: "Take love"—stretching toward me a cupped hand as if love, like a nesting bird, was in it, her voice rising to an unpleasant pitch.

Her husband put his head out and said wearily: "Such noise! How can one work?" and disappeared. Mrs. Zamoshkin lowered her voice to a hoarse whisper. "I ask you to consider love! What have they done to love—your priests, your rabbis, your governments? They have tied it hand and foot with marriage. When I told you Grisha was my husband, I was using a word meant for slaves. Yes, he is my husband. But he is more!" Again the husband poked his head through the door. This time he said nothing, but he looked at his wife threateningly. "All right, all right, *Golubchick* (Dove)," she cried as he again vanished, "I'll be quiet." Then to me hoarsely: "Artists *need* quiet. The soul *needs* silence. Someday you will understand. But how can they get silence in a city? The noise of the horse-cars—the screaming of children—the barrel-organs . . ." Mrs. Zamoshkin went on in this manner for some time, during which I learned that she had been a pupil of a pupil of somebody called "the Great Anton Rubinstein," who, it was well known, had never practiced—just played—sometimes missing notes, but what of that! Also that she had met her husband five years previously in Russia, that they had fallen in love instantaneously and had eloped to America, that there was a slight difference in their ages—"but love laughs at time"—that poetry did not pay, and that she was the sole support of the house. Furthermore, Mr. Zamoshkin was frail, subject to colds, and altogether unworldly. "If left to himself," she confided, "he would be unable to boil a kettle of water for tea—he would perish." Each time I politely rose to go, Mrs. Zamoshkin had some fascinating detail of her life to relate. However, the practical upshot of my visit was that I was to leave Miss Taffel and accept a scholarship from Mrs. Zamoshkin (I told her I was in no position at the moment to pay for my lessons), provided that I would give myself whole-heartedly to her "Freedom" method in piano-playing.

The more I thought of the benefits of the "Freedom" method, the more I considered my meeting with Mrs. Zamoshkin providential. I saw ahead of me a limitless repertoire of music which would be mine without drudgery of fingerwork and long hours of practice. I explained the new method to my mother and Molly and paid a visit to Hannah to acquaint her with it. They did not quite grasp Mrs. Zamoshkin's philosophy of piano-playing, but confessed that they were in no position to judge it. Hannah thought I had a duty to Miss Taffel, and that I must not mention Mrs. Zamoshkin or the "Freedom" method to her, but tell her that I could no longer raise the money for lessons. That, Hannah said, would give Miss Taffel the chance to proffer a scholarship. Knowing Miss Taffel's disposition well by then, I had no fears that she would offer me free tuition. And so it proved. For after I had my next lesson I told her I could no longer study with her, pleading poverty. Miss Taffel said she was sorry, but I would have to find another teacher. I left the basement much relieved and went straight to Mrs. Zamoshkin.

Mrs. Zamoshkin held that the "Freedom" method carried with it for the pupil the privilege of choosing the music to be studied. Seeing me at a loss for the moment, Mrs. Zamoshkin suggested the overture to *Poet and Peasant*, the music of which stood on the music rack of the piano. I was taken with the title and readily acceded; but when I opened the music, I saw that it bristled with unusual technical problems and several time changes. Mrs. Zamoshkin laughed away my fears and offered to play the overture for me to prove how easy it was. "People pay too much attention to notes," she said, as she composed her large frame and her dressing-gown (she dressed fully only when she went out), "and not enough to the spirit. The great Anton Rubinstein always played wrong notes and nobody cared. Why? Because he always brought out the soul of music.

Anybody can play the right notes, but how many can bring out the Soul!"

Mrs. Zamoshkin played the overture daringly and recklessly, I thought. I turned the pages. In my eagerness to keep up with her I sometimes turned a page too soon or too late. My teacher never paused or hesitated, but composed a few measures of her own on the spot. As I listened and watched the music at the same time, I realized that the impromptu interpolations had a wild, gypsy character that contrasted violently with the more classic style of the overture itself. How closely she had modeled herself on the art of the great Anton Rubinstein! For she quite disregarded, for the most part, the printed notes, especially in intricate or rapid passages! In the slower, lyric sections, she brought out what I presumed was the soul. On these she lingered, caressing some notes by raising and depressing her wrist, while her face assumed a pained expression and she shook her head ecstatically, as if the beauty of the moment was too much for her to bear. When she arrived at the last page she pressed the loud pedal down and kept her foot on it remorselessly, and with flashing arms and fingers let loose a babel of sound such as I had never before heard. Though it had little relation to the notes on the page, it was a stirring finale in itself, and when it was over I saw that Mrs. Zamoshkin's face was triumphant, though covered with sweat. "You may have noticed," she gasped, wiping her face with a large handkerchief edged with torn, black lace, "that I left out some of the notes. But I didn't leave out the souls of the Poet and Peasant! No! *That* I didn't." To this I assented, though it seemed to me she had been more successful with the soul of the Poet than with that of the Peasant.

In the half year that I studied with Mrs. Zamoshkin I "interpreted" at least two dozen compositions, most of them transcriptions of orchestral works or arias and songs. Mrs. Zamoshkin denied the existence of pianistic difficulties or, at any rate, treated them summarily when she herself met them. When I found that I was unable to negotiate certain passages, she would tell me to regard the spirit, not the letter, and, brushing me off the piano stool, would demonstrate how to achieve the one without engaging the other. The effects she conveyed were always dramatic. They excited in me a kind of uneasy admiration for her self-confidence and daring. I learned to rely on the loud pedal in critical technical moments, and while the results were unclear, Mrs. Zamoshkin soothed my doubts by admiring the "impression" I had created with seemingly recalcitrant notes. As for octaves, thirds, sixths, arpeggios, and all the other problems of piano-playing, Mrs. Zamoshkin called them "a bag of tricks" for the amusement of the superficial, but promised that if I really wanted to acquire them they would come to me of themselves easily with age and experience. In the meantime I must not feel intimidated when the music called for them, but do the best I could.

The news of the "Freedom method" spread quickly in the neighborhood, and Mrs. Zamoshkin was soon besieged by pupils, both beginners who looked forward to a speedy conquest of "pieces" without much practicing and students of the piano who had hitherto believed that one had to work hard to master the instrument and were delighted to find they had been quite wrong, and that "methods" existed that dispensed with the drudgery of work. Mrs. Zamoshkin was charging twenty-five cents a lesson. Notwithstanding this high fee, she was quickly making inroads among the students of teachers like Miss Taffel, who charged only ten cents and offered an hour's practice time.

I enjoyed the distinction of being her only scholarship pupil, and indeed I came to be regarded as a member of her household. She continually played and sang her settings of her husband's gypsy songs for me, gave me tea and "broken cake," and made me a confidant of everything that appertained to her husband and herself. She loved Mr. Zamoshkin inordinately as both her husband and her "child," as she called him, explaining that she had never had a child of her own, and that her husband, because of his youth and temperamental nature, was in many respects a child to her. Certainly no child I had known was ever so indulged and coddled. There was hardly a moment when Mrs. Zamoshkin was not preparing something for him to drink or eat, and in the middle of a lesson she would say: "Keep right on playing, dear, while I boil some milk for Grisha." Mr. Zamoshkin kept to his room mostly, and I saw him only at such times as he would put his head out to complain about something. It was a mystery to me how he managed to write his poems amid the never-ending sound of lessons and practice. He wrote only in Russian, considering the English language harsh and unmusical, and Yiddish hopelessly vulgar. Mrs. Zamoshkin called him a genius and prophesied that someday his works would be published and he would be recognized as another Nekrassov or Lermontov. I shared Mrs. Zamoshkin's indignation at the neglect her gifted husband was enduring, for my own efforts to have Mr. Katz publish the gypsy songs had come to nothing. Mr. Katz, to my astonishment, did not find the gypsy poems and their musical setting "real." They seemed real enough to me. Indeed, they had a savagery that invoked gypsies of the hottest blood imaginable.

Besides saving money on piano lessons, I was put in the way of earning a substantial sum through the kindness of Mr. Katz. Perhaps he wished to atone for his rejection of the gypsy songs by doing something handsome for me. One day when I went in to pay him an installment on the money I owed him for music, he told me that Cantor Feinstein—a great name on the East Side—was holding auditions for choirboys, and that the pay for those boys who were accepted would be two dollars and a half for the Rosh Hashonah and Yom Kippur holidays. I lost no time in getting to the basement of the Madison Street Synagogue, where the auditions were being held. I had a

flexible alto voice, and I read music easily at sight. After a
short test I was engaged. For six weeks before the holidays
we had lengthy rehearsals after school. The music of the
choir, in four-part harmony, was craftily integrated with the
solos of the cantor, and required a great deal of practice on the
part of the choir both alone and in conjunction with the cantor.
I enjoyed these rehearsals very much, especially those with
the cantor, whose flights of coloratura were breath-taking.
While his voice soared away into the topmost reaches of the
vocal scale in a hazardous display of trills, runs, and scales,
like an acrobat doing impossible feats on a high trapeze, we
would sustain beautiful solid chords underneath his daring
flights. The cantor had written the music himself, and had
most sensibly provided himself with moments of rest. During
these the choir held forth with ordinary diversionary passages,
so as not to erase from the minds of the congregation the more
important virtuoso contribution of the cantor.

Three or four days before Rosh Hashonah, one of the older
choirboys called a secret meeting at the fountain on Rutgers
Place. When we had all assembled, he got up on one of the
stone benches and addressed us. He told us that the Madison
Street Synagogue was raising the price of tickets for the holidays, mainly to meet the increased demands of our cantor for a
higher fee. Why shouldn't we, he asked, share in this raise?
The cantor couldn't do without us. Furthermore, we had
worked very hard, and our expert support would contribute
to his success. Our leader therefore proposed that we go to
the cantor at once and ask for a fifty-cent raise. Should the
cantor refuse, we must be prepared to strike.

The suggestion was put to a vote and unanimously approved. The cantor, realizing that the imminence of the holidays would not give him time to form a new choir, reluctantly
acceded. And on Yom Kippur night I triumphantly brought
home three one-dollar bills, the first money I had ever earned.
Though the day had been long and there were moments when

my head grew light from lack of food I found a great satisfaction in singing with the most celebrated cantor in America and in wearing the shiny skullcap and beautiful silk tallis (prayer shawl) the cantor lent to his choirboys. Furthermore, I saw at first hand the splendors of a "temple," for the Madison Street Synagogue was a far cry from the poor, dilapidated hired room where the average East Side congregation worshipped.

The previous year on Yom Kippur I had accompanied my father to his synagogue on Henry Street, and had scarcely survived the ordeal. At least one hundred men and boys were packed in a room that could not have accommodated fifty. Like every Yom Kippur I had known before or have known since, this one was unbearably warm and humid. I had taken the precaution the day before of buying a tiny phial of "Yom Kippur drops" for a penny, and whenever I grew faint I would take a whiff of the drops and feel better for a while. But in the late afternoon there came a moment when the men removed their shoes and prayed in their stocking feet. Inured to individual odors only, I was unable to tolerate the massed onslaught. I fainted dead away, and had to be carried outdoors and revived with many applications of "Yom Kippur drops" and dashes of cold water on my face. How different was the roomy temple on Madison Street, where open windows on opposite sides of the room provided a slight crosscurrent of warm air, and the congregation did not remove its collective shoes!

My three dollars could not have arrived at a more opportune time. My mother's teeth had been troubling her for years, and many of them had been extracted. On her most recent visit to the dentist on Rivington Street she had been advised to have the rest of them removed and replaced by an artificial set. This she agreed to on the representation that she would then be done with dentists forever. The new teeth would be costly, but the dentist was willing to undertake the

job on an installment arrangement of fifty cents a week. Two
of my dollars went to the dentist as an advance, fifty cents
went to Mr. Katz, and the remaining half dollar I was allowed
to do with as I pleased. I felt proud to be able to contribute so
large a sum toward my mother's new teeth. The parents of
some of my playmates had complete sets of teeth, which they
removed at bedtime and put in a glass of water for the night.
Now I should also be in a position to boast about my mother's
"plates." A gold cap was of course more ostentatious and
therefore more desirable. But a whole new set of evenly
matched teeth, removable at will, was the next best thing, for
while they did not command, like a gold cap, instant attention,
there was no possibility of mistaking them for one's natural
teeth, because of their whiteness and regularity.

With my own half dollar I began to assemble a library of
books. My taste had suddenly taken an unusual turn away
from the classics of poetry and short tales we read in school
and toward a new and more exciting literature of adventure.
The Rutgers Streeters were, by and large, reading the works
of Horatio Alger, the adventures of Nick Carter, the detective, the weekly serial *The Liberty Boys of '76*, and, in a lesser
measure, Oliver Optic and George Henty. All these appeared
in paper covers and were rotated among those of the gang
who contributed to their purchase. The Alger books cost
eight cents apiece, the weekly serials two cents, and all were
bought second-hand. With my very first Alger book I felt
that a new horizon had opened for me, for they were not only
embodiments of action, but action prompted by the highest
ethical principles. Then, too, they vindicated Mr. Silver's
philosophy of sturdy, aggressive individualism. Horatio Alger
convinced me through art that poor and rich were alike indispensable to a great country like America.

I now became aware of America, where before I had been
aware only of a few square miles in New York's East Side.
The America of Horatio Alger contained, curiously enough,

no Jews. There were no divisions of "classes" and "masses." There were rich and poor, but the rich could suddenly become poor, and the poor gradually became rich. It was a country of limitless opportunity for the moral, the virtuous, and the industrious. The poorest, the obscurest boy could aspire to the richest, the most beautiful girl. As I read my very first Alger book, I fancied that the author was writing about me. How did it happen that this great writer knew the secret aspirations of a young boy he had never seen? *I* was the "Erie Train Boy." I did not sell candy and peanuts on a train, but I had the Erie Train Boy's desire to better myself and, above all, to help my mother. My mother was not a widow; but if she had been, I would have been as loving and considerate a son as the Erie Train Boy had been. And what extraordinary insight into the mind and heart of a boy Mr. Alger revealed! He had endowed his hero with all my characteristics. I, too, hated bullies and was quick to right injustice. The only differences between us were owing to the difference in bringing up and environment. The Erie Train Boy had never questioned the social order because there was no Mr. Strassmeir to influence him to question it. For him the social order was composed of good and bad people, and what else could people be but good or bad? Extraordinary, too, was Horatio Alger's belief in the existence of luck, especially in the lives of the poor and deserving. How often had I daydreamed about being accosted by a man who would place a wallet, fat with money, in my hands and—saying: "I know you are good and are in need; take this and ask no questions, nor ever try to find me" —would disappear! How often had I (out of compassion) given my penny allowance for candy to a tattered, misshapen beggar, with the secret hope that I should someday be the beneficiary of his accumulated wealth, for it was well known that the worst-looking mendicants left the largest legacies!

A recurring daydream had me stopping a runaway horse and carriage, thus saving the life of its only passenger, a lovely young lady belonging to a rich family. And now, marvelous to read, I saw my hopes and dreams coming true in Horatio Alger's books. Here on the printed page before me a poor boy stopped a runaway equipage and saved the life of a beautiful young lady whose father was miraculously yet justly the president of an important bank. What insight into the soul of a boy! And what a country America was for a boy to grow up in! I do not recall worrying about the absence of Jews in the America of Horatio Alger. Certainly so democratic a country could be counted on to embrace and cherish people of all faiths. The fact that all the Alger heroes were Christians was merely accidental. I had little doubt that I, too, could have been an Erie Train Boy. I knew I should have behaved exactly like the one in Horatio Alger's story.

On the other hand, I often thought I should have preferred living in America during the period of the Revolutionary War as one of the Liberty Boys of '76. Business opportunities were scarcer in those days, but nobody required business opportunities at the most crucial moment in American history. What the boys of that fateful year desired exclusively was the opportunity to serve their country, and those opportunities could not have been more abundant. I could never have imagined that the Revolution owed so much to the American boy—not the soldier in uniform, but the younger boys who could not bear the thought of sitting idly by while their country was desperately engaged in throwing off its foreign yoke. Even General Washington leaned heavily on the courage and resourcefulness of these boys out of uniform. This nation would never have been freed without their aid. At Valley Forge, at Trenton, at every great crisis of our Revolutionary cause, these Liberty Boys saved the day. They exposed the traitorous Aaron Burr and captured the suave Major André. They were everywhere except, curiously enough, in the history books!

The future held several interesting possibilities for me, and

I escaped into it frequently, especially at those times when the present began to show a forbidding side, as it did in the alarming decline in the profits of our delicatessen store. There were weeks when the store showed no profits at all. And as with our living-quarters, the first of each month again became a day to be dreaded. My parents held many consultations on the advisability of selling the store or, if no one should offer to buy it, of dissolving the business and returning the fixtures to the Mandlebaum Sausage Factory as part payment of our debt. We could never hope to repay Mr. Beylinson, but that was not a serious consideration. My mother believed that Mr. Beylinson, out of sentiment, did not expect to be repaid. My parents would no sooner have decided to abandon the store, however, than there would come an unexpected spurt in sales, which my mother chose to regard as a trend and an augury of future prosperity. Whereupon plans for its sale or dissolution were hastily abandoned.

Fortunately, during this time of indecision my father completed his rabbinical studies and became free to set up as a shochet and mohel and to perform marriage ceremonies. My brother-in-law, the house-painter, painted a small tin sign that read: "Morris Chotzinoff, Practical Mohel (Circumciser), 1st Floor Back," which, with the janitor's permission, he nailed to the wall in the entrance hall. My father was averse to the change from Moshe Baer to Morris, but, anticipating this, Joe had made the change on his own initiative as a gesture toward Americanization, and my father was presented with a *fait accompli*. At home and among his friends he was called Moshe Baer. As for the adjective "practical," Joe had merely copied it from the signs of other East Side mohels. According to these, all mohels considered themselves "practical," and I, and presumably everyone else, assumed that that was what mohels had to be to invite patronage. "Practical" of course meant "practicing." Yet I used to doubt the necessity of the adjective on the signs of the neighborhood mohels. It seemed to me supererogatory; for if a mohel was not practicing, he would hardly put up a sign to that effect.

My father's first circumcision came through the recommendation of Zalman Reich. Mr. Reich's six sons were most prolific, and my father was constantly invited to the Reichs' to celebrate the birth of a grandchild with a glass of *"schnapps"* (whisky) and a piece of herring. On the arrival of another male grandchild, Zalman Reich told my father that he had ordered his son to engage him as mohel, but that he had permitted the mother of the baby to assume that my father was a "practical" mohel of long standing. My father made much of this proof of Zalman Reich's absolute power over his children and his trust in the steadiness of the new mohel's hand.

A week after the birth of the Reich grandson, my father and I repaired to the son's house. I went in the capacity of assistant and aide. The house was full of friends and neighbors to witness the ceremonial operation, and I felt very important as I made my way through them behind my father, carrying the case of knives, the whetstone, and the cotton wadding. To prevent the baby from catching cold, all the windows had been shut tight, though it was midsummer and very hot. We went into the bedroom, where the mother, with her breasts exposed, reclined sideways on a beautiful iron bedstead ornamented with numberless shiny brass globes. The baby, smothered in long clothes, lay at her side and sucked greedily at her right breast. *Mezuzahs* were tacked to the door to ward off evil.

A woman removed the child from the bed, placed him on a small pillow, and carried him into the front room, where the circumcision would take place. The mother was loath to give up the child. She cried a little and begged my father not to hurt him too much. In the front room the pillow with the baby on it was placed on a table and the baby's garments and diapers removed. I opened the case of knives and handed one to my father, who examined it critically and tested its sharpness by deftly cutting a hair from his hand. A basin of water and a towel were brought. The spectators, with the *sandak* (godfather) at their head, formed a circle around the table and my father and me. The woman who had brought the baby in now held him down firmly by the shoulders, and the *sandak* held down his legs. My father then performed the act of circumcision with astonishing swiftness for a first attempt. The baby began to wail and the mother in the bedroom set up a sympathetic weeping. The woman replaced the diaper and long garments and took the baby, still crying weakly, back to its mother. Cakes and wine were passed around, and the gathering grew merry. I replaced the knife (after my father had wiped it clean) and felt very professional and quite superior to some boys of my age who clustered around me admiringly.

Zalman Reich's son gave my father three dollars for the operation. This was the standard fee for a circumcision, but we thought it was handsome, considering the inexperience of my father. Two circumcisions a week would about bring in as much profit as the delicatessen store made in its best weeks. But it might be years before my father's skill would be well enough known to bring him so large a number of circumcisions.

Some weeks later my father was engaged to slaughter sixty chickens at a butcher's shop in Scammel Street for the Purim holidays. The price agreed on was two chickens for a nickel. On a Saturday evening I accompanied my father to the butcher's. My job was to take each doomed chicken from its coop and pluck out its feathers in the vicinity of the jugular vein, preparatory to my father's slitting its throat. The noise set up by the chickens was deafening, and the small basement shop appeared snowing with feathers. My father, with his jacket off and his sleeves rolled up, stood with a knife held between his teeth, in front of him a large tin vat. As I handed him each cackling, reluctant chicken (I can still see their glassy eyes fixed on me reproachfully), he bent its neck back-

ward with his left hand until the throat almost snapped. With
his right hand he took the knife from his mouth, made a single
pass with it over the jugular vein, and held the fluttering bird
directly over the vat, which now received its spasmodic spurts
of blood. I soon got used to the baleful look the chickens gave
me before they expired, and I prepared them for the knife as
rapidly as my father finished them off. The slaughter was over
by midnight, when we washed the blood from our clothes and
hands and left for home, a dollar and a half richer.

My father was pleased with his new activities, and our
future began to look rosier. On the other hand, the delicatessen store was now a definite liability, and its liquidation could
no longer be postponed. My mother gave notice to the landlord that the store premises would be vacated by the end of
the month, and the Mandlebaum Sausage Factory was advised to remove the store fixtures before that time. At this
moment in our affairs my brother Solomon arrived from
Waterbury, Connecticut, with good news. He had succeeded
in obtaining a position for my father at a slaughterhouse on
the outskirts of the city. The wages were twelve dollars
and four pounds of meat a week. We would move, rent-free,
into the upper story of a house Albert and Solomon owned in
one of the best neighborhoods. Thus all our troubles would be
over, and we could live in comfort and security in a fine Connecticut town for the rest of our lives.

My father and I greeted this plan with enthusiasm. My
mother was more reserved, though she did not oppose it. I
figured that she was loath to leave Hannah and Molly. Indeed,
she would have been hard put to it to find any other grounds
for opposing the plan. Molly, as a marriageable young girl,
would, of course, be better off in New York than in a country
town whose Jewish population was negligible. On learning
about our plans to remove to Waterbury, Hannah invited her
sister to make her home with her in her apartment on Seventh
Street, between Avenue B and Avenue C. By the end of the

month the store had been dismantled; on the very day we left for Waterbury a junk-dealer bought the entire contents of our own apartment (except for the few household items we would need) for the sum of fifteen dollars. Considering that the dealer, on first looking the things over, announced that he couldn't in honesty offer more than two dollars and that he wasn't even sure he could realize that sum on a resale, it seemed to me that my mother had taken advantage of him. Several times he left the house in indignation, but he always returned a few minutes later with what, after consigning my mother and her furniture to perdition, he swore was his final offer. When he advanced his offer to ten dollars and vowed that if that was turned down we should never see him again, I implored my mother to close with him before it was too late. But she knew better. And as the dealer reluctantly counted out fifteen crumpled and soiled dollar bills into her hand, she threw me a contemptuous glance.

CHAPTER TWELVE

❧ A Connecticut Interlude—1

W<small>E WENT</small> to Waterbury by water and rail. Early in the morning we walked to the foot of Gouverneur Street. A pushcart bearing our clothes and bedding, our pots and pans, our cutlery, and such household odds and ends as my mother wished to take along had preceded us to the pier. The boat went no farther than Bridgeport, but we checked our baggage direct to Waterbury. At Bridgeport we walked to the railroad station, which was close by, and after an hour's wait the Waterbury train came along and we climbed aboard it in haste, so that we might find seats together.

Children between the ages of six and twelve required a half ticket, but no ticket of any kind was bought for me. I was cautioned to slump down in my seat when the conductor came along and try to look as young as possible. As we left each station and the conductor came in to punch the tickets, I slid down in my seat as far as I could and remained in a cramped and uncomfortable position until my mother signaled that the coast was clear. Once the conductor looked at me sharply and asked how old I was. My mother gave him a charming smile and said: "Baby!"—one of the few English words she knew. Fearful that the man's suspicions would only be confirmed by an exaggeration so gross, I hastily interposed and said I was five and three-quarters, in the most childish voice I could muster. The conductor, still looking dubious, passed on, and I waited until I heard the door of our car shut behind him before I thought it safe to sit up. But he gave us no further trouble.

It was the longest train ride I had ever taken. I sat close to the window and watched the lovely countryside come into view, unfold for me in a semicircle, and roll off somewhere behind the train. After an hour my mother produced the inevitable *kuchlech* for herself and my father, and corned-beef sandwiches with pickles and mustard for Sarah, my little sister Goldie, and me. Many passengers had left the train at the frequent stops we made, and we had almost the entire car to ourselves by the time the conductor announced "Naw-gatuck! Naw-gatuck? Next station, Waterbury!" We left Naugatuck, and the train ran alongside a riverbank. We came in sight of a field where boys were playing baseball. The river, which had at first been clean and sparkling, became muddy and shallow. Pieces of rusty iron stuck up from its bottom and lined its banks. In the distance we saw long, low buildings with tall chimneys from which poured heavy smoke and live cinders. The train slowed up. The conductor opened the door and shouted: "Water-bury! Water-bury? Waterbury!" We gathered our belongings and moved toward the door.

Flanked by my mother and father, who tried to hide me from the conductor, I walked with my knees bent and my shoulders hunched in a final effort to look my alleged age. The conductor was now on the station platform giving a help-

ing hand to the people leaving the train. I doubled up, climbed
down the steps onto the footstool, then stepped to the ground.
Nor did I straighten up until the train began to move and the
conductor hopped aboard it.

Albert and Solomon were waiting at the station with a horse
and wagon. There was some delay in getting our baggage, but
it was presently piled on the wagon and we started off. We
drove through wide streets, tree-lined, and up a steep hill,
turning in to Burton Street, where we were to live. Burton
Street was wide, too, and tree-lined, and each wooden house
was painted white and had a front lawn and a back yard.
Many years later, longing to see Burton Street again, I re-
visited it and was amazed to find the street rather narrow than
broad, as I had remembered it. But it looked very wide when I
first set eyes on it, very leafy, and charmingly rural. When
contrasted with Rutgers Place, it was *country*.

Our house had a white picket fence around it. There were
a downstairs and an upstairs porch, both open, and a great
horse-chestnut tree stood close by, its branches almost touching both balustrades. Our apartment occupied the second
story. Its size and splendor took my breath away. Solomon,
looking very pleased, conducted us from room to room. He
had furnished it completely except for bedding, and apparently
had spared no expense. He took us first into the kitchen, by a
back entrance. There stood a large, shiny black stove ornamented with elaborate nickel facings. Linoleum covered the
entire floor. A large, open, white cabinet held a complete set
of dishes, brilliantly colored and set out in tiers. There were
three sunlit bedrooms (I had always thought bedrooms were
obliged to be sunless and dark), one with a double brass bed,
the others with two single wooden beds in each! The dining-
room was vast. A large pot-bellied tin stove stood in the
center, its stovepipe rising halfway to the ceiling, then bend-
ing and continuing straight across the room to a hole in the
wall above a window.

With a feeling for climax, Solomon left the front room for the last. When he threw open its door, we were dazzled by what we saw. Our eyes were first of all drawn to the floor by a brilliantly flowered carpet, so vivid as to nullify everything else in the room, even the wallpaper, whose colors and design would by themselves have been overpowering. And right against a wall, near a window facing the street, stood a *piano*, a shiny, tall, upright piano of unmistakable mahogany, as solid as any I had seen on display in Spector's store on Grand Street. Quite overcome with emotion, and forgetting my secret, I ran to the piano, seated myself on the revolving stool, and launched into *The Burning of Rome*. It was only when I arrived at the moment of Nero's appearance on the balcony of his palace that I remembered that no one but my mother and two sisters knew that I could play. I stopped abruptly and wheeled around. To my surprise, my mother was smiling. My father and my brothers looked quite bewildered, and regarded me with curiosity. My mother appeared to enjoy the sensation I had caused. "Don't stop," she cried. "Go on! Go on!" And I turned back and finished *The Burning of Rome* with an extra show of bravura.

When I finished, my mother revealed the story of my secret musical studies. It was a carefully doctored version, in which there had never been an outlay of a single penny on her part, for either tuition or music books, both of which grateful and enthusiastic teachers had been only too happy to contribute. Indeed, my dash and agility at the piano gave her story plausibility and reduced my father's grievance to mere petulance at having been kept in the dark about my inexpensive accomplishment. As for the presence of the piano in our new home, Solomon explained that he had acquired it along with all the other household furnishings as a result of a "foreclosure," a mysterious event that he did not deign to explain, but in which my mother professed to see the hand of providence.

For days I could not bear to be away from the piano. I knew that I must not play it when my father was *dovening* (praying). But the moment he took off his prayer shawl and phylacteries in the morning, I went into the front room, closed the door, and began to play. But before a week had passed, my father complained that my never-ceasing "banging" had become unendurable. "And where will it end?" he demanded, a question my mother brushed aside with the flat assertion that a child must have some amusement and with the disturbing statement that there were less innocuous pastimes than music a young boy might be tempted to pursue. What these might be she would not tell.

Playing the piano on the Sabbath was at first out of the question. But after a month of strictly observed Sabbaths, I could no longer resist the temptation to play on the forbidden day. And one Saturday morning from a front-room window I watched my father turn the corner at Burton Street into North Main Street. When he was out of sight, I boldly sat down at the piano and began to play. I expected my mother to rush in to tell me to stop, but to my surprise she left me undisturbed for a long time. When she came into the room, it was only to warn me that my father would be returning home at any moment. She must have pledged my sisters and my brother's family downstairs to secrecy, for I continued to play the piano Saturday mornings without my father's knowledge.

The "Freedom method," apart from releasing me from the drudgery of ordinary practice, also solved the problem of a teacher. For the nature of the method was such that, once it had been grasped, a teacher could prove a hindrance to the development of one's individuality. I knew, at the moment, no piano teachers in Waterbury. In any case a provincial city, hours distant from New York, most likely had never even heard of the "Freedom method" and of its two exponents, Mme Zamoshkin and the Great Anton Rubinstein. I felt confident that I could learn to play the most difficult music of the past and present without the aid of a teacher. The problem was how to obtain the music. I knew my small repertoire by heart, but I felt the need of adding to it continually, both for my own profit and for the pleasure of my audience, who might, I feared, soon get tired of the three overtures, *The Burning of Rome*, and the half-dozen smaller programmatic items I kept repeating. This problem, however, soon solved itself, and in the most unexpected fashion.

Since the London days my father had suffered much from headaches. Having seen a remedy advertised called "Bromo-Seltzer," he sent me, one day, to purchase a bottle at the drugstore on North Main Street. When I paid the ten cents, the clerk not only gave me a bottle of Bromo-Seltzer, but asked me to choose one piece of sheet music from a large assortment piled up on the counter, explaining that the Bromo-Seltzer people were giving out a printed musical work for the piano with each purchase of the remedy. I examined the pile and was astonished at the variety and range of the compositions. I should have liked to carry away all the numbers. Choosing only one posed a heartbreaking problem. At last I decided on the *"Miserere"* from *Il Trovatore* because it recalled my London and Stanton Street days, when I followed the hurdy-gurdies from street to street. The excerpt was an easy arrangement, but it included the words of the chorus, and Manrico's aria. "Ah! I have sighed to rest me" was printed above the notes of the aria, and I understood for the first time why the melody had so moved me. Whatever else he was in Verdi's opera, Manrico in his "Bromo-Seltzer aria" was melancholy to an unbearable degree, even though in a major key. Wherever he had languished when he sang the aria in the opera, he must have been nobly and mellifluously unhappy. I was consumed to know why, but there was no enlightenment beyond the expression of his unhappiness in the words and music. And what did the opening chords of the chorus, minor and softly massive, identified only hazily by words in a strange language (presumably Latin), picture? A Christian church perhaps, but grander than the one on the corner of Rutgers and Henry streets, from which, on Sunday mornings, I used to hear, over an organ foundation of sound, voices chanting, but in unison, crudely, not in somber chords as in the "*Miserere*."

My gratitude to the Bromo-Seltzer people for their largess was unalloyed for the time it took me to master and commit to memory the "*Miserere*." When I had done that, I realized with a shock that the growth of my musical repertoire would be dictated by the frequency of my father's headaches. I saw, with a sinking of the heart, that a single bottle of Bromo-Seltzer held sufficient powder to relieve the recurring headaches for a month, while I was able to learn a new composition in a matter of three or four days! I took to watching not only my father but the rest of the family for signs of migraine. My mother, unfortunately, suffered from maladies beyond the scope of Bromo-Seltzer to alleviate. I took to withdrawing a teaspoonful of the white substance secretly now and then, and so hastened the purchase of a new bottle. My mother sometimes wondered at the extraordinary rate of the family's consumption of Bromo-Seltzer. Over a period of a year, however, I acquired, through the agency of my father's real and my own simulated headaches, more than a dozen compositions of the most piquant variety. I learned them quickly, ascribing my skill to the liberating properties of the "Freedom method." In later years I discovered with a sense of shock that the Bromo-Seltzer people had simplified the pieces to the lowest common denominator of current proficiency on the piano.

Burton Street and the neighborhood around it were Christian territory, but across the car tracks on North Main Street, in the rear of the Waterbury Brass and Foundry Company, there was a ghetto-like area called Jerusalem, where most of my brothers' friends resided. In due course these families became our friends, and we were invited to Jerusalem to visit and drink tea. My brothers had built up the greater part of Jerusalem. With no capital of their own they had erected a dozen or so two-story wooden houses, each with a porch, and had rented the apartments to those of their friends and acquaintances who had previously lived dispersed among the Christians of the town. My brother Solomon was a habitué at the Feinsteins', a family who lived on the first floor of one of these houses, and we had not been long in Waterbury before he presented us to them. The Feinsteins had two daughters, Bernice, a young lady of marriageable age, and Hannah, a girl of about my own age. It was clear that the Feinsteins regarded my brother Solomon as a suitor for Bernice. Mrs. Feinstein praised her elder daughter extravagantly to her face in my brother's presence, attributing to her all the virtues of an efficient wife and several purely ornamental accomplishments such as piano-playing and the writing of poetry. Bernice, a pretty, plump brunette, who, it seemed to me, could inspire affection with her looks alone, was sincerely modest and always decried her mother's fulsome praises, which she would interrupt with "Oh! Stop, Mamma!" or "Don't be silly, Mamma!" Mrs. Feinstein loudly brushed aside her daughter's protestations. "Oh! Stop, Mamma!" she would mimic. "Why should Mamma stop? Is Mamma telling lies? No! Is it wrong for Mamma to say that you are an educated girl? (She graduated from high school with the best marks!) Is it wrong to tell the world you can recite? Is it wrong to say you play the piano? Play for Solomon *The Eight Sufferers*."

In the end Bernice always did what her mother bade her. She turned back the flaps of the gray rubber sheathing that completely encased their upright piano, opened the lid, screwed the piano stool up as high as it could go (I noticed that girls and women always sat high at the piano), and launched into *The Eight Sufferers*. I liked *The Eight Sufferers*, and I was hoping that Bernice would lend the music to me so that I might learn to play it by heart. The composition, by a composer whose name I have forgotten, was a memorial to eight anarchists who had figured in the "Chicago strike" in the year 1886. This unfortunate octet were tried for murder and found guilty, and four were executed. On learning the details of the tragedy I at once took the side of labor against capital, and, like the composer of *The Eight Sufferers*, fiercely resented the martyrdom of the eight. The Feinsteins, too, were on the side of the martyrs, but Bernice's interpretation of the piece lacked, I thought, the pathos inherent in the terrible situation of the eight during their trial and the nobility of soul implicit in their defiance of capitalism.

The impact of *The Eight Sufferers* on my brother was, naturally, modified by the circumstance that he himself was something of a capitalist, though in a small way. By nature timid, retiring, and sentimental, he was, however, also moved by the sufferings, if not by the ideology, of the eight. During her daughter's performance Mrs. Feinstein watched him narrowly for signs of a favorable reaction to the performer. She could not, of course, know that his heart at that period belonged to his own foster sister, Molly. Molly had herself intimated as much to me and, indeed, I had observed Solomon's marked attentions to her when she came to Waterbury to spend a week's vacation with us. My mother favored the alliance, but Molly herself could feel nothing for Solomon "in that way," and accepted his invitation on Sunday afternoon to take a buggy ride to an amusement park beyond the city limits only on condition that I would go along. I was, of course, invited to accompany them, and I spent an unforgettable afternoon.

I had not seen an amusement park since we left Russia. This one was a large tract of forest, with long tables and benches for picnickers who brought their own provisions. There was an open-air theater, and Solomon paid thirty cents for three tickets. We sat on a long bench close to the stage and enjoyed a variety show that lasted more than two hours.

There were vocalists, wire-walkers, trick bicycle-riders and comedians, and, for a finale, a minstrel show. The black-face artists interested me most, and their songs opened for me a new world of careless, ingratiating music, while the "lyrics" painted the Negroes as a jolly, pleasure-loving, humorously fatalistic people. I saw "soft shoe" dancing for the first time, and I gave myself up to the enchantment of its effortless rhythms. "Please go 'way, and let me sleep. Don't disturb my slumber deep," a black-face pair of men, clad in identical checked suits, with starched collars, straw hats, and canes, intoned dreamily and improvisationally, sometimes hurrying a word, sometimes drawing it out, while their feet tapped out soft, insistent rhythms, strictly in time. It was my introduction to "rubato," though it would be years before I could thus identify this strange relationship of melody and rhythm.

We moved to Waterbury sometime in August, and school did not begin until the second week in September. I had more than a month for idling and getting to know the city, time to make friends, practice the piano intensively, and explore the fields and forests that lay about a half-hour's walk from Burton Street. Burton Street itself was "country" enough for me. Its grassy front and back yards, little flower gardens, and great horse-chestnuts and elms very nearly approximated the pastoral scenes that climaxed the excursions Molly and I had used to embark upon at the foot of Montgomery Street on hot, sticky summer mornings. Directly opposite our house began Elm Street, which after about two hundred feet of level ground suddenly rose as a steep hill and continued so for a quarter of a mile. Its summit, bare of houses, marked the beginning of virgin country. Standing there, one could not see the city below, so thick was the vegetation, so tall and close together the trees. I found a small clearing, where I decided to build myself a rustic hideaway, something like the houses of boards and pine branches my father and some neighbors put together in the back yard of our tenement in East Broadway during Succoth. I borrowed a saw, a hammer, and nails from Solomon, and in a single morning I constructed a small sylvan retreat. There I used to sit for hours at a time listening to the birds and imitating their music in the hope of drawing them down to visit me. I told my mother that I communicated with many birds, but most intimately with one who sang "Bobwhite." And I fibbed a little and said that the bobwhites and I were now on the most agreeable footing and that I must not forget to take along with me a roll soaked in milk with which to feed my new friends, carrying out the promise I had made them in bird language. I did, indeed, scatter tiny pieces of a milk-soaked roll in the vicinity of my hut, but when I kept watch, no birds appeared to eat them, though I could hear their notes in the trees above me. The next morning, however, I could find no traces of the bread. I hoped that in time they would overcome their shyness and not wait until I was gone to pick up the crumbs I scattered. But they never did, and at length I grew impatient and angry with them. And when Chubb, a boy who lived in a house across the street, invited me one morning to go bird-hunting with him, I accepted his offer.

He carried a long, evil-looking gun with two barrels, and when we came to my hut on the top of the hill he taught me to aim and fire it. At my first attempt I fell on my back from the recoil of the gun, and my shoulder ached. But Chubb made me try again and again, and at last he pointed to a sparrow on a twig in a copse some distance away, and I fired, shutting my eyes as I did so. Chubb ran into the bushes and returned with a tiny, rigid bird in the hollow of his hand. I saw to my horror that the little head lay open and spattered with blood. I felt sick and was forced to turn aside and vomit. Chubb asked me if I had eaten something that had made me ill, and I said I had and that I had better go home and lie down. When I got home, however, I felt better, and boasted, to my mother's bewilderment, of having killed a bird. She had understood, she said, that the birds were my friends, and she wondered why I should want to kill my friends. I began to cry, and I promised her (and myself) never again to harm a living creature. And I kept my promise, though I could not resist accompanying Chubb on his frequent hunting expeditions.

Chubb was about thirteen, a tall, gangling boy, loosely built. He always looked as if he had slept with all his clothes on and had only just got out of bed. Yet he was very strong. He wielded an ax on a cord of firewood with great efficiency and, if I happened to be present, with exaggerated flourishes. He liked to wrestle and fight. Of course I was no match for him, and I was always quickly thrown. When I was down, he would dig his knees into my back and wrench my arms backward until I cried for mercy. Sometimes on our walks in the country he would suddenly stop in his tracks, square off, and command me to defend myself. We both knew the command to be insincere, but there was nothing for me to do but clench my fists and make a show of guarding my head and chest before I fell, overwhelmed by the force of his powerful blows. When I got to my feet again, he brushed my clothes with his hands and erased all signs of our encounter, behaving like one who bears no malice.

Yet it was Chubb who first made me aware of anti-Semitism in Waterbury. Unlike New York, where I believed that most Christians were bottled up in Cherry Street and on the water-front, Waterbury was entirely Christian except for the hand-ful of Jews residing in Jerusalem. Thus far our neighbors on both sides of Burton Street had shown politeness and some-times even cordiality toward me. Mrs. Calahan, Chubb's mother, often invited me in for a cookie and a cup of coffee when I came over to play with her son or help him cut the lawn. His older sister Jessie, a senior in high school, was a large, pretty, blonde girl, with whom I fell in love at first sight as she sat on her front porch and chewed gum lazily, drawing the aromatic tape to and from her lips like an elastic in ever longer and thinner stretchings. Jessie liked to tease me, but she always took my part in the quarrels her brother and I continually engaged in.

On our side of the street, where it began its decline toward the intersecting Elizabeth Street, was a firehouse with two beautifully equipped and shining vehicles—a hook and ladder, and an engine and hose. They stood side by side, with the harnesses for the horses suspended by wires from the ceiling. Mornings at seven and evenings at six a bell would ring for a fire drill. Unless prevented by illness, I never missed these exciting tests. At the sound of the bell the hitherto quiet place suddenly came to life. Half-dressed firemen slid down a pole from some upper region in rapid succession. Five big white fire-horses came clattering from their stables and took their places under their harnesses, which then descended on them and were quickly fastened by the firemen charged with this task. The drivers leaped into their lofty seats and seized the reins, while all the other firemen, in their undershirts, but helmeted and with axes in hand, sprang on the running-boards of the engines. At that crucial moment the bell rang again. The firemen jumped off the running-boards, the drivers in front and the steersmen behind scrambled down; the trappings of the horses were unbuckled, the harnesses ascended half-way to the ceiling. The drill was over. But the demonstration, witnessed by many children of the neighborhood and a sprinkling of grown-ups, was always breath-taking.

At other times I used to chat with the chief fireman, who generally sat on a stool in front of the firehouse and beguiled the time with a paper-bound book. People were cheerful and pleasant with me. Our next-door neighbor to our right said "Good morning" to me when we met in the early morning, he carrying a lunch basket on his way to work, I returning home from the fire drill. He had two little girls, aged about three and five, and a beautiful wife who seemed to love flowers more than any of her neighbors did. Every clear day at sundown she watered her geraniums and nasturtiums while she kept an eye on her children playing on the lawn. The three would wait for the father to come home from work. And when they descried his tall, thin, bent form in the distance, they would go to meet him halfway and then walk back together, not speaking to each other, but looking contented. After supper the man would come out alone, attach a hose to a spigot at the front of his house, and water his lawn, painstakingly slaking the thirst of every blade of grass. He would call out to me to say what a nice evening it was, and ask if I continued to like Waterbury, and wasn't Burton Street pretty?

Then Chubb disturbed the serenity of my first summer in Waterbury. One morning when we were wrestling on his lawn, while Jessie sat reading and chewing gum on the steps of their porch, I gained the advantage over him for the first time in all our battles. I had him flat on his back, and I exerted all my strength to pin his shoulders to the ground and so win the match. Jessie, seeing how close I appeared to be to victory, spurred me on with words of encouragement and made me determined to conquer, if only to gain favor with her. I had already firmly pinned his left shoulder down with my knee when Chubb screamed: "No you don't, *sheeny!*" The appellation had its intended effect. My grip relaxed, and the next moment Chubb had rolled over me and had me under him, both my shoulders securely touching the ground. As I rose and dusted myself off, his sister cried: "Shame on you, Chubb!" and Chubb retorted: "Well, he *is* a sheeny!" And to me: "You are, you know! *You* killed Christ, didn't you?" I denied the charge vehemently. Chubb went on: "Well, if you didn't, your *father* did. He's got a beard." I stood helplessly shaking my head, and Jessie came over and put her arms around me. "Stop that, you brute!" she screamed at her brother. But he wouldn't be stopped. "Your grandfather—your great-great-great-great grandfather did it. *He* killed Christ. Yes he did.

And on Passover you drink Christian blood. Everybody knows *that!*" I broke away from Jessie and ran up Maple Street, my heart pounding with impotent rage. I made for my hide-out on the hill. There I threw myself on the ground and wept bitter tears.

I knew that it was forbidden to speak of Christ in an orthodox Jewish house. In cheder he would be mentioned derisively by the name of "Yoshke Pandre" (Yoshke was the diminutive of Joseph, but the meaning of "Pandre" I could never discover), a renegade Jew who pretended to be God and deservedly crashed to the ground when in his foolish pride he attempted to fly in the air like a bird. I was smarting under Chubb's wild accusation, however, and I decided to brave my father's wrath and learn, once and for all, the truth of the matter. After supper that evening I boldly asked him if it was true that the Jews had killed the Christian God.

The question displeased him. He began shoving the crumbs on the table in front of him away with the back of his hand, an infallible sign of after-dinner petulance. After a long silence he said: "A foolish question! How could anyone know? It is even doubtful if there ever was such a person. In any case he's had his revenge. Yes, yes—he's had his revenge!"

Some time later, on a Saturday, he brought back with him the rabbi of the synagogue for a *schnapps* and a morsel of herring and bread. The rabbi was a thin old man with a long white beard that completely hid his collar and tie. He stayed awhile, and then from an open window in the front room I watched him leave our house and walk slowly and feebly away. He had not proceeded a hundred feet when two boys who were walking on the other side of the street picked up a handful of stones and began pelting the old man. I ran downstairs and out of the house, grabbed a handful of stones and pebbles, and attacked the boys in turn. The old man, holding his hands to his head, accelerated his walk, but did not otherwise appear surprised. I fought them until the old man had safely turned into North Main Street and was lost from view. By then the battle was going against me. I turned back and ran home zigzag fashion, to confuse the aim of my assailants. Once in the house, I slammed the front door behind me and turned the key. After shouting: "Come out of your house, sheeny!" several times, the boys went on their way, leaving me breathless and bewildered by the wanton cruelty I had witnessed.

Now for the first time since we had come to America I felt alien. I had thought that, with the exception of the hostile edge of the New York ghetto, America was my home. I could not mind being called a sheeny in Cherry Street, because Cherry Street represented a small, self-contained, violently antisocial perimeter that threatened me only when I invaded it. But to be called a sheeny in Burton Street obliged me to re-examine the image of America I had pieced together from the security of the New York ghetto and from the absence of any racial discrimination in the books of Horatio Alger. I had seen two boys attempt to stone an old man, seemingly because he had a beard. But I had met Christian men with beards who walked the streets of Waterbury unmolested. It was not, then, the beard of the rabbi that had offended his assailants, but the Jew behind it. It was clear that in Burton Street, and no doubt in every other street in Waterbury except those in Jerusalem, Jews were not considered Americans. The boys I had battled did not consider them Americans, nor did my friend and neighbor Chubb.

On the other hand, Chubb's mother and sisters did not seem to mind that I was a Jew. They were invariably kind to me. Our neighbor with the lovely wife and two little children was civil. But who could tell what they really thought of me, of all Jews? I looked back with longing to my former un-clouded life on East Broadway and in Rutgers Place. There Jews with beards walked not only with impunity, but with pride in their ancestry and beliefs. Rabbis were respected, even by the children of anarchists and atheists. Yet I could not conceal from myself that but for the difference in the status of Jews, Waterbury was a more desirable place to live in than the ghetto, especially in summer. There had been nothing in the ghetto so pleasant as the window-boxes and little flower gardens on Burton Street, and the great horse-chestnut tree in our front yard. When it rained softly in the evening, I sat on the porch alone and heard the drops make their silent way through the foliage. The tree stood breathless, absorbed in filling up every pore and vein to meet the onslaught of the morning's thirsty sun. Instead of fetid tenements, there were individual houses set at a polite distance one from another. Windows were curtained, and at night front parlors were lit softly and deeply by gas lamps with shades of subdued colors over them.

There were even more beautiful streets than Burton Street, lovelier and wider, where the very rich lived in large, spreading houses with flat tin roofs painted black or green. Some had glass-enclosed porches and high towers. These mansions were set in the midst of expansive lawns and gardens, and many of them had drive-ins for carriages. On one leafy street stood St. Margaret's School for girls, a beautiful, rambling, wooden structure, more like a rich home than a school. There, I learned, young ladies not only were educated, but were resident eight months of the year. It was aptly called a "boarding"-school. I marveled at the expense these young ladies were to their parents, and I also wondered at the young ladies' willingness to leave their homes and families (they came from many states), for they must surely be homesick. I should be homesick away from home.

From Chubb I learned that America was full of boarding-schools for boys, and that he himself would prefer a military academy to the educational schools that prepared the wealthy youth of the land for college. On hearing this, my mind went back to the gang wars on the East Side, and I recalled the pleasures of battle and the adulation of my fellow warriors. Perhaps Chubb was right! A military academy was the proper school for a courageous American boy. I was curious about what such military preparation might lead to, and Chubb said to a military career, and went on to tell me about West Point, which produced both Robert E. Lee and Ulysses S. Grant and other great generals and presidents. Chubb said that it was easy to get detailed information about the country's military boarding-schools. All one had to do was to send a postcard, and a booklet would arrive by return mail. He showed me a page he had cut out of some magazine listing military academies. I read fascinating names and places, and then and there I decided on a military career. I dispatched penny postcards to four institutions whose advertisements caught my imagination, and in a week there arrived, addressed to me, four booklets, profusely illustrated and completely informative. I had not written to West Point. I had heard with a sinking of the heart of the difficulties attendant on an appointment there. In any case, West Point lay far ahead in the future. It had, perforce, to wait on my graduation from a preparatory military school.

I devoured the contents of these booklets in my hide-out. In a few days I knew practically by heart the terrain, the buildings, the requirements for entrance, the fees, the courses of study, the privileges, the prohibitions, the number and dates of the holidays, and even the signed endorsements of famous military figures in the United States Army. But I found each of the academies so glamorous in its own special way that I began to despair of ever making a definite choice.

One school situated close to the field of Gettysburg in Pennsylvania appeared irresistible for its historical association. The booklet asked parents to evaluate the effect of such proximity to the field that became the turning-point in the Civil War and was the scene of President Lincoln's famous address. As a Northerner I felt I was obligated to choose the Gettysburg Academy. I found myself attracted also, however, to the Staunton Military Academy in Virginia. This school, its prospectus pointed out, was situated quite close to a famous academy over which General Robert E. Lee had presided until his death. Virginia sounded deeply romantic. Virginia had been, I hastened to inform myself, the head and front of a Lost Cause. This in itself drew me to it, even though the cause that was lost had for its misguided objective the perpetuation of Negro slavery. I weighed the two alternatives: on the one hand, years of residence in a Northern academy in the inspiring atmosphere of the Great Emancipator; on the other, the prospect of pupilage in the romantic terrain of the defeated yet lovable champion of slavery, Robert E. Lee.

I was particularly taken with the Virginia school's insistence on discipline, perhaps for the perverse reason that I was prone to resist any form of coercion. Then, too, I was attracted by the enumeration of a long list of prohibitions, defiance of which could bring about the instant dismissal of the student. Among these one stood out for its noble, though vague, implications. "Conduct unbecoming a gentleman," the prospectus stated, "will not be tolerated." "Conduct unbecoming a gentleman" invoked in a single phrase all the things that the heroes in Horatio Alger and the *Liberty Boys of '76* scrupulously avoided. It was, of course, unthinkable that I should ever be found guilty of it. The future seemed clear enough. Upon graduation from the Staunton Military Academy, I would apply for an appointment at West Point. I inquired the name of the Congressman from Waterbury with a view of making a direct application to him at once, and to suggest that he stand by for the time, about six years hence, when I should be ready for admission to the national military school.

If I entertained the thought that a military career would lead to the Presidency, as it had in several instances in American history, it was not for long. Chubb told me, with ill-concealed satisfaction, that no foreign-born male was eligible for that supreme office. There appeared to be nothing in our Constitution, however, to prevent the rise of a foreign-born American to the highest rung of the military ladder. I would, perforce, content myself with a lieutenant-generalship. The pay, I learned, would be ample, with a suitable residence, an orderly, a saddle-horse found, besides the privilege of purchasing victuals at the army stores at cost. Half of my pay I would give my wife for the upkeep of the household, and the other half I would distribute among my mother and my sisters, Hannah and Molly. Hannah, as the neediest, would receive a larger share than either my mother or Molly.

Hannah never complained, but Molly's letters from New York hinted at an unusual slump in the fresco-painting business. Week after week Molly voluntarily filled up the hole in the household economy. Hannah accepted this additional aid with the utmost reluctance, and her husband breezily promised to return the money as soon as the art of interior decorating took a turn for the better, a direction that to him appeared imminent. Though I respected my brother-in-law's art, I longed to free my sister Hannah from its business vagaries.

The brochures from the military academies did more than satisfy my curiosity about the practical aspects of military training. As they were in the form of booklets, sometimes bound in cardboard, they were, in a sense, books, and therefore, also in a sense, literature. I had appropriated a small unused storeroom in the attic. This I had fitted up as a den sacred to myself and not to be entered by my mother, my little sister, or even Molly when she came to visit us. I had nailed an old egg crate to one wall, which I pretended was a beautiful bookcase. My library was as yet negligible, consisting of half a dozen paper-bound Horatio Algers and a pile of *Liberty Boys of '76* which I had brought with me from New York. The *Liberty Boys* I stood up erect in the crate as if they were real books, and to these I now added the prospectuses of the military academies. But there still remained a whole shelf to fill up. At this point Chubb, who, while not a reader of books himself, took a friendly interest in filling my bookcase, suggested that a postcard to the U. S. Department of Agriculture would result in my being placed on that Department's mailing list. At Chubb's dictation I dispatched the following card to the Secretary of Agriculture in Washington:

> *Dear Sir:*
> Please send me all your books on Agriculture. I am a farmer.
> > Yours truly,
> > *S. Chotzinoff*
> > 79 Burton St., Waterbury, Conn.

To my delight the postman one morning delivered a weighty bundle addressed specifically to me. Inside I found a number of pamphlets on many aspects of farming, and a large, beautifully bound volume entitled, if I remember, *The Apple in America.* The book was more than three hundred pages long, the paper heavy and shiny, and the print large. But what pleased me most were the twenty-five plates illustrating the Apple in America in actual colors. Some plates featured a single apple, others an apple sliced in two, with the black pits showing. So realistic were the apples in color, rotundity, and texture that my mother swore she could have mistaken the pictures for the real fruit. Some time later, and quite unsolicited, the Secretary of Agriculture sent me two companion volumes: *The Pear in America* and *The Peach* of the same territory. I desecrated the books by cutting out three plates—an apple, a pear, and a peach. These I framed in pieces of wood I picked up in a new tenement my brothers were building, and hung up on the wall opposite the bookcase. I now could boast of both an art collection and a library.

My great objective was eventually to eliminate all paper-covered volumes and replace them with "real" books bound

in cardboard, cloth, or leather. My taste, too, was again under-
going a change. Rarely now did I take down an old Horatio
Alger to reread the history of the average, indigent American
boy. *The Liberty Boys of '76* languished, erect, on my bookshelves. My reading for a while was factual, and I was absorbed in the publications of the Department of Agriculture.
At my fingertips I had complete information about every
variety of fruit grown in the United States. At night I was kept
awake by reviewing, mentally, the contents of the prospectuses of the country's military schools. At the same time
I was conscious of a hiatus in my life, formerly occupied by
books of the spirit.

When school began in September, this lack was partly
modified, for I was placed in the sixth grade, and our readers
contained much poetry and some short stories appropriate to
our powers of comprehension. I was particularly impressed
with *The Rime of the Ancient Mariner*, which I committed to
memory. I marveled at its economy of language. It seemed an
easy poem to have written. Yet if *I* had written it, it would
have had to be twice as long. I recalled Tennyson's *Enoch
Arden*, over which I had wept in Mr. Strassmeir's class, and
I compared it with *The Rime of the Ancient Mariner*, to the
disadvantage of the former.

It was a new world of poetry that Coleridge opened up.
There seemed to be a pictorial, emotional, or spiritual reason
for each word in the poem. To my delight, the poet eschewed
precise information. Where Tennyson had told us in detail
about Philip and Annie and Enoch, their background, their
bringing up, and their relation to each other, Coleridge struck
out simple images, leaving me to fill in or speculate upon the
details as I chose. I was overwhelmed by the boldness of the
opening lines: "It is an ancient Mariner, and he stoppeth one
of three." *I* should have said: "*He* is an ancient Mariner,"
not "*It*." But how much better "*It*" was! And how imaginative the lack of ordinary identification in "one of three"! And

a moment later, when the identification comes, it is as vague as the previous "one of three," yet more impressive for its vagueness than if we had been told his name and history.

And who was the Ancient Mariner? I never knew, except that he was "one" who survived an eerie, soul-searing voyage in strange seas, and returned with loving-kindness in his heart for his fellow men, "both man and bird and beast . . . all things both great and small." And to my astonishment my eyes filled with tears at the mention of "him who died on cross." I hardly dared to dwell on the lonely image so startlingly placed before me. Could a Jew permit himself to weep over "him who died on cross"? Because of him, Jews in countless numbers had suffered and died. I myself had seen them suffer, and I had suffered to see them reviled and stoned. Yet the crucified image hovered before me and brought on tears. Perhaps I ought to find out more about "him"! "He" could not know what crimes had been committed in his name! If he could know, he must disapprove, else why should my eyes fill with tears when I thought of him? I must find out about him, secretly, of course, why "he died on cross." I could not ask Chubb, who was always hinting that I was, by association, responsible for his death. But I could read "their" Bible and find out.

On South Main Street, close to the railroad station, stood the public library, a lovely, dark-red, ivy-covered brick building. I passed by it often and wondered who that Howard Bronson was who had given his name to it, as a large plaque near the entrance door testified. I walked in boldly one day and discovered to my surprise a different situation from that which I had known in the Aguilar Free Library in the Educational Alliance on East Broadway. I found myself in an enormous room lined with books, and on the floor several long tables and chairs. Through another door I saw another room with countless rows of heavily-laden bookcases. Boys and girls, men and women browsed among the shelves as freely as if they were in their own homes. They selected a book, or several books, and walked over to a desk near the door, where a kind-looking gray-haired lady stamped their cards and conversed amiably with each borrower. I waited until the gray-haired lady was alone; then I politely inquired if I might look at a Christian Bible. She gave me a pleasant smile and said of course I might. She went to a bookshelf, found the Bible, and invited me to sit down at one of the oblong tables and read it. But when I opened the book to the first page, I was startled to find in English the very words I had studied in cheder: "In the beginning God created . . ."

I took the book back to the lady at the desk and said that I thought she had misunderstood me, that she had given me "our" Bible, not "theirs." She looked at me oddly and then leafed the pages to a place toward the back which read "The New Testament of our Lord and Saviour Jesus Christ," and said that what I was looking for began there. I took the book to the table and began to read. I felt afraid. I looked around to see if I was being observed. What would my father say if he was told I had been reading the forbidden book, the forbidden name with the bold claim of "our Lord and Saviour"? No one was looking at me. I could read on and no one would know. I must find out about him, who he was, where he came from, whom he had saved.

As I read I could hardly believe my eyes. He was "the son of David," it said, "the son of Abraham" (but, I realized, only in the sense of being a descendant). For "Abraham begat Isaac; and Isaac begat Jacob." I counted forty-two generations between David and him. With such an important *Hebrew* lineage, why did Jews proscribe him? His life had been exemplary, his death noble and pitiful. Many things baffled me as I read the Gospel according to St. Matthew. What was the Holy Ghost? Why should his death save "us"? Why did God permit his crucifixion? But I forgot such perplexities in the "personal" beauty of the tragedy, in the vivid details, in

the unflickering radiance of the central figure. I closed the
book in a ferment of conflicting emotions. I thought of my
grandfather, and I felt sure that he would have understood
Jesus Christ. For his heart, too, went out to pitiful people and
he had never thought of himself at all. I would not be afraid
to tell my grandfather about him. Perhaps even my mother
would understand! But I would have to think twice about con-
fiding in her; for all her goodness, there was no denying that
she was an uneducated person. I felt that only an educated person like myself could rise above prejudice and custom to understand him. It was true that she condoned my breaking the
Sabbath with my playing the piano. But could she consider
dispassionately a point of view that my father would regard
as sheer apostasy? It was hard to tell. I must wait for a favorable moment to test her. In the meantime I must learn more
about Christ and Christianity.

With this in mind, I went back to the Howard Bronson
Library to read more in the Christian Bible. But what I found
was only a retelling of the story I had read, with some unimportant differences. After finishing the Gospel according to
St. Mark, I decided that the reports of the remaining two
disciples would not enlighten me further. Outside, on the
curb, I saw a pushcart overflowing with books. A sign on a
stick advised that the books had been discarded by the library
because of age, and the price was two cents a volume. I picked
up one at random and opened it at the title page. *Oliver Twist*,
it said, *the History of a Foundling*, by Charles Dickens, Esquire. On the opposite page was a drawing. It showed a little boy sitting in a comfortable chair in a pleasant room,
absorbed in a picture book spread out on his knee. A window
looked out on a garden. I caught sight of a man peering at the
boy from outside this window. He was an evil-looking man
with a thin, swarthy face, a long, sharp nose, and gimlet eyes.
He wore a large felt hat and an old-fashioned cape. He had
evidently come a long way. His presence, I felt, boded no

good for the little boy. Underneath the picture it said "Oliver is visited by the Jew." The evil-looking man was the Jew. Therefore the boy, Oliver, must be a Christian. I was aware of the racial juxtaposition of the two. Apparently the hero of a story, being kind and good and brave as in the books of Horatio Alger, or merely young and innocent, as in *Oliver Twist*, could not possibly be a Jew. Only a villain could properly be one. Yet I knew Jews were good—that is, with a few exceptions. I had never met an evil Jew, one who looked as crafty and sinister as the man in the picture.

I felt that in making this character a Jew, Charles Dickens, Esquire, the author, was being unfair and unjust. There could be no possible resemblance between this terrible man and me, though we were of the same race. Still, in spite of the author's bias against Jews, I was taken with the mystery of the re-lationship between the man and the boy in the illustration, and I longed to read the book without delay. Fortunately, I had two cents in my pocket. And, the purchase made, I began walking slowly home, reading as I went. It was my first encounter with realism in literature, and I found it both re-pellent and absorbing. Here was poverty in a guise that I knew only too well, though the settings and the characters were un-familiar. Years later when I read in *Cranford* that one of the characters became so absorbed in reading an installment of a Dickens novel as he walked in the streets that he was run over by a horse and killed, I thought of my walk from the library to Burton Street with my eyes glued to the pages of *Oliver Twist*, and I marveled that I had not been run over at some street-crossing. Once in my house, I closeted myself in my attic room and read *Oliver Twist* until my mother called to me to come to supper.

As I read, I forgot my unhappiness about the author's un-fairness to Jews and gave myself up wholly to the story and its gallery of strange and fascinating people. I was relieved to find Christian villains along with the Jew, Fagin. Bill Sikes

was evil and cruel, though less subtle than Fagin, and Monks
was even more forbidding and certainly as crafty. I was delighted with the humor of some of the characters. I had never
before encountered such humor in books. I laughed till I cried
at the antics of the Artful Dodger and his haughty bearing before the police officer: "Were you re-dressing yourself to me,
my man?" The author seemed to know people most intimately. He also knew how to relieve the reader's tension just
when it was at the breaking-point. When my eyes swam with
tears and my heart ached unbearably at a crisis in Oliver's
misfortunes, the next chapter would set me laughing at the
pomposity of Mr. Bumble or the drolleries of the Artful
Dodger. When, happy and satisfied with the outcome of the
tale, I closed the book and looked up at the paper-covered
Algers on my bookshelves, I realized that Charles Dickens
knew life and people in a more comprehensive way than did
the author of *The Erie Train Boy*. I saw that both writers had a
passion for justice, but that there was an undefinable warmth
in Dickens that was missing in Alger. I realized that Oliver
had not the drive and ambition of the Erie Train Boy. And I
wondered if perhaps this very lack made Oliver more attractive, more heart-warming, more *living*, more *real!*

The more I compared the two authors, the more startling
became their differences to me. Dickens knew, and through
him I knew, too, the importance of language. Hitherto I had
not been conscious of it. Horatio Alger, I was forced to concede, was not. I was eager to read more of Dickens, and also
more of poets like Coleridge, who also used language in a
special way.

Yet if I should decide to become a writer, I thought, I
would favor poetry over prose. I realized it was the more
difficult medium of expression. For one thing, one had always
to be on a lofty plane of thought and feeling in poetry. I
should like to be aways on a lofty plane. Poetry permitted no
relaxation of thought, and the necessity of rhyming interfered

with one's natural flow of words. Another obstacle in writing poetry was the need of a knowledge of horticulture. Almost all poems spoke familiarly of flowers. But I knew very little about them. Yet, in spite of these difficulties, I *would* be a poet.

One afternoon during a study period in school, I wrote my first poem. I called it "Evening." It had six stanzas of four lines each. Several times I was forced by the exigencies of rhyming to change a thought or an image, but I finally succeeded in recalling and conveying the emotions I felt as I sat on my stoop underneath the horse-chestnut tree in the quiet of a starry night. I was enchanted with the poem, and tears came to my eyes at the beauty and felicity of some of my lines. "The flowerets," I had written, "sadly droop their heads." I was pleased with having chosen "flowerets" instead of "flowers," which would have been prose. The final couplet, besides being unusually lofty in sentiment, had a rather dexterous rhyme: "And yet to them [the flowerets] a Hope was given, a Hope as if sent down from heaven." Miss Quinn, my teacher, seeing me occupied in writing instead of studying, came up behind me and read the poem over my shoulder. Miss Quinn was redheaded and uncongenial. She asked me if I had copied the poem out of a book. When I said that it was my own, she gave me an incredulous look and walked away. Later, when school was out, I showed the poem to some of my classmates and was most gratified by their praise. At home I read it to my mother. Knowing only a few English words, she could not, of course, understand it. But she was touched by the tremor in my voice as I read, and the tears came to her eyes as they did to mine. She said it "sounded" good, especially the end words. She thought I should make copies and send them to Hannah and Molly in New York.

One day, accompanying my mother to the Woolworth's Five and Ten Cent Store, I walked idly among the counters while she rummaged around for needles and for thread of certain colors she wanted. Near the entrance on East Main Street was a wall lined with shelves on which stood rows of books, all bound in light pink boards. They were priced at ten cents a volume. My heart leaped at the sight of so many books, so uniform in color and size. I reached up for one and opened it. *Treasure Island*, by Robert Louis Stevenson, I read on the cover. It was the most provocative title I had thus far encountered, and I hastily turned to chapter one to see if I could find enlightenment there. Nothing could have excited me more than what I read in the very first paragraph: "Squire Trelawney, Dr. Livesey, and the rest of these gentlemen having asked me to write down the whole particulars about Treasure Island, from the beginning to the end, keeping nothing back but the bearings of the island, and that only because there is still *treasure not yet lifted* [italics mine], I take up my pen in the year of Grace 17, and go back to the time when my father kept the Admiral Benbow Inn, and the brown old seaman, *with the sabre cut* [italics mine], first took up his lodging under our roof."

At this point my mother, having completed her purchase, saw me and came toward me. I replaced the book and we left the store. I could hardly wait for her to enter our house before I ran back at full speed to East Main Street and Woolworth's, but when I looked for *Treasure Island*, it was not on the shelves. Someone must have bought it during the half-hour it took me to go home and return. I was utterly disconsolate, and was deciding to run over to the Bronson Library to see if there was a copy there, when the title of another book attracted my attention. *Kidnapped*, by Robert Louis Stevenson, the author of the missing *Treasure Island*. Perhaps *Kidnapped* was a sequel, and I could learn what became of the brown old seaman *with the sabre cut!* It wasn't. It was quite another story, but in its way as exciting as *Treasure Island*. And while I was deep in the opening chapter of *Kidnapped*, a store official came along trundling a little wagon full of the pink volumes. He filled the gaps in the bookshelves and left. To my delight, he had replaced *Treasure Island*. Then and there I knew that the two books must be my very own or I would never be happy again.

I could perhaps borrow them from the Bronson Library, though as yet I had not filled out a library card. But it was not alone an eagerness to know the outcome of both stories that possessed me. Indeed, I did not wish to know the outcome too quickly. If I owned the books I would limit myself to reading one chapter a day, the better to savor and prolong the great adventures and the probably startling denouement implied in the succinct titles. My passion at the moment was to *own* the books, and without delay. To buy them, if I could some-how borrow the money, would mean delay, and I dared not take the chance of the books being sold out completely beyond replacement by the storeman with the little wagon. I would steal the books. I saw no alternative. And someday when I had twenty cents I would pay the store and explain the nature of the delayed transaction. They would understand that I was not an ordinary thief, else I would have stolen chocolate-covered walnuts, which I never tired of eating. But I must take the utmost care not to be caught, for I should then not only lose the books, but render my family miserable and myself liable to imprisonment in jail or the reform school near Watertown which Chubb had pointed out to me on one of our walks. My desire to own the books outweighed all con-siderations of possible exposure and punishment. I set about planning the theft for the following day, which would be Saturday. There being no school, I should have at my disposal unlimited time. I would need to wear my overcoat, though the days were warm, for I could slip the books between it and my jacket. I would then saunter out with an air of innocence, my right arm pressed to my side to hold the concealed books in place until I should be safely out of the store.

I had no appetite at supper that night and ate very little. My mother felt my head, thought it warm, and put me to bed early. But I could not sleep even after everyone else had retired and the house was dark. And once I felt sick and had to rush to the toilet to vomit. But I was careful to make as little noise as possible, so as not to wake my mother. I lay with eyes open in the dark, and I saw myself in Woolworth's store at the bookshelves, waiting for the moment when I would be the only one there. Suddenly I imagined I stood at the gate of the reform school near Watertown, a policeman at either side of me. Then the scene changed to my attic room, and there on the shelf on the wall stood my two coveted pink volumes erect between *Oliver Twist* and *The Apple in America*.

Notwithstanding the agonies and hallucinations of that interminable night, my determination to carry out my plan never faltered. And soon after the opening of the store in the morning, I was on East Main Street, looking casually into shop windows and passing the great doors of Woolworth's with no apparent interest in the shop. I walked to the end of the street, crossed to the other side, and from a sheltered doorway watched customers go in and out of the five-and-ten-cent store. I was waiting for a lull, and about noon it came. I left my position and began to walk, and to allay the suspicions of anyone who might have seen me in the doorway and wondered at my loitering there, I made several detours and came into East Main by way of North Main.

When I entered the store, there was no one at the bookshelves. I made my way to the hardware department at the extreme end of the store, looking around for an article I pretended I could not find, and walked determinedly toward the entrance. There I paused as if I had accidentally caught sight of the pink books on the shelves. Leisurely I took down *Treasure Island* and glanced through it. From the corner of my eye I saw that I was unobserved. I closed the book and slipped it inside my overcoat. No one had noticed me. I took down *Kidnapped*, perused it for a while and slipped it, exactly as I had planned, under my coat, not *over Treasure Island*, but on a level with it, so that my chest should not bulge suspiciously. I pressed my left arm against my body just below *Treasure Island*, and with my right hand held together the two ends of my stand-up overcoat collar. I felt certain the books could not be seen from above or slip out below. I then walked slowly and calmly out of the store, looking neither to right nor to left.

Outside, I paused a moment to look at some of the wares in the window, then proceeded slowly toward North Main Street. When I turned the corner, I broke into a desperate run. As I ran, a passage from *The Rime of the Ancient Mariner* came suddenly to mind, spelling out my agonized plight:

> *Like one that on a lonesome road*
> *Doth walk in fear and dread,*
> *And having once turned round walks on,*
> *And turns no more his head;*
> *Because he knows, a frightful fiend*
> *Doth close behind him tread.*

I did not stop until I gained my attic room. There I hid the books in an old suitcase, which I then concealed in a closet. That done, I ran downstairs and took up a position on the front stoop, where I could survey the entire street.

I sat quiet and frightened, and pretended not to notice passers-by. I dreaded the possible sudden appearance of a policeman, but I also knew about "plain-clothes" men. Any ordinary-looking passer-by might well be one of them. Once a man who walked past our house rapidly stopped suddenly, turned, and came back. To my horror, he opened our wicket gate and advanced on me. I sat paralyzed with fear and waited helplessly for the blow to fall. But when he spoke he asked the way to the Brass and Foundry Company. In gratitude for this reprieve, I vowed never again to play the piano on Saturdays and holy days and not to take so much as a drop of water on Yom Kippur.

At noon my father returned from schul, and my mother called out to me to come to dinner. But though cholent (a potato stew) was my favorite dish, I dared not leave my post on the stoop, and I pleaded a headache and want of appetite. Toward evening I felt less apprehensive. On Saturdays the stores closed at nine. I gave myself an hour's leeway before I could feel it reasonably safe to retire. Yet lying in the dark, I fell a prey to the hallucinations of the night before. And in the morning I felt really unwell and was unable to get out of bed. My mother was much agitated and considered calling the doctor. But my father said that I must have eaten *chazerei* (unkosher food) and ordered castor oil. I languished, queasy and uncomfortable, for two days, and one night I grew delirious and my mother said I spoke wildly about policemen and prison. But I soon was quite well, and when I went out of doors again, I felt free of all fears and did not even bother to scrutinize passers-by. Before another week had passed I felt secure enough to look into the Woolworth store window, though I could not summon enough courage to enter.

That same night I took the pink books out of the suitcase and placed them on my shelves. As I had expected, they looked beautiful standing erect, flanked by a fat volume on either side. Unfortunately, I could not boast of my new acquisitions, nor show them to anyone, at least for a long time. Each morning before going off to school I paid them a visit to assure myself that they were still there. During school hours I daydreamed about them and was often inattentive to what Miss Quinn was telling the class. At home on late afternoons I read a little in each book, but not too much, for I had determined to keep a tight curb on my curiosity and to dole myself out only two or three pages a day. It was months before I finished the books. By then the world of Jim Hawkins and David Balfour had become so actual for me that I could not long bear to be outside it; and a few days later I took the pink books down from their shelf and began to read again from the beginning.

CHAPTER THIRTEEN

A Connecticut Interlude—2

THE Webster Grammar School was a pleasanter place than No. 2 on Henry Street. It stood on a hill on the edge of town, and around it were big trees, a variety of shrubs, and large lawns to play on. Recess time came between eleven and eleven fifteen in the morning, when the whole school was let out at the same time. We played games, and some of the older boys paired off with the girls. There had been no girls in No. 2, and no one had missed them. But now, unaccountably, it was agreeable to have them in one's class, to talk to them during recess, and sometimes to walk home with one of them after school.

Yet, for all its pleasant surroundings, the Webster School was not exciting. For one thing, there were no teachers with the colorful personalities of Mr. Strassmeir and Mr. Silver. Unlike No. 2, where promotions took place every half year,

grades in Webster School were on a yearly basis. In my
three years at Webster I had only three teachers. I remember
Miss Quinn better than the other two because she was my
last teacher there and because of her red hair and her aloofness from the three or four Jewish pupils in her class. It is
true that she called her pupils by their first names, a practice
that should have pleased me. At No. 2 I had been Chotzinoff,
young as I was. This cold appellation had been an insurmount-
able bar to the intimacy I longed to establish with Mr.
Strassmeir and Mr. Silver. Miss Quinn called me Samuel, yet
she managed to make my first name sound as impersonal as
Chotzinoff. It was Dorothy Wiener, a Jewish girl who sat in
front of me, who first called my attention to Miss Quinn's
frigidity to her Jewish pupils. On the day before Rosh
Hashonah, Miss Quinn told the class that those who preferred
to stay at home on Jewish holidays could do so and would not
be marked absent. At recess Dorothy spoke bitterly to me
about Miss Quinn's choice of the word "preferred," and I had
to agree that the word was unfortunate in that it put our
observance of an important holy day on an elective basis.
Miss Quinn never told the class that those who "preferred"
to observe Easter or Christmas would suffer no punishment.
Dorothy also asked me to note how often the Jewish pupils
were made to stay after school, while others who might have
been just as guilty of an infraction of the rules got off scot-
free; this was also true. Yet I could have forgiven Miss
Quinn's hostility if she had shown a passion for art and
socialism like Mr. Strassmeir, or for individuality and conservative patriotism like Mr. Silver.

Miss Quinn was animated by passion, but I could not
determine its nature. She moved about the classroom in a
state of secret, pent-up agitation that never came to a head.
She had authority, and taught us with efficiency in what
seemed to me even then a correct and standardized way. But
she brought no illumination to bear on the subject that inter-

ested me most, literature. Where Mr. Strassmeir would have directed his imagination like a searchlight to a poem or a story and would have exposed under-surface beauties and called attention to subtle expedients of poets and writers in their pursuit of "effect," Miss Quinn was content to follow the story-line relentlessly, as if the "story" alone was the aim and end of art.

I could not love Miss Quinn, perhaps because I felt that she could not love me. But her unfaltering command of her powers as an administrator impressed me greatly and forced me to admire her. She seemed never in doubt as to what to do. She never hesitated in meting out her cold censure or praise. There was even something magnificent in the assurance with which she disregarded the decisive elements of poetry and imaginative prose. Nothing ever caught her unawares. Her decisions followed automatically on events, sometimes terrifyingly so. When Howard Haskins, one of the boys, failed to appear in class two days running, she dispatched two fellow pupils to his house to find out the cause. And when they reported that Howard was ill of diphtheria, she sent the boys instantly back to their own homes to be quarantined for their own protection and that of the class. And when news came a week later that Howard had died, Miss Quinn commanded the class to bow its head in silence for a minute out of respect to the "departed." When we had done that, she said that the class must send flowers and that she expected each of us to bring five cents in the morning to pay for them. In the meantime she would herself lay out the money for the flowers, which, she said, should be roses with long stems, and she would inscribe a card saying: "To Howard, from his sorrowful friends of the Eighth Grade."

Miss Quinn's quick and realistic response to so disturbing an event cushioned the shock of it, at least for me. At the same time I was lost in wonder at her seeming insensibility to death. "And *now*," Miss Quinn said a moment later, "we

must get on with our *work*. I am sure Howard would *want* us
to." How could she, how could anyone be sure what Howard
would want? After school we argued about that in the yard
and on our way home. Some of the boys thought Miss Quinn
should have dismissed us for the day. That, and not a minute
of silence with heads bowed, would have been a "real" mark
of respect for the dead. Others shouted and played tag and
teased one another, quite as if nothing unusual had taken
place. Only the girls huddled together and spoke self-
consciously in whispers and looked at the ground a great deal.

At home I created, as I had hoped, a sensation with the
news of Howard's death. My mother grew pale, and her
hands trembled as she helped me off with my jacket. Even my
father was impressed, for he stopped reading his Talmud and
said: "*Takké?*" in a doubting tone of voice, as if he wished I
would deny what I had just said. I pretended a greater sadness
than I felt, perhaps because I had not known Howard intimately. But the thought of death could always bring tears to
my eyes. And the possibility, now so sensationally proved,
that a boy of my age could die and be ruthlessly severed from
his friends and his family forever was hardly to be borne.

Miss Quinn had arranged for the class to attend Howard's
funeral in a body. The class was to have a spokesman who
would express our sense of sorrow to Howard's mother. It was
well known that I excelled in elocution, and Miss Quinn,
properly putting aside her prejudice against me in the interest
of the class, selected me as spokesman without a moment's
hesitation. She then gave me a little speech she had written,
which I was to memorize and make to Mrs. Haskins later
that afternoon.

At four o'clock Miss Quinn marched us in a body to Mrs.
Haskins's house. I walked at the head of the procession,
trying to approximate the solemnity of the occasion by
stooping a little and keeping my eyes on the ground. Indeed,
notwithstanding my feeling of importance, I had been unable

to shake off the oppressive reality of juvenile extinction, and the prospect of coming face to face with it in the house we were approaching filled me with dread. I was afraid of seeing the anguish on the faces of the dead boy's friends and relations and of hearing their lamentations. The East Side funerals I had witnessed had left with me painful memories, which sometimes induced a feeling of hopelessness that it might take hours or some new and exciting diversion to dissipate.

Outside the Haskinses' house several closed carriages and a hearse stood at the curb. I had always avoided looking squarely at a hearse, and I quickly averted my eyes from the significant vehicle. Strangely enough, no sounds came from the house—no screams, no loud words of stern comfort from outsiders, no wailings from the bereaved. Even before Miss Quinn could grasp the knob, the door was gently opened from the inside by an unseen hand. Miss Quinn had briefed us on what we were to do, and the class now followed her into the parlor.

I was bewildered by what I saw there. A neatness, a silent decorum, as of a genteel, muted party in progress, prevailed. In the center the coffin stood on a raised platform draped in black. Close to the walls many people sat silently on little gilded chairs. And in the doorway stood Mr. and Mrs. Haskins, both dressed in black, waiting to receive us. They were not weeping. Mr. Haskins said: "Come in—come in," encouragingly. Mrs. Haskins looked a little tired, but showed no outward signs of grief. She smiled at me rather kindly when I made my speech, thanked me in a sweet voice, and said we must have a last look at Howard. We filed around the coffin, and each of us stood a moment gazing into it. I was determined not to look, and I stood my moment with head bent and eyes closed. We then filed out as we had entered. Mr. and Mrs. Haskins were greeting an incoming line of visitors, and we had to pass through the door sideways to give them room.

This, then, was a Christian funeral, the first I had ever

seen. I had been brought up to believe that Christians had no feelings. On the face of it, what I had witnessed was sufficient to confirm my belief. Yet I couldn't be sure. Until that day I had never doubted that Mrs. Haskins loved her son. Once I had walked home with Howard, and his mother saw me from a window and invited me in. Howard was a frail, skinny boy, and his mother appeared much concerned about him. She made him drink a large glass of milk and eat a big slice of bread and butter against his wish. (In winter he would come to school bundled up to his ears, and we could see that he felt unhappy at being so carefully and warmly wrapped.) In her concern for her son Mrs. Haskins resembled my mother, who tried, but without success, to have me wear too many clothes in winter. And now Howard lay dead in the parlor, and his mother behaved strangely, just as if she didn't care. How different my mother would be in such a situation! She would shriek dreadfully and tear her garments and throw herself on the coffin and resist being dislodged. Indeed, I did not see how she could go on living without me. Sooner or later she would disappear, and be discovered one day lying dead on my grave.

Yet it was impossible that Howard's mother should not love him. Could she have been dissembling in the parlor? Christians were curious people. They made no outcries. But sometimes even *they* must cry. Perhaps when she returned alone with Mr. Haskins from the cemetery Mrs. Haskins would cry. Perhaps they were like us, but only when they were *alone*. If so, I pitied Mrs. Haskins. For Howard was an only child, and she must have wanted to cry dreadfully. I knew then that under affliction it is easier to be a Jew than a Christian.

For a while Howard's death robbed me of my feeling of unquestioned security about my own immortality. I had quite forgotten the playmate I had lost long ago in Russia, but now he came to mind, and I saw that death took no account of race or even intellectual superiority, and might not even spare a Jewish boy so sensitive and intelligent as I. What was the good, then, of all my daydreams, my appreciation of the lovely universe with its music and books, my awareness of my own tenderness and the tenderness of those I loved, if at any moment I could be made insensible to them forever!

And, as if further to impress me with his undiscriminating power and to batter down the doors of my own fancied immunity, Death continued to strike flagrantly all about me. Diphtheria was everywhere in the city. Everywhere on houses one read the warning sign: "Under Quarantine." Cases appeared on Burton Street. Late one afternoon I saw the lady in the next house who loved flowers come out to water them. But she was alone, and when her husband appeared with his lunch box at the end of the street, she did not go to meet him, but waited for him to come to her. Together they silently entered the house. The next morning I saw the dreaded sign on their front door. I watched the doctor come and go, sometimes twice a day. And one morning as I came from the fire drill (the watchers had dwindled to myself and another boy), I accosted our neighbor with the lunch box and asked him how his children were. He said: "Poorly, poorly," as if to himself, without looking up from the ground, and went on, his tall, skinny figure more bent than ever. That night, before I went to sleep, I prayed God to spare the man's children. But in the morning the man failed to appear. I ran to Chubb's house, where I learned that both children had died during the night. I went to sit on my porch and tried to picture the desolation in the afflicted house, whose whiteness, relieved by the pink of geraniums and the deep blue of pansies in the window-boxes, now sparkled in the morning sun. As at the Haskinses', not a sound came from the house.

Two days later I watched the funeral from a window of my house. There were fewer people than I had seen at the Haskinses', and only one carriage. When the husband and wife came out of the house, I saw that they were not crying! They were both dressed up, he in a spring overcoat and a black derby, she in a suit and hat, with a dark veil over her face. She carried a bunch of geraniums. When she came to the carriage door she faltered as if she had accidentally missed a step, and her husband raised her up and helped her in and got in after her. Strange people, as strange as the Haskinses!

The sign was removed from their house, and the next morning the man passed the firehouse carrying his lunch box as usual. And that afternoon and for about a week the lady came out to water her flowers, and a little after six o'clock her husband came through the wicket gate and they went indoors without saying a word. Then one day the sign went up again on their house. I was astonished to see it there, for I had been told that diptheria attacked only the young. But Chubb's mother said that this case was an exception, that the woman had taken her children's death so "hard" that she was left with little "resistance" to anything "in the air." I wondered how Chubb's mother could know all that. At the same time I was relieved to hear her say it. It strengthened my desire to believe that *they* were as *human* as *we*, though *they* perhaps regarded as a weakness any outward show of pain. Undaunted by my failure to save the little children, I again prayed God to spare their mother. I could not imagine what would become of the man without any family at all.

The next morning I could not get out of bed, though I tried several times to do so. When I failed to come down to breakfast, my mother went to my room and found me "on fire," her standard phrase for a temperature. In view of the epidemic, my father himself went at once for the doctor, and when the doctor came and said, even before he examined me, that I had caught the infection, my mother began to cry loudly in the Jewish fashion, and my father, looking, I thought, troubled himself, commanded her sternly not to be "a woman." I found this and the general commotion my illness induced around the house reassuring. In my lucid intervals (my mother in recalling her days of anxiety boldly stated, science to the contrary notwithstanding, that my temperature, fluctuating crazily, once reached the incredible height of 108 degrees), I took pleasure in the contemplation of the animated despair around me. When I passed the crisis and began to mend, I felt as if I had done something handsome and generous for my family. And I suffered myself to be interminably caressed, and my every want anticipated, with a show of impatience which I thought justified by the miracle of my survival and even becoming in one on whom the happiness of an entire family depended.

For weeks I had been so preoccupied with myself that it was only when I was permitted to walk about the room that I remembered the lady next door and asked about her. My mother, with many asides adjuring the Almighty to keep such visitations from all Jewish homes, but especially from ours, told me that our neighbor had died the day after I was taken ill. Soon after the funeral her husband gave up his house and went to live in another town, my mother did not know which. A new Christian family had moved in, an old lady and her niece, also not young. They had brought a piano, on which the niece played occasionally. My mother said the niece played well, but she played only one piece, over and over again.

I went to the window to look at the familiar house. The window-boxes were in the same place, and in them were the same flowers. The lawn was cut. The white clapboards of the house and the green tin roof glowed in the sun. Nothing had changed. Yet it seemed such a long time since I had watched the dead lady watering her flowers, the dead children playing near her on the lawn, and the tall, bent man with the tin lunch box in his hand walking toward them. To my surprise, I did not feel sad. The remembered picture caused my heart to contract with a delicious ache. It was so beautiful and *right*, like the memorable groupings and scenes in stories and poems that I had stored in my mind and could recall whenever

I chose, thus experiencing at will the exquisite pang of my
first coming upon them. From this storehouse I now conjured
up several affecting moments as companion pieces to the
once actual, now remembered, grouping on the lawn, and I
was gratified by their æsthetic kinship. I recalled the picture
of Evangeline and Gabriel Lajeunesse, their *not* meeting as,
unaware of their proximity, they passed each other on a river
on a starless night, to be lost to each other forever; of Enoch
Arden, who, after witnessing the happiness of his wife,
returned to his lonely room to live through his "dark hour"
unseen; of Oliver Twist dozing off happily in his pleasant
room in the country, unaware of the evil forces closing in on
him; of the open-eyed, blind Pew tapping loudly with his
stick on the gravel outside the Admiral Benbow; of the peril
of David Balfour as a flash of lightning revealed him poised on
the uncompleted, treacherous outside staircase of the House of
Shaws. All these had a kinship of beauty or emotion or both.
They all moved me to tears, but I knew them for tears of joy.
In myself, too, I felt a joy in an upsurge of strength, an arro-
gant pleasure at having been chosen to survive when so many
had died. And now the sound of a piano penetrated my reverie
and presently usurped all my attention. It was the old lady's
niece playing in the next house. She was playing a pleasant
tune in waltz time, a piece I had never heard before, one that I
felt I should like to learn. I hoped it was a "Bromo-Seltzer
piece." If not, and if my mother's report was accurate, I
would probably hear it often enough to enable me to play it
without ever having to see it.

Because of our economic prosperity, the atmosphere of our
home in Waterbury was less tense than I had ever known it to
be in New York. The twelve dollars a week my father
brought home was sufficient to warm, feed, and clothe us. It
also enabled my mother to dispatch a few dollars now and then
to relatives in Russia, though still without the knowledge of

my father. An attempt was made to begin payments to Mr. Harris in London on the debt we owed him. But he returned the five dollars with a note in which he said he never had any idea of lending us money, that he had meant his "contribution" as a gift, and had told us it was a loan for fear that we would otherwise refuse it. He begged us to accept the money as our "small inheritance," for in his will he was leaving everything to "Palestine," and he was certain that so endearing and enterprising a family as ours would have no trouble in making their way in America. He could not, of course, know the trouble we had had in making our way in New York. My mother, out of pride, never complained to Mr. Harris in her letters to London. And here in Waterbury neither of my parents was obliged to be enterprising. Life for all of us was reasonably pleasant.

On the matter of my religious upbringing my father showed a forbearance which, in the light of his former intransigence, I found it hard to understand. However much I had tried to conceal it in New York, in Waterbury my religious skepticism was quite apparent, and my interest in music and literature had the effect of highlighting my indifference to Hebrew studies and the strict observance of ritual which absorbed my father. Perhaps he had given me up as hopeless in those directions. At any rate, the piety of his eldest son was sufficient to guarantee the welfare of his soul in the world to come. I was not made to attend synagogue except on important holidays. And while he never suspected that I played the piano at home on Saturday mornings, my father pretended not to notice minor infractions of Sabbath rules which I permitted myself.

He must have guessed that I went on Saturdays to a matinee at the Jacques (pronounced Jakes) Vaudeville House on West Main Street, for on coming home from the theater I was so full of what I had witnessed that I could not resist repeating some of the jokes and imitating the characteristics of the headliners. Having once tasted the delights of vaudeville in

the outdoor theater at Lakewood, I had implored Solomon to
finance a weekly matinee for me at Jacques. With a view to
fostering an ally in his courtship of Molly, or perhaps out of
unmotivated kindness, Solomon gave me fifteen cents every
Saturday—ten cents for a seat in the gallery and five for an
ice-cream soda. I had hinted to Solomon that those of my
friends and schoolmates who attended the Saturday matinee at
Jacques always capped the afternoon with an ice-cream soda
after the show.

My Saturdays were now full to overflowing. I played the
piano in the morning. After a deliciously heavy Sabbath
dinner at noon, my father and mother would take the traditional Sabbath after-dinner nap. I would slick my hair and tidy
myself up, for all the young patrons of Jacques looked neat
and clean. It was good to walk the mile to Jacques and feel
myself a part of that recognizable stream of well-attired
youngsters which, fed from side streets, was converging on
the theater. Inside, Jacques was very unlike the Grand Street
and Windsor theaters in New York. Before the show began,
the patrons were somewhat noisy. But there was no confusion
in the matter of seating. Only the popcorn- and candy-
vendors running up and down the aisles reminded me of the
Jewish theaters. And the moment the lights went out, all
noises ceased abruptly.

Though the performers (except the pianist) changed
weekly, the ingredients of the show never varied. The overture came first. A spotlight would isolate the upright piano in
the pit (there was no orchestra), and the never-changing and
ever-popular and admired pianist would emerge to deafening
applause, bow many times, seat himself, and launch into the
"overture," a potpourri of the tunes of the period, ornamented
with runs and arpeggios, and concluding with a great display
of virtuosity. This done, and rapturously greeted by the
audience, a uniformed attendant would appear from the wings
and remove the cardboard sign with the numeral I from an

easel standing at the extreme left front of the stage, revealing a card marked II. With No. II the show was on in earnest. For three hours one sat entranced through acts by acrobats, trick bicyclists, soft-shoe dancers, hilarious skits in which real pies were prodigally expended, sweet singers of ballads, and raucous singers of ragtime, dog acts (my favorite was the canine response to a fire-alarm in which small dogs slid down poles and clambered aboard miniature fire engines, which, accompanied by a great clanging of fire-bells, were then raced off the stage by other dogs harnessed to them), and well-known actors or actresses in scenes from their Broadway successes.

A block away from Jacques stood Poli's, the theater of concerts and serious drama. The posters on the billboard of Poli's pictured important moments in the different plays that followed one another twice a week. I longed to see them, but the price of admission was more than double that prevailing at Jacques, and I did not think it wise to overplay my role of go-between in my brother's love suit by an additional demand for money. I was destined to witness my first play in English without his help. One morning the postman delivered a letter addressed to the "Reverend Morris Chotzinoff." It was in English, and it advised the "reverend" addressee that a box at Poli's had been placed at his disposal for the opening performance of one of the greatest dramas of all times, enacted by a celebrated Broadway cast. *The Ninety and Nine* was the mystifying name of the play. The letter went on to say that *The Ninety and Nine* featured effects of a most sensational character never before seen on any stage, and that its theme was religious, embracing all creeds, and bearing a clear message of faith and hope for all humanity. The producers of the play hoped that the "reverend" gentleman and his family would accept their invitation and that perhaps he would express his approval of the play to a gentleman who would interview him after the final curtain.

The great day came at last. We all wore our Sabbath
clothes. As my father was going in his role of "Reverend,"
we decided he must wear his new, shiny stovepipe. The lobby
of Poli's was full of wall-to-ceiling mirrors that reflected us
flatteringly from every side. We took our places ostentatiously in the box. I had never before sat in a box, and I was
happily conscious that people in the pit were looking up at us,
some through telescopes. But I was startled to find the boxes
on the other side occupied by priests and clergymen in black.
They had doffed their hats. I glanced at my father's stovepipe,
which sat imposingly on his head. This, I felt, made us
conspicuous and marked us out for Jews. For the first time
in my life I experienced a desire for conformity. I called my
father's attention to the hatless clerical gentlemen on the other
side. He took the hint, removed his stovepipe, and placed
it on the floor beside him. He then took out the skullcap he
always kept in his pocket and covered his head. But the skullcap, being a rarity in Waterbury, was even more conspicuous
than the stovepipe, and attracted much more attention. I could
do nothing further, for my father never went bareheaded
except to bed. Fortunately, the lights suddenly went out, the
orchestra began to play music. To my delight it proved to be
the *Light Cavalry* Overture, which had used to ring up the
curtain of the Grand Street Theater. Now all eyes were
turned toward the stage.

The drama did indeed live up to the promise of the letter to
my father and the colored billboards. In retrospect it appears
to have been an up-to-date version of the parable of the
Prodigal Son. Its features are dim in my mind. But quite vivid
still are the two scenes illustrated in the posters, for which I
waited expectantly and which on the stage were breath-
takingly realistic. What looked like a real engine, propelled
by real engine wheels, raced through a real fire. The tattered
hero had one hand on the throttle, and with the other clanged a
great bell. The combined sounds of the hissing of the flames

and steam, the motion of the wheels, and the clang of the bell achieved a crescendo that was almost insupportable. At its peak it was overpowered by a fearful grinding of brakes. The engine slowed down, the fire was left behind, glowing faintly in the distance, the huge machine came to a halt, and the exhausted engineer descended to the ground, where a throng of anxious people shook his hands and praised him for his courage and daring.

The next and final scene depicted the church I had seen on the posters. The tattered engine-driver walked in and, finding it deserted, made straight for the organ, at which he seated himself and began to play. He played beautifully, and I began to be affected by the soft, lofty, impersonal organ sounds, when my father rose precipitately and, declaring that we had been tricked into witnessing a heathen rite, left the theater. We had no choice but to follow him, and I never knew how the play finally ended. At home my father, still irate, called for a basin of water and a towel and solemnly washed and dried his hands, saying that he had committed a sin and was cleansing himself of it. I never knew what he thought of the play.

It was also in Waterbury that I heard my first purely instrumental concert. A billboard at Poli's one day proclaimed the only appearance in our city that year of the celebrated Creatore and his celebrated band. The price of tickets ranged from one dollar to twenty-five cents. Fearing to miss this single opportunity (who could tell where I or the band would be next year?), I did not hesitate this time to approach my brother. To my delight, Solomon was himself eager to hear the famous band. He bought two seats in the balcony, in the very first row. On the day of the concert I worried so lest we might arrive late that Solomon and I were at the theater half an hour before the doors opened. By that time I was in such a turmoil of expectation that, forgetting we had reserved seats, I ran ahead of my brother, to be among the first to get in. As I

ran I became aware of a boy of about my own age and size
running toward me. I tried to dodge him, but whenever I
veered to the right or left he did the same. Inevitably he
must run into me, and suddenly he did, and we collided, my
forehead bumping with a loud noise against his. The blow
sent me reeling backward. At the same time I realized that I
had run headlong into one of Poli's full-length mirrors. The
boy I had seen running toward me was my reflection! Solomon
now appeared, laughing at my odd mishap. With the blade of a
pocket knife he always carried with him, he flattened down a
great bump that had arisen on my forehead, and we made our
way less hastily to the balcony.

From the moment Creatore emerged from the wings, I
forgot all about my accident and the bump on my forehead.
The celebrated leader had on a uniform of blue with white
trimmings, as did all the members of his band, except that his
trimmings were more plentiful and whiter. He was bareheaded. His hair was long and fell in disorder around his head
and the back of his neck. I thought he looked every inch a
high priest of music. He began with the *William Tell* Overture, which I was to hear for the first time—it was, strangely,
not among the overtures in Madam Zamoshkin's repertoire.
The piece was electrifying. I knew the story of Tell from one
of our school readers, and now I heard it unfold in its broadest
outlines in orchestral sound: the pastoral Swiss background
against the sudden loosing of the War of Liberation. And
Creatore himself was magnificent. Like a general who aims to
leave nothing to chance, he took command of every phrase,
even of every note (he beat out each note of the English horn
solo in the pastoral episode, at the same time weaving and
suggesting a variety of nuances with his baton). In the final
"War" episode the great leader outdid himself in directions to
the several sections of his band, turning with lightning agility
from side to side, releasing cascades of notes from the flutes
and piccolos, exciting the cornets to more stentorian vehe-

mence, pleading with the trombones for piercing, golden sound, and whipping up the whole to a frenzy of musical carnage of almost unbearable magnitude.

Yet, brilliant as he proved himself in the *William Tell* Overture, Creatore was even more compelling in the *"Miserere"* from *Il Trovatore*, which followed it. Here he was dealing with emotion, with the human heart, not with peace and war, and his behavior to his men underwent a startling change. Even before he signaled the soft opening chords, he assumed an air of hopeless dejection, which communicated itself gradually to the audience. His head fell on his chest, his shoulders rose to his neck in a hunch, and his hands were outspread, frozen in a gesture of resignation. After standing motionless in this attitude for the time it took the house to achieve a startling silence, Creatore released a down beat with the most mournful of gestures. I could imagine nothing sadder than the sounds that forthwith issued from the trombones.

But I was already anticipating Manrico's solo: "Ah, I have sighed to rest me," and wondering how Creatore would treat that noble aria, which, I was certain, would be played by a cornet. Indeed, when it arrived, a cornet did play it. But he had hardly begun when Creatore stepped down from his podium, sank to his hands and knees, and crawled through a maze of music stands and players' legs to the solo cornetist. There, still on his knees, he straightened up and beat time in great sweeping motions, almost in the cornetist's face. The cornetist, raising his instrument and his head toward the gallery, blew soft, sad, tawny notes in my direction, while Creatore begged and implored him to give of himself and his art without stint. The effect on the cornetist was hypnotic, for he played with an extravagance of emotion which went to the heart.

Later the same player was entrusted with a lively theme and variations, which he tossed off with the utmost dexterity and brilliance, quite as if he were not the very same person who a moment earlier had given such poignance to Manrico's plaint. I treasured my first concert at Poli's, and decided to show my gratitude to Solomon by picturing him in my next letter to Molly as a patron of music. This, I hoped, might induce Molly to feel "in that way" about her foster brother.

I was approaching my thirteenth birthday. At thirteen a Jewish boy becomes a man in every sense of the word, and his dedication to a responsibility to God and man for his acts is celebrated with the solemnity appropriate to so momentous an event in his life. So far I had known very little of personal responsibility. But as to becoming a man in the physical sense I had for some time had intimations of a mysterious and disturbing character. These intimations ran parallel with my discovery of and interest in a new kind of literature, whose existence I had never even suspected.

Since I had first looked into the adventurous world of Robert Louis Stevenson in Woolworth's on East Main Street, my favorite authors had grown in number. I craved adventure in a world of action, and my instinct led me to authors who provided it. Chief among them was Alexandre Dumas, whose works I encountered accidentally while browsing in the public library on West Main Street. Milestones in my life were *The Count of Monte Cristo* and *The Three Musketeers*. I saw at once that French intrigue was both subtler and bolder than English. Besides, there were women in Dumas, a sex Stevenson had neglected in his books, though, to be sure, it was an omission I had not noticed. They were a new kind of women, attractive in a way to make a boy of twelve or thirteen feel grown-up and important. They were not "good" women in the usual sense, and it was rather disconcerting to realize that their very want of conventional goodness was not the least part of their attraction for me. The attractive women in Dickens were all good. Even Nancy was a good woman, in spite of her association with criminals and her betrayal of Sikes. What a totally different creature was the little seamstress in *The Three Musketeers*! I had heard vaguely, in the conversations of my sisters, about "loose" women in literature who had been unfaithful to their husbands. Madame Bonacieux, the mercer's wife, not only was unfaithful to her husband, but laughed and joked about her infidelity as if it was no sin! Nor did d'Artagnan, her lover, take the situation seriously. What a far cry d'Artagnan was from the equally immoral, but guilt-tortured hero of Chernishevsky's *What is to be Done?* The Frenchman took everything with levity—adventure, peril, love, but a strange kind of love, ephemeral, not founded on affection, easily discarded and forgotten—love, in short, as adventure. This kind of love seemed natural in the life of a Frenchman. Why shouldn't it be natural in the life of all men, Jews included, who aspired to be brave and generous?

In all my life I had not met a girl or woman so alluring as Madame Bonacieux. I wondered whether she could flourish only in an era as brave and careless and chivalrous as the France of the last four Louis, and was now extinct as a type. Yet equally fascinating was Milady, though for different reasons. Milady was beautiful, haughty, inscrutable, and, alas, evil, and she deserved, I reluctantly admitted to myself, her dreadful fate. But when I began to read the scene describing her execution on the bank of the river, I could not bear it and was obliged to put down the book for the moment. For I loved Milady, with all her faults, and I also loved Madame Bonacieux. And if I had to choose between them I should not know what to do, because (I dared not admit to myself) I wanted them both!

The women in *The Count of Monte Cristo* were not exciting, like those in *The Three Musketeers*, but the Count more than made up for this. The idea of vengeance, conceived and executed on a scale so grand as that of the poor, wronged sailor, was absolutely breath-taking. Ever since I could remember, I, too, had planned revenge after every wrong or injustice inflicted on me. I had thus far not suffered evil machinations of the magnitude of those that sent Edmond Dantès to a dungeon in the Château d'If. But I had harbored ideas of revenge as devastating as those devised by the Count of Monte Cristo. I had even contemplated patricide. Fortunately my father had abandoned naked cruelty as a weapon against a part of his family, and there were moments now when I could even feel affection for him. Ideas of revenge, however, persisted in my mind. I hoped that misfortune would overtake the anonymous boys who had stoned the rabbi of the synagogue. I dreamed about challenging Chubb to a fight and felling him with the first blow. And some day when the world would have proclaimed me its greatest poet, I would visit Miss Quinn at the Webster School and remind her of her hostility to my youthful verses at a time when encouragement was so vital to my development as an artist. However—and I counted it not as weakness, but as the magnanimity of a true poet—I would leave behind me a copy of my latest book of poems, inscribed simply: "To my teacher, from her pupil, S. C." I could picture her surprise, her feeling of gratitude, not unmixed, I hoped, with one of guilt.

But this literary world of intrigue, revenge, bravery, magnanimity, of reckless, generous men and earthy women, was soon to be eclipsed by a new world, one less artistically and realistically meritorious, but more exciting for an adolescent boy. One fateful day, hunting for book bargains in a second-hand shop, my eye was caught by the titles of two paper-covered novels in a heap marked one cent apiece. The first book, *A Mad Love*, promised a sensation. *Dora Thorne*, the second, I found irresistible because of the illustrated cover showing a young woman and a man in a passionate embrace at the edge of a lake on a moonlit night. I had no wish to own the books, but I felt an urge to read them, if only hurriedly. My curiosity satisfied, I would then, perhaps, resell the books to the second-hand dealer for a penny for the two.

At home I locked myself in my attic room and consumed both books rapidly, with a kind of guilty relish. I was at once aware that they differed glaringly from the other books on my shelves. They gave me a consciousness of my physical being, and certain parts made me feel warm and brought the perspiration out on my forehead. I was puzzled at this effect on me, for the two stories were surprisingly high-minded and moral, not at all like *The Three Musketeers*. The heroines of both were, if I can trust my memory, simple English country girls who were seduced by men of wealth and station. Though themselves innocent in soul, they reaped the wages of sin, the one committing suicide in the lovely Swan Lake of her seducer's country estate, the other murdered, I believe, by whom and by what means I cannot recall. From every moral and ethical standpoint both novels were exemplary. Yet their effect on me was disturbing. Why was it that the trysts of d'Artagnan and his paramour made pleasant reading (though I could guess at what must have occurred at them) while the meetings of Dora Thorne and her noble lover at night in the magnificent park of his country place sent the blood rushing to my head?

Now my nights were disturbed by dreams of seductions in silent parks. I became the licentious hero of each book, and I felt myself drawn to both innocence and its spoliation. Madame Bonacieux, once so desirable in a jolly, open way, seemed no longer interesting. I would not, like d'Artagnan, cross swords for her possession. But the innocence of Dora Thorne, her unconsciousness of the danger around her, the sweet, trusting surrender of body and soul to her lover, made her desirable. For hours at a time I sat rereading *Dora Thorne* and *A Mad Love*, returning again and again to the trysts at night and the seduction scenes, my senses luxuriating in unformed, nameless, yet somehow shameful desires. Nor did the influence of these stories vanish when I put the books down. The sensations they induced persisted throughout the day, in school and at play. I tried reading my old favorites again, but my mind wandered from the characters and incidents that once had absorbed me completely.

Only music could free me from the pleasurable oppression of awakening desire. There was so much to think about while playing the piano—technique, phrasing, tone-color, dynamics! Feeling and emotion had to be built up coldly and deliberately out of many elements. In the process one forgot everything else. Even in performing before an audience one could not succumb to the emotions one was building up, without endangering the structure of the music. In those troubling days of my thirteenth year, I rushed from my oppressive sessions with *A Mad Love* and other novels of that nature which I sought out and purchased in second-hand stores and junk shops, to the cerebral release of piano practice.

A month before my thirteenth birthday arose the delicate question of my *bar mitzvah* (ceremony of confirmation). The question was a delicate one because my father had permitted me a certain laxity in the observance of Jewish ritual. My skepticism about religion in general, as yet undefined, was nevertheless apparent, and for reasons of his own my father did not choose to try to break it down. I suspect that my mother was not without influence in his decision not to attempt coercion. Whether because they had grown older or because of the necessity of closer family ties in an environment predominantly Christian, or through release from economic pressure, the relations of my parents were now equal. Indeed, my mother's influence on my father and on family matters had become dominant, though its manifestations were so subtle that I doubt my father was at any time conscious of not having the upper hand. And now it was not my father, but my mother who approached me on the subject of my *bar mitzvah*. Pointing out that unlike most Jewish boys I had not been required to go to *Talmud torah* (school of higher religious studies), she implored me to please my father (and ease her own situation) in the matter of the *bar mitzvah* ceremony. I could not deny my mother anything, and I undertook to learn the prescribed chapter in the *Shulkhan Aruk*, and the commentaries on it. The thin old rabbi whom I had saved from being stoned taught me a Hebrew oration, which I committed to memory, though I did not understand its meaning.

In the morning of the important day, I accompanied my father to the synagogue, where I put on phylacteries and a prayer shawl for the first time. Both were a present from my father. My mother's gift was a lovely silk bag for the phylacteries, which she had herself sewn and embroidered. At home I was greeted by an assembly of our friends and personages from the synagogue. At a signal from the old rabbi I delivered my Hebrew speech. The rabbi then solemnly spoke to me in Yiddish, telling me that I was now a man, eligible to be one of a *minyan* (quorum), that my father was no longer responsible for me to God, but that henceforth I should be held accountable by the Almighty for my sins. I was then congratulated on all sides and my mother dispensed whisky, wine, and *teglich* (small fritters). I could not help being moved by the ceremony at the synagogue (adjusting the phylacteries was fun) and at home. Yet I knew that my elation was transitory and that my true pleasures were not in ritual, which everlastingly complimented God, but in "goyish" books, music, and the expression of life in art. I began skipping morning prayers and the "laying" of phylacteries; and one day I put the little silken bag away for good. My father pretended not to notice, and our life went on as it had before I had been inducted into Jewish manhood.

My graduation from the Webster School was approaching. One morning in May, Miss Quinn told us that it gave her pleasure to announce that the class would graduate in a body. Committees were appointed to get out the class book and to decide on the shape and color of the class pin. The graduation exercises were to be held at Poli's Theater. They were to consist of choral singing, a piano solo, a selection on the cornet, a valedictory, a recitation, and speeches by the principal and one or two political figures of the city. The girls were all to wear white dresses, the boys blue suits. I was selected to be the class orator, and Miss Quinn gave me a long poem to memorize. To my dismay, the piano solo was allotted to a girl of fourteen who had been studying the piano for the last eight years. This girl, unacquainted with the "Freedom method," played mechanically well, but without imagination. Miss Quinn said she was sorry to disappoint me in the matter of the solo, but that it would be unfair to the rest of the class to have me occupy too prominent a place in the graduation exercises.

As soon as I had committed the poem to memory, Miss Quinn helped with "elocution" and "gestures," both essential, she maintained, to an adequate public performance. The poem, called "Winning Cup's Race," seemed to me, after consideration, a happy selection. It was both a romantic and a dramatic poem. Its tone was conversational, something quite new in poetry to me, and at first I was displeased with its jaunty air. But I quickly caught on to its dramatic possibilities. Miss Quinn said it called for subtlety in inflection and broad realistic gestures if the audience was to get the full flavor of its dramatic story.

Miss Quinn had planned my interpretation in every detail. "You, Samuel," she said at the beginning of our rehearsals, "are telling something that once happened to you. You are a jockey on a great estate in England. It's a strange tale, and you are telling it directly to an English Lord. Now, Samuel, you must imagine that every person seated out front in Poli's is the Lord you are addressing. Of course no jockey ever spoke poetry, so you must pretend that this is not a poem, that you

are just saying what happens to come to your mind." For all
that, I found it difficult to pretend that "Winning Cup's
Race" was not a poem. Its meter, which resembled that of
Evangeline, seemed to defy any attempts at conversational
delivery:

> *"You've never seen Winning Cup, have you? Stroll
>   round to the paddock, my lord;*
> *Just cast your eye over the mare, sir; you'd say that,
>   upon your word,*
> *You ne'er saw a grander shaped 'un in all the whole
>   course of your life.*
> *Have you heard the strange story about her, how she won
>   Lord Hillhoxon his wife?*
> *No? . . ."*

Miss Quinn bade me forget all about the rhymes, but I
couldn't. "Don't pause after 'upon your word,' even though
there is a comma," she said, "but go into the next line quickly
—like: 'you'd say that, upon your word you ne'er saw'—
And, Samuel, move a few steps to the right when you say:
'Stroll round to the paddock, my lord.' In other words,
Samuel, stroll to the paddock, and pretend the Lord is strolling
to the paddock with you. And now we have the first gesture.
When you say: 'just cast your eye over the mare, sir,' point
to the mare," and Miss Quinn stuck out a forefinger at an
imaginary mare, "and at the words: 'you ne'er saw a grander
shaped 'un in all the whole course of your life,' outline with
both your hands the shape of a beautiful horse—like this,"
and Miss Quinn drew in the air with both her hands the belly
and back of a large horse.

I spoke the lines in an offhand manner and made the
gestures. It had not the confidence of Miss Quinn's delivery,
nor the definition of her gestures. But she made no comment,
and I continued:

> "*. . . I'll tell you why Winning Cup, here,*
> *Has lived in this lazy grandeur since the first time they*
>   *let her appear—*"

I paused, compelled to do so by the rhyme.

"Don't stop," Miss Quinn shouted at me; "go on—go on! Appear where? Appear what?" "On a racecourse," I hastened to add. Miss Quinn told me to go back and run the two lines into each other, conversationally. This I did.

> "*. . . Has lived in this lazy grandeur since the first*
>   *time they let her appear*
> *on a racecourse—to run for a wife, sir—the loveliest*
>   *girl in the land. . . .*"

Miss Quinn worked hard with me every afternoon after school, and in a few weeks "Winning Cup's Race" was whipped into a dramatic monologue of obvious vividness and force. I copied all of Miss Quinn's gestures faithfully. At home I had my mother stand up in front of me as "my lord," and I recited the poem and executed my gestures straight at her. Long before graduation came around I was letter-perfect, and I moved my body and my arms in strict synchronization with the words. Miss Quinn signaled the completion of her task by telling me one afternoon after I had gone through the poem: "It will do."

My mother was more enthusiastic, though I could not be sure that she comprehended the drama of "Winning Cup's Race" as I paraphrased the poem for her in Yiddish. And, truth to tell, I was hazy about the story myself even as I boldly reconstructed it for her. Young Lord Hillhoxon had ruined himself and his ancestral estate by gambling. His jockey, Bob Doon (that is, I), foreseeing his master's ruination, had secretly trained the foal, Winning Cup, to run in a race that would restore the young Lord's fortune and win him the lovely Lady Constance for a bride. That much was clear.

But as the devoted jockey deplored gambling, I could not see how the winning of the race could accomplish what it did. I did not, of course, disclose my perplexity to Miss Quinn. If I had, Miss Quinn would have exclaimed at my obtuseness. As for my mother, I stressed the running of the race itself. This she understood. She found my gestures evocative of the excitement and tension of the race. My performance as a whole had, she said, the overtones of a *"Lebensbild"* (portrayal of life) as vivid and heart-warming as a serial novel of high life in a Jewish daily.

The expense involved in being graduated was considerable, and I was again obliged to appeal to Solomon. He gave me five dollars, which paid for a graduation suit, the class book, and a blue enamel class pin. The class book looked in all respects like a regular book. It had many pages, and it was bound in glossy white linen-covered boards. Everything in it, with the exception of an article by the school principal, was the work of the graduating class. For some reason never told me, I was not represented in the book. This omission was hard to explain to my family and friends, who knew me for a poet through my own frequent representations. I could not deny, however, that the poem of the class poet in the book was a worthy production. It was, in essence, a hymn to the future of the graduating class. It pointed out, ringingly, the high moral quality of our training at Webster School and called on us to be forever worthy of the school's tradition of learning, honor, and good citizenship.

Good as the poem was, I thought the prose in the class book of a higher order. I was particularly taken with a humorous story called "Jones's Dog," contributed by a quiet boy who had hitherto been notably unproductive (in class) in a literary sense. In the story, Jones, an impeccably dressed youth, took his dog for a stroll around the town one Sunday morning after church. The dog was described as gentle, though slightly frisky, and his master as polite and well-bred to a painful degree. Yet the moment they emerged on West Main Street both of them were overtaken by the most extraordinary, comic misfortunes. Jones's dog broke his leash and ran into side streets and alleys, followed by his anxious master. Mishaps piled up at a sidesplitting rate and achieved on the last page a climax altogether unexpected and pathetically hilarious. For just as Jones had succeeded in shooing his dog out of a deep puddle of dirty water, who should turn the corner of the street but Jones's best girl, dressed in her Sunday clothes. To Jones's (and the readers') horror, the dog, recognizing the young lady and desiring to show his pleasure at the meeting (so the author intimated), made a flying leap at her and spattered her with mud from head to toe. Needless to say, Jones, unable to face so appalling a situation, fled homeward, presently to be followed by his wretched but well-meaning pet. And there the author left him, cleverly refraining from resolving the unhappy Jones's marital future. I translated the story to my family and they agreed that I had *not* exaggerated its comic values. My father, who disliked animals, nevertheless laughed at the tale, and said: "What else could one expect of a dog?"

In the midst of my preparations for graduation, the slaughterhouse where my father was employed shut down for lack of sufficient business. My mother, not at all disheartened, said it was high time that we returned to New York and civilization. What, she inquired, could become of me in Waterbury? What outlets were there for my various talents? Must I grow up to become a laborer in the Waterbury Brass Co. and daily take my lunch along in a tin box? And what was my father's future in this provincial city? Should he fail to get employment in some other slaughterhouse, he would have to depend for a living on a very limited number of Jewish weddings and circumcisions. The shutting down of the slaughterhouse she recognized, as she had so often done with calamities in the past, as a blessing in disguise.

My father was not really loath to leave a city that had

proved as injurious to his health as London had, a city, more-over, where Jews were practically nonexistent and the wear-ing of a beard was a real hazard. He took a satisfaction, how-ever, in hinting that my mother's eagerness to move back to New York was not unrelated to her desire to be near her daughters. This was true enough. Hannah's baby was pres-ently due; and Molly seemed perversely to be uninterested in marriage. My mother could only feel she was needed on both fronts. Yet she thought fit to deny my father's insinuation and offered to swear upon the head of her only son that she was speaking the truth. Notwithstanding my growing agnosticism, it was with a feeling of apprehension that I heard my mother airily lying to God. I half expected immediate annihilation by a shocked and outraged deity. And, as so often in the past, I wondered if my mother was really the devout, old-fashioned Jewish wife we thought her.

At any rate, she began at once to prepare for New York. Molly was empowered by letter to find a suitable apartment of three or four rooms, perhaps in a neighborhood less thickly populated than the East Side ghetto. For our sojourn in Water-bury had given my mother a feeling for space and cleanliness which the cramped conditions of the East Side could hardly gratify. She suggested Harlem as a region that had begun to draw the better-class Jews. There my talents might be better nurtured. And my father would find fewer competitors and more young people who might be eager to marry and beget male children.

Graduation day arrived at last. In the afternoon we had a final rehearsal on the stage of Poli's. I could hardly believe that I stood on the very boards that had accommodated Creatore's band and the realistic mechanical wonders of *The Ninety and Nine.* When my turn came to recite "Winning Cup's Race," I felt nervous as I advanced to the edge of the stage and faced a dark, empty, silent, menacing auditorium. What if I should forget a line, a word? My voice trembled throughout. But I got through the poem without forgetting anything. Miss Quinn spoke no word of praise or blame.

At eight that evening we again took our seats on the raised platform in front of a painted backdrop depicting the junction of North, South, and East Main Street, with Apothecary's Hall, the city's most impressive building, in the foreground. A few minutes later the curtain rose, revealing the auditorium now brilliantly lighted and completely filled. I at once sought and found my family. They were sitting quite close to the stage. My father wore his skullcap, and his shiny stovepipe hat rested on his lap. My mother had on her "good" dress, and over it a spangled shawl, another one of Solomon's "foreclosure" trophies.

At a signal we rose and sang "Shoulder to Shoulder," a martial setting of a poem describing the valor, camaraderie, and determination of Napoleon's Old Guard. This was followed by a lyric ballad, "By the Side of a Mossy Bank a Modest Violet Grew," celebrating reticence not only as a virtue but as one that pays off well, for at the end of the song the retiring violet triumphed over bolder flowers. I sang along with the class mechanically.

While I sang I went over "Winning Cup's Race" in my mind several times from beginning to end. I was letter-perfect. Yet when Miss Quinn motioned to me that my turn had come, I could not recall the opening words. And as I rose and stood still by my seat for a moment, looking straight at my teacher in what must have seemed to her utter bewilderment, she formed her lips in patterns that I recognized. "You've never seen Winning Cup, have you?" her lips said in an exaggerated manner, and her face looked ridiculously contorted, like mine when I made faces at myself in the mirror. Instantly the succeeding words came to my mind.

I advanced to my appointed place near the footlights. I felt millions of eyes probing my face. At the same time I *knew* that Miss Quinn was staring right into the back of my head, *willing* me not to forget, not to bring disgrace on her and the class. I looked up at the gallery, seeking refuge there from the staring eyes around me. The gallery presented a wavy, unidentifiable mass, soothing to my troubled senses. I felt that I must look only at the gallery or I would be lost. It now seemed like an age since I had taken up my stance at the rim of the stage. Miss Quinn must be reaching the limit of her patience with me. I should begin at once; if only I could remember the opening line, the others would follow. An oppressive quiet was circulating in the theater like pervasive, humid air. Suddenly I remembered Miss Quinn's puckered face, and the opening line came to me with a rush. Mechanically I stuck my right hand out toward the gallery and took a few steps forward, as Miss Quinn had taught me to do. "You've never seen Winning Cup, have you?" I heard myself say, though the voice I heard was not at all like mine. "Stroll round to the paddock, my lord." On, on the voice went, while my hands and feet and my body made the expected motions.

The story of Winning Cup's race unrolled itself more rapidly than I had rehearsed it. Yet I heard, with astonishment, the unfaltering voice discharge every word with the expected inflections. In spite of the speed of the recitation, it took a long time. There were moments when my thoughts wandered and I forgot to listen to what the voice was saying. At those times extraordinary irrelevancies filled my mind: Chubb, and his sister Jessie, the fire drills, the sound of *Valse Bleu* from the house next to ours. Yet when my mind returned to listening, the story of Winning Cup's race was at the point where it should have been by then. At last I heard myself shouting: "For God's sake, Winning Cup, *now!*" And I leaned forward at a perilous angle, like a jockey making a last desperate effort to inspire his mount to an ultimate exertion. Thus I hung, frozen for a moment. Then my body relaxed. " 'Twas over," the voice said calmly, "we'd won by a head!"

There was a moment of utter silence. Then I heard a noise

around me like the sliding of egg coal down a narrow chute.
My eyes left the balcony and looking downward I saw hands
clapping. They were applauding rather listlessly, I thought.
I bowed, as I had been taught to do in such an event, and returned to my place. I sought Miss Quinn's face for some sign
of approbation. But Miss Quinn was looking on the floor. The
principal rose and began to distribute the diplomas. Each
recipient was applauded. I expected to be singled out for a
special demonstration. But when my name was called and I
advanced toward the principal, the applause that greeted me
was even smaller in volume and intensity than that bestowed
on the graduates who had preceded me!

The exercises ended with our singing of "My Country,
'Tis of Thee" and *The Star-Spangled Banner*. By prearrange-
ment I met my family in the theater lobby. There I was
warmly congratulated by my brothers and sisters. But I
managed to persuade my mother to reserve her more physical
demonstration of affection for the privacy of our home. Once
there, though I could not shake off a feeling of uneasiness, I
suffered myself to be kissed and embraced by her, and I experienced a sense of relief when she said that I looked and
sounded like a great actor.

From the English-speaking members of the family I elicited
more detailed praise. And to assure myself that they had not
missed any of the fine points and subtleties I had hoped to
convey, I recited the poem again, pausing at certain spots to
inquire if I had used the same intonation and gesture in the
theater, and to be assured vehemently and enthusiastically
that I had. I then craved their indulgence for another performance, this time without interruption. In the security of
our front room and surrounded by affection and admiration, I
recited "Winning Cup's Race" with a skill, an ease, and a
brilliance that overwhelmed both my family and me. Compared with it my performance at Poli's was admittedly unas-
sured, pale, and stilted. I read in the troubled eyes of my
audience that they, too, understood the difference, but a tacit

delicacy obviated any reference to the comparison. From myself I could no longer hide the feeling that "Winning Cup's Race" had been a fiasco in the theater. That, and not her personal hostility to me, was why Miss Quinn had not returned my inquiring look, and why there had been no crescendo of applause when I rose to receive my diploma.

The memory of my first public failure embittered my last weeks in Waterbury. When I met a schoolmate on the street, I suspected that his greeting, whether cordial or indifferent, concealed either pitying condescension or malicious triumph. Indeed, my feeling of guilt increased with the passing of time, and the picture of my frightened self staring at the gallery in Poli's Theater and waiting for the once so familiar, but now elusive opening words of "Winning Cup's Race" to take shape in my mind grew more and more vivid and terrifying. Could I ever again face an audience? Whether in music or in drama, the great man I expected to be would have to demonstrate his powers, not in the security of his home, but in the threatening, hostile impersonality of the concert hall or the theater.

What else could I aspire to that held no such threat to my vulnerable sensitiveness? Poetry, perhaps. The poet was not a public figure. But how could the poet know the pleasure his works gave to the world? By counting the number of books he sold? But how impersonal was such a reward! Better, perhaps, the promise of even such a partly satisfying moment as when, at the conclusion of my nightmarish recitation, I identified the rattling sound of coal moving down a chute as reluctant applause than the poet's cold knowledge that some unseen persons were reading his works. My fears were great, but my yearning to shine in public was even greater. Besides, *music* was my forte, not recitation. I could not be frightened playing the piano in public. For one thing, I did not have to look at anything but the keys. I must henceforth set my will to banish fear or else become reconciled to an inglorious future at home.

CHAPTER FOURTEEN

Widening Horizons

WE HAD hardly installed ourselves in New York in a railroad flat in a house on Madison Avenue, at the corner of 112th Street, when the alarming news arrived from Waterbury that my brothers Albert and Solomon had "failed." The details of this catastrophe were not touched upon in Solomon's letter to my father, which left us to add "failed" to our limited and uncertain vocabulary of business terms like "chattel mortgage" and "foreclosure." What Solomon had made plain was that they had lost everything and were contemplating a removal to California, a state, in his opinion, eager to encourage the building trade. There, being unknown, they could start anew. Fortunately, they had salvaged enough from the wreck of their fortunes to get them to the small but thriving town of Mariposa, which they hoped would be but a steppingstone to the greater city of Los Angeles. The implication of this news for us was plain. We could no longer in a pinch count on my brothers for financial aid. And in a pinch we decidedly were at that very moment.

In a family council held immediately upon the receipt of Solomon's letter, it was decided that I must find a job of some sort and for the duration of our financial crisis pursue my musical studies on the side. I scanned the want ads in the *New York World* for jobs in our neighborhood. This would save me both carfare and time. There seemed to be a few such, particularly in the offices of doctors and dentists. The latter, especially, appeared to be in need of boys of my age to sweep out their offices, answer doorbells, and do a variety of chores that required little skill, and they were prepared to pay wages of between three and three and a half dollars a week for the "right" boy.

When I appeared in these offices at eight in the morning, the stated time for interviews, I found, to my dismay, the waiting-rooms crowded with applicants. No matter how early I arrived, there was always a crowd ahead of me. In weeks of answering suitable advertisements I was able to achieve an interview only once. After a brusque inquiry into my background and an examination of my qualifications my name and address were noted down and I was dismissed with the promise that a decision would be communicated to me by mail. The letter never came.

In the meantime my mother had established credit at a butcher's shop, a fish store, and a grocery. The last was located, most conveniently, in the house we lived in. Two years of freedom from financial worries had not dampened my mother's buoyancy and general optimism, nor her powers of persuasion. And she now proceeded to establish relations with tradespeople as easily as she had done before we moved to Waterbury. I was not present at her initial interview with the grocer; but it had been highly successful, and the grocer had given her an oblong-shaped notebook in which he recorded all our purchases. She had agreed to weekly payments. Each Saturday night, for a month, she asked for a reckoning and paid it in cash. Thereafter her payments tended to grow irregular, and one day when I was sent to the store to do the shopping, the grocer, to my embarrassment, refused to fill the order and in the presence of several customers declared vehemently that my mother had exhausted his patience, that he, too, had to live and buy provisions and pay rent, and that, in short, he could not extend us further credit without visiting the greatest injustice on his wife and children. On hearing about this my mother went downstairs at once and returned a quarter of an hour later with the provisions I had failed to get. There were times, too, when the butcher failed to deliver meat, and the baker, bread and rolls. But a visit by my mother to their shops always set things to rights, and the stream of provisions resumed flowing. We ate very well indeed.

Learning of our return to New York, relatives and friends began visiting us in large numbers, as in the old days. They generally arrived just before mealtime. My mother, even before greeting them, would pour a quart or so of water into the soup kettle, and I would be dispatched to the various stores for an extra can of herring in tomato sauce, another rye bread, and a chunk of hard salami. When Nochum and Chaie Rive Flayshig and their two boys paid us a visit, my mother would not hear of their returning to their home in Brooklyn (a journey of at least two hours) late in the evening, and the visitors were put to bed in a body on the floor of the front room. The following morning Chaie Rive rose early, washed and dressed the twins (their curls had given way to high pompadours, but their hair still required their mother's attention), and put on their jackets, preparatory to leaving. Her preparations took a long time, as if she were reluctant to depart, as indeed she was. At that delicate moment my mother remarked that it must be indeed an unfeeling parent who would take her young children on a long journey to Brooklyn on an empty stomach. And Chaie Rive, loudly protesting, allowed herself to postpone their return until after lunch.

My father plainly showed his annoyance with my mother's excessive hospitality and Chaie Rive's delaying tactics, and when the guests finally left, my mother upbraided him for his want of delicacy, denying his accusation that she put herself out only for *her* relatives, and calling on God to absolve her of any display of partiality. This led to a quarrel, and for days the atmosphere in the house was oppressive with animosity. To escape it, Molly and I went for walks in Central Park after supper or visited Hannah, who lived on Ninety-fourth Street near the East River, five flights up in a house facing George Ehret's brewery.

Hannah had grown very large, but her pregnancy had made her face more beautiful than ever. She now seemed indifferent to the things that had used to trouble her, such as the hardships and calamities of friends and our economic plight. Her own situation was, at the moment, rather favorable. Her husband had captured an impressive "job" of fresco-painting which would take many months to complete and net him three hundred dollars. Half of the sum had been paid in advance. On the advice of friends who knew and feared the fluctuations of her husband's profession, Hannah invested ninety dollars in a diamond ring. As against the insecurity of banks, whose failures were periodic, a diamond ring was as safe as anything possibly could be. Indeed a "stone" (as it was familiarly called) had an intrinsic value not subject to economic ills. Economic depressions even had the curious effect of appreciating the value of a "stone." At the worst, a diamond could be instantly translated into cash at the pawnbroker's.

Negotiations for the purchase of the ring were carried on privately with a friend of Jake's who had a friend in the diamond business. One Sunday Hannah summoned my mother, Molly, and me to her house to help her choose a stone from among an assortment that Jake's friend's friend was bringing over. The stones, spread out on a velvet mat, were dazzling. The dealer delicately picked out the diamonds with a pair of pincers and held them up to the light and turned them around to let us see them sparkle. The stone we finally chose was priced at one hundred dollars. My mother made one of her best efforts to bring this down to seventy-five. But she reluctantly settled for ninety when the man exclaimed: "If you won't buy it for ninety, you don't *want* a diamond," and brusquely poured the jewels into a small paper envelope that he shoved into the inside pocket of his jacket with unmistakable finality.

The purchased stone was then taken to a jeweler's on Grand Street and mounted on a gold ring. Henceforward the presence or absence of the diamond ring from the fourth finger of Hannah's right hand served as an index of her economic state, as well as of that of her family and friends. At those rare periods when Jake was doing well, Hannah was glad to lend the ring to friends in need, who pawned it and then redeemed it at the first opportunity. Emergencies might arise in her circle while the ring happened to be out at the moment for the benefit of somebody. At those times Hannah would do her best to redeem the ring herself and pass it on to the neediest of the moment. An emergency operation, a lying-in, the instant requirement of a dowry as an inducement to a youth to marry a friend's daughter whom he had got in "trouble," required the intervention of Hannah's diamond ring at the shortest notice.

Hannah's baby, a boy, was born at a time when the ring was in her possession. The night before, Jake appeared at our house to tell us that Hannah's pains had begun and that he had already summoned the doctor. My mother went back with him to stay the night, and early the next morning I ran to Hannah's house.

I was permitted to go into the bedroom with Jake. Hannah lay in bed with the baby close at her side. The infant was swaddled in several layers of clothes, and only his thin, shriveled, crinkled, ancient-looking profile was visible. He made no sound. Hannah looked very pale and serious, and when she saw me she stretched out her right hand toward me. Her fingers were bloodless, long, and thin, and on one of them the diamond ring sparkled, a tiny point of radiance in the darkened, silent room. I kissed her hand and sobbed for joy, for I had heard of women dying in childbirth. Then Jake said she must sleep, and we left.

Sometime later an apartment in our house fell vacant, and at my mother's insistence Hannah moved into it. The proximity was beneficial all around. I spent a good deal of time in Hannah's house playing with the baby and watching Jake make water-color sketches for his big job. The baby had grown young-looking and had lost his wrinkles. I began to take pleasure in his company, and was happy when I was permitted to hold him or take him out for an airing in his carriage. In no time at all he became everybody's preoccupation. Even my father showed a mild interest in him, though he said we all gave him exaggerated attention. As for Hannah, the baby absorbed all her waking hours and, when he was indisposed or ill, her nights as well.

My mother, having seen Hannah through childbirth, now addressed herself to the problem of getting Molly married. Solomon had been written off. Molly swore that never, under any circumstance, would she consider marrying her foster brother. Several men whose acquaintance she had made in New York during our stay in Waterbury visited our house and were closely examined by my father and mother for their eligibility as suitors. Molly seemed heart-free, but she showed a slight preference for a Mr. Glanz, a quiet, well-spoken man of about thirty-five, who was in the insurance business and seemed prosperous. Mr. Glanz took Molly to an occasional concert and ball, but always brought her home before the ball began. He did not care for dancing, and said as much. For all his quiet demeanor, my parents did not feel comfortable in his presence. "He behaves," my mother once remarked, "like a man who is hiding something. . . . I wouldn't be surprised if he had *traveled!*"

A man who traveled much was a legitimate object of suspicion. It wasn't even possible to make inquiries about him. How could one know what he did in distant places! He might even have a wife somewhere at the ends of the earth! One night as Mr. Glanz was sipping a glass of tea my father looked up from his book and directed a loaded question at him. "Am I right, Mr. Glanz, that you have seen something of the world?" Mr. Glanz smiled and did not answer immediately. My mother looked much concerned. Mr. Glanz was obviously well-to-do and might yet prove to be an ideal match for Molly. But when Mr. Glanz finally spoke, he might just as well have exploded a bomb in our kitchen. "Yes," he said, "I have seen a bit of the world in my youth. I once spent a year in China."

My mother gasped. "In *China!*" she repeated incredulously. "In China," Mr. Glanz affirmed. "Another glass of tea," my mother suggested, rising hastily and taking up Mr. Glanz's glass and saucer. My father resumed his book, and after drinking his second glass of tea Mr. Glanz politely took his leave.

"I knew he was concealing something," my mother said sadly. "My heart told me. Yet he seems nice."

My father nodded. "One never can tell," he said. "China! *Imagine!*"

Molly put up a half-hearted defense of Mr. Glanz. A good man, she argued, need not necessarily succumb to corruption even in so distant a place as China. But, not really caring for Mr. Glanz, she let the matter drop, and the next time he called she was quite short with him and declined to go walking in Central Park. Mr. Glanz, perhaps as a result of his travels, was no fool. He took the hint, and we never saw him again.

With the elimination of Mr. Glanz, my mother's concern for Molly's future became acute. My father, who, since our

return to New York had reverted to his old attitude of coldness and sometimes even of hostility to my mother and her
children, began referring pointedly to Molly as a *"mahd."* A
mahd was a *maedel* who had passed the freshness of youth.
While not wholly a spinster, a *mahd* was so dangerously close
to being one as to cause her family the utmost concern. Molly
was twenty-one, going on twenty-two, and perilously close
to the age limit of a *maedel*. My mother made it a point to
strike up an acquaintance with the women she met in the
grocery and at the butcher and fish shops and learn in a casual
way about the composition of their families. But when she
hinted to Molly that the son of a neighbor or acquaintance was
eager to call on her, my sister flew into a rage and accused
her mother of lacking pride. She even threatened to move
away.

At that period Molly, no less than my mother, was in a
nervous state. The basement shop on Vesey Street where she
worked was gloomy, and the Armenian proprietor, who was
the only occupant of the premises besides herself, made her
feel uneasy. It might take a long time to find another job, and
we could not afford to do without Molly's wages even for a
week. It was decided that I should accompany Molly to work
and find out for myself whether there were grounds for her
fears. I thought it only prudent to supply myself with a
weapon with which to meet the situation that Molly feared.
In a vacant lot on Fifth Avenue I found a brick. I put it in a
paper bag and tied a cord around it to make it look like a box
lunch. Armed with this and a book to while away the time, I
went along to Vesey Street with Molly one morning.

The "factory" was indeed a gloomy place. The room in
which Molly worked was underneath the sidewalk, and the
window, which let in an uneasy light, was close to the ceiling.
A single gas burner fixed to one wall threw an eerie light on
two workbenches and several stools and cardboard crates.
The proprietor sat at a workbench manufacturing cigarettes.

Near the bench stood a low stool that held a phonograph with
a very large horn. The appearance of the man was odd and,
to me, frightening. He was tall, thin, and stoop-shouldered,
and his long, unkempt hair was black streaked with gray, like
a mixture of black pepper and salt. His hands were yellow,
bony, and gnarled, his eyes deep-set and smoldering.

Molly said: "Good morning. This is my brother," but did
not explain my presence. The Armenian gave me a piercing
look over his shoulder and murmured something unintel-
ligible. Molly took off her hat and gloves and sat down at her
bench on the other side of the room. I found a rickety stool,
sat down between Molly and the Armenian, and opened my
book.

Presently the Armenian reached under his bench and picked
a cylindrical wax record from a half-dozen standing there. He
fitted it on the phonograph, which he wound up. After some
preliminary rasps the horn began to emit the strangest sounds
I had ever heard. The voice struggled out of the horn as
if under desperate compulsion to escape from the confines
of the cylinder, filling the wretched apartment with the
screeching and wailing of a soul in torment. Now soft and
pitiable, then suddenly raucous like a cry of pain at some
dreadful hurt, the voice hurled itself at the damp walls and
gathered force from the rebound. It flashed through my mind
that this could be the "woman wailing for her demon lover"
in *Kubla Khan*, Coleridge's strange poem whose imagery I
felt, but whose sense I could not make out.

When, following a piercing coloratura flourish, the music
stopped, the Armenian removed the cylinder and said in my
direction and in a strange accent: "Nice—you like?" He then
chose another record. This, with some slight difference,
sounded like the first. The records followed one another, and
when he had played the lot he began over again. So the
morning wore away. At noon Molly and I went outdoors and
ate our sandwiches while walking the streets. When we re-

turned, the Armenian was gone. In the afternoons it was his custom to visit tobacconists' and restaurants and take orders for his brand of cigarettes.

That night we held a family council, and I described the Armenian's basement and the Armenian himself so vividly that it was agreed that the danger to Molly was greater than our need of her wages. I accompanied her, still armed with the brick, to Vesey Street for the rest of the week. And when she was paid off on Friday, she told the Armenian that she would not be back. Even as we stood in the doorway I feared an assault, and I clutched the brick with both hands. But the Armenian said nothing and made no move. When we reached the sidewalk we heard the sound of one of his records seeping through the transom. We broke into a run toward the streetcar as if we feared pursuit.

Molly soon got another job in more respectable surroundings. No longer needed as a protector, I could turn my attention to finding some lucrative work for myself. Through my mother's skill at blandishment and at advertising my merits as a pianist and musician, I obtained my first pupil. This was a sad-looking, squint-eyed spinster who had definitely passed into the category of *mahd*. My mother had made her acquaintance in the grocery store and had cleverly turned her thoughts to studying the piano. I suspect that my mother stressed the importance from a man's point of view of music among the accomplishments of a young lady. And, indeed, a plain-looking young lady who played the piano had an edge, in the matrimonial market, over those who didn't. Piano-playing was noted down as an asset in the shadchen's little notebooks.

This *mahd* had no ear for music, and her fingers were too old and ungiving for the piano. But she paid me fifty cents a week for two lessons and an hour of practice a day on our piano. At the very first lesson I realized that I could regard her only in a monetary light. The lessons were a chore for both of us.

In addition to being untalented, the spinster was nervous and ill at ease. She could not concentrate on fingering and counting out loud. Her thoughts seemed to be on other things, and her eyes were often on the door, as if she expected the entrance of the prospective groom my mother had probably guaranteed. For a year, at least, she persevered. Then, nothing in the way of a suitor having materialized, she abandoned the piano. Sometime later I heard, with astonishment, that my former pupil had succeeded in obtaining a husband. My mother did not hesitate to attribute the good fortune of the *mahd* to her having studied the piano with me. To hear my mother talk, one would think that she had herself arranged the *shiddach* (match).

Another and more unexpected source of income was brought to my notice by my old friend Mr. Katz, the owner of the music shop on East Broadway. I acquainted Mr. Katz with my need for earning money, hoping that he would recommend me as a teacher of the piano to beginners. He told me that the teaching field was overcrowded and that even beginners now aspired to be taught by the top men in the professions—noted virtuosi and teachers like Montana and Ivan Tschirsky. I asked Mr. Katz whether Madam Zamoshkin was also numbered among the outstanding teachers. He said that the Zamoshkins had disappeared two years previously, leaving many debts (including a large unpaid bill in his own shop) and the suspicion that Madam Zamoshkin's "Freedom method" was as controversial as her claim that she was legally the wife of Mr. Zamoshkin.

Mr. Katz thought that an educated boy like myself could make money teaching English to immigrants who desired to learn the language in the shortest time and were willing to pay for it. He knew of a newly arrived brother and sister who were on the lookout for a cheap young teacher, and he would take pleasure in recommending me. As to the fee, he counseled me to be bold and ask for twenty-five cents a lesson *per person*.

Mr. Katz was as good as his word and arranged an interview. My boldness in the matter of my fee so impressed the brother and sister that there was no need of bargaining. Twice a week I journeyed to Norfolk Street, where they lived, and taught them how to read, write, and pronounce English. They made good progress. And soon they induced two of their friends to give up night school, where progress was slow because of the large classes, and take the short cut of private lessons with me.

My teaching activities in piano and English brought me two and a half dollars weekly. With this and Molly's and Sarah's wages, my mother now had fourteen dollars a week with which to run the household. The actual cost of running the house came to a great deal more, but my mother juggled the fourteen dollars in a masterly way, paying so much on account here and promising full payment a week later there. Sometimes she would advise me to avoid passing the shoe store on 116th Street for a fortnight, or she would caution all of us not to loiter on our stoop for the time being. Then we surmised that the grocer's bill was long overdue and that he would be on the lookout to intercept one of us to obtain what satisfaction there might be in airing his grievance publicly and putting us out of countenance before the neighbors. Notwithstanding my mother's warnings and the precautions we took, the grocer once confronted Sarah as she was turning into the house laden with provisions from a rival grocery. In the hearing of neighbors and passers-by who had collected around the stoop, he abused my mother for an ungrateful, scheming, and unprincipled woman who, not content with running up enormous bills at his store, added insult to injury by taking her custom elsewhere, where she and her methods were as yet unknown! The following Saturday night my mother entered his store as if nothing had happened, paid a few dollars on account, and proceeded to give a large order, which the grocer dutifully filled.

Our economic situation, while leaving my mother unruffled, had a depressing effect on Molly and me. It seemed to me and to Molly (Molly was quick to accept and adopt my ideas and opinions, despite the disparity in our ages) that the wealth of the world was unevenly and rather stupidly distributed. This unreasonable and unfair distribution was also proof to us of the validity of atheism; for a deity would certainly have ordered it otherwise. In the *New York American*, which Molly and I read assiduously, there were stories and photographs of people who had no need to work and who spent their time arranging lavish and costly entertainments for one another. We read about the Vanderbilts and the Goulds, and we resented them, though we were avid to learn the details of their frivolous lives. We followed the course of dazzling international marriages with concealed relish, while openly excoriating the rich Americans for buying foreign titles and the noble foreigners for selling them.

In Central Park Molly and I took pleasure in calling out insults to the beautifully dressed ladies and gentlemen as they drove past us in their carriages and electric landaulets, or rode in pairs on horseback on a bridle path that ran the length of the Park. What an affront to the poor was this bridle path, created and maintained for the pleasure of a useless minority! Yet many of the pampered ladies I watched go by me were lovely to look at, and I had daydreams (which I did not confide to Molly) in which a beautiful lady in a carriage would on seeing me command her coachman to stop. I would be invited to ride in the Park, with the explanation that something in my face had caught her attention. The adventure ended in my marrying the lady if she was not too old or, if she was, her daughter, whom I was to meet at supper in the family mansion on Fifth Avenue, adjacent to the Vanderbilt house. Then having acquired my wife's fortune, I would spend a good deal of it in helping the poor, especially talented young boys. I would roam the poorer districts of the city incognito and listen for the sounds of piano-playing. And when I discerned arresting musical qualities in the performer, I would reveal myself and make him and his family independent for life.

My own piano repertoire had grown considerably. I had left far behind me pieces like *The Burning of Rome*, *The Eight Sufferers*, and *The Alpine Shepherd's Evening Call*, which now seemed to me insufferably juvenile and sentimental. In Katz's music store I bought the first volume of Beethoven Sonatas. And having read somewhere the legend of the origin of the "Moonlight" Sonata, I committed that composition to memory.

It was an unusually difficult piece, but its alleged "program" and the Freedom method helped me to ignore its technical hazards. True, the music did not quite conform to the details of the legend. I had read that the great composer, wandering at night through the streets of Vienna, had heard the sounds of his own music coming from a lowly cottage. Entering the house, he discovered a blind maiden at a piano. He introduced himself. The blind girl, overawed, asked him to play. As Beethoven seated himself at the instrument a ray of moonlight fell athwart it. Then and there Beethoven improvised the "Moonlight" Sonata, to the unutterable delight of the blind girl and posterity.

In the sonata, the story related, the composer depicted gentle spirits dancing on a moonlit lawn. The image guided me in my interpretation of the first movement, though I could not help wondering at the extremely slow tempo of the spirits. But what did Beethoven depict in the violent, stormy last movement? I could find no clue in the legend, so I arbitrarily made up a scenario to fit the dominant mood of the music. In my version Beethoven improvised only the first two movements for the blind girl. He then took his leave. On the way home the moon suddenly disappeared and a violent storm ensued, with peals of thunder, flashes of lightning, and torrents of rain. On reaching his home Beethoven, drenched to the skin but creatively inspired, rushed to the piano and improvised the last movement, incorporating in it the drive and fury of the storm and, in the intervals of its cessation, invoking the tender image of the blind girl in the cottage. As a complete contrast to the "Moonlight" Sonata, I added Liszt's Second Rhapsody to my new repertoire. The tremendous technical problems of the Rhapsody succumbed to the Freedom method and its wonder-working aid, the loud pedal. My rendition of these two compositions, so utterly different in quality, never ceased to move and excite my audience.

Apart from the members of my family, our relatives, and friends, my audience now included the Finkles, a family that lived on the third floor front in our house. The Finkles were a father and mother, two daughters, and a son. My mother made the acquaintance of the elder Finkles in the grocery store. The elder Finkles were a remarkable couple. They were of the same size and age, their features were almost alike, and they were inseparable. Mr. Finkle had no visible occupation, and, indeed, he did not require one, for his children all worked and earned more than enough for the needs of the family. Mr. Finkle accompanied his wife wherever she went. Never were they seen alone. On their shopping tours he carried the basket and some of the parcels. At home Mrs. Finkle did the cooking while her husband swept the rooms, washed the dishes, and peeled the potatoes and onions.

The elder Finkles were very proud of their children. They had, to be sure, every right to be. The girls, Naomi and Reba, were schoolteachers and the son, Harry, the oldest of the three, was, most incredibly, a member of the great Metropolitan Opera House chorus. I had read about the Metropolitan Opera House in the *New York American* and had seen pictures of some of the stars. But it was hard to believe that a member of the company actually lived in our house. I longed to know him and to talk to him. And one night his sisters brought him to us and he asked me to play. I played Liszt's Second Rhap-

sody (it was by now called "*The* Rhapsody" by my family
and friends).

I was less confident of my powers before a member of the
Metropolitan Opera House, and my playing reflected my
nervousness. To my delight, Harry Finkle said: "Bravo!"
which I understood to mean approval, and clapped his hands
with the rest of the audience. Yet I was sure that he had
noticed the inadequacy of my octaves, and I waited for his
judgment.

"Sammy," said my mother, turning to Mr. Finkle, "wants
to take more lessons. From what you heard, don't you think,
Mr. Finkle, that he doesn't have to any more? Don't you think
he's finished?"

Mr. Finkle smiled. "In music," he replied, "*nobody* is ever
finished. At the Metropolitan"—the august word startled
me—"many of the greatest singers go regularly to teachers."

"Do you go too?" my mother persisted.

"I, too," Mr. Finkle said gravely.

Later, over a glass of tea, Mr. Finkle was induced to talk
about himself and his glamorous duties at the Metropolitan.
No life could be more exciting. One night he was a courtier at
a Duke's palace helping to abduct the lovely daughter of the
Duke's jester. Another night he was a *bon vivant* playing for
high stakes in a Parisian gambling-house. He felt at home in
every variety of wig and costume. He was on the most familiar
terms with the Metropolitan stars. They conversed with him
in the wings and during intermissions. He related anecdotes
both serious and amusing. Some in the latter category I found
rather disillusioning. "One night, in *Faust*, my friend de
Reszke pressed an egg into Marguerite's hand—I think Eames
was the Marguerite. Yes, it was *Emma*—during their love
scene. Poor girl! She was afraid to open her hand until the
curtain came down." I liked the serious ones better, especially
those which told of last-minute substitutions of untried and
unknown singers for indisposed veterans of the opera house.

Mr. Finkle himself knew every bass role in the Metropolitan's repertoire, and was ready at a moment's notice to replace any scheduled star.

I could have listened to Mr. Finkle forever. But Hannah, who had come down to our apartment to hear me play for our important neighbor, managed to bring the conversation back to me and my future. She agreed with Mr. Finkle that I required further study, and asked him to recommend a teacher. Mr. Finkle had several suggestions to make, among them Ivan Tschirsky and a certain Mr. Plesch. The latter, Mr. Finkle said, was a Romanian musician and pianist of the highest repute, though as yet not so well known as Tschirsky. Hannah took down the addresses of both. When the Finkles left, she said that I must lose no time in seeking out one or the other of the pedagogues. And when my father raised a skeptical eyebrow, Hannah said that she would herself pay for my lessons and glanced significantly at the diamond ring on her finger.

My first choice was Ivan Tschirsky, whom I had once seen for a moment in Katz's music store. Tschirsky looked like Beethoven and was thought to be the illegitimate son of the great Anton Rubinstein, a rumor that he himself had started and carefully fostered. Mr. Finkle made an appointment for me, and one morning I stood, with beating heart, in Tschirsky's presence in his studio on 116th Street. On closer inspection he resembled both Beethoven *and* the great Anton Rubinstein. I thought it rather a pity that he couldn't be the illegitimate son of both. Before he asked me to play for him, Tschirsky inquired if I had seen his new suite for piano, *O Russia!* recently published by Katz. And without waiting for a reply he sat down at the piano and played *O Russia!* for me. The suite was in many movements, each bearing a colorful title and a sentence or two of description—"Russia, cradle of my soul . . . a village at twilight . . . hark the dogs! . . . the peasants dance and sing . . . they are happy . . . the storm . . . hark the thunder! . . . " He played with every show of emotion, tossing his dark, long, coarse hair and breathing hard. He seemed to be in the grip of an over-whelming nostalgia for the country of his birth. At the same time, he exploited the realistic touches in the suite, making the piano bark like dogs and resound with rumblings like distant thunder.

When I had complimented him on his suite and his per-formance, he suddenly told me point-blank that his fee was two dollars a lesson and asked me if I was prepared to pay it. I suggested that perhaps he should hear me play first. He said he considered an audition a lesson, and lessons were to be paid in advance. I had brought no money with me. In any case, two dollars a lesson was prohibitive. At that rate Hannah's ring would in no time be liquidated. I tried bargaining. Would he contemplate a dollar a lesson? Mr. Tschirsky grew angry and shouted that he was an artist, not a fish-peddler. But when I started to leave he advised me in calmer tones to make every effort to raise the two dollars and return. He then autographed a copy of *O Russia!* which he took from a large pile of the suite stacked up on the floor and presented it to me.

Hannah was in favor of my taking at least a few lessons from Tschirsky. But I had been put out by his commercialism, and I wished to try Mr. Plesch. Mr. Plesch lived in Bay Ridge, but one day a week he taught his New York pupils in their own homes. Harry Finkle wrote to him about me, and Mr. Plesch replied, naming a day when he would call at my house and hear me play.

I was quite unprepared for the kind of man he turned out to be. I could see at once that he was a Christian. He was thin and sandy-haired. His blue eyes were clear, yet they looked troubled and inquiring. They appeared vitally concerned with me, or my mother or father, or anyone he talked with. His face was small, each feature delicately formed, the skin tightly stretched over an exquisitely fashioned bone forma-tion. He *looked* like an artist. He wore a formal gray Prince

Albert that he did not button and, underneath, a checked vest
and striped trousers. His starched collar was turned down and
its front obscured by a large dark-blue flowing tie. His voice
was slightly husky, and he spoke English with a strange, ingratiating accent. His gentle manner and unselfconscious
politeness put us all instantly at ease. No one so handsome, so
artistic, so *individual*, and so *alien* had ever come to our house.

I played for him, surrounded by my anxious family. He
pronounced me talented, and said he would be glad to teach
me. When Hannah asked him about his fee, he blushed and
said it was a dollar usually, but that the matter was inimpor-
tant, and we needn't worry, that it would be all right whatever
we could pay or even if we couldn't pay at all. Hannah said a
dollar would be all right. Mr. Plesch said we must start to
build up my technique; and the next time he came he brought
with him a volume of Clementi's Sonatinas and a book of finger
exercises with the curious name of the *Little Pischna*. The *Little
Pischna* was an introduction to the *Big Pischna*, which posed
the ultimate in finger problems.

I was rather taken aback by Mr. Plesch's choice of the
Clementi Sonatinas. Compared with works like "The Rhapsody," the "Moonlight" Sonata, and the overtures in my
repertoire, the Sonatinas were juvenile from both a technical
and a musical standpoint. But I was so drawn to Mr. Plesch
that I said nothing. To my surprise, he insisted on my using
the fingerings set down in the music and forbade altogether,
for the time being, any use of the loud pedal. When I mentioned the "Freedom method," he laughed and said it was more
a "crime" than a "method." With the *Little Pischna*, and eventually with the *Big Pischna*, I would acquire the strength and
facility to play virtuoso pieces like "The Rhapsody." Until
that time I must practice and play only what he prescribed.
This was a blow, for it obliged me to forgo the little concerts
I played for my family and our neighbors. No longer could my
mother say of an evening, when the Finkles were assembled in

our front room: "Play something, Semeleh—play 'The Rhapsody,'" and when I played watch the faces of the listeners narrowly for pleasurable reactions.

Mr. Plesch must have sensed our poverty, for he never asked me to purchase music and always brought along what I needed. And his diffidence in accepting his fee led me to the subterfuge of slipping the dollar bill under his hat, which he always placed on the lid of the piano. This saved us both from embarrassment. Once when I was ill I had Molly send him a letter stating that I would be unable to take a lesson that week. But he appeared at the usual time, bringing a bag of oranges for me. I was both happy and dismayed to see him, for the house had not been tidied up as it always was when he was expected.

He seemed oblivious of the disorder around him. He sat at my bedside and talked of music and his favorite composers, Richard Wagner and Richard Strauss. I had known about Wagner for a long time through three pieces—"To the Evening Star" and the March from *Tannhäuser*, and the *Lohengrin* "Wedding March." But Strauss was quite new to me, and I asked if he happened to be the Strauss who composed "The Blue Danube Waltz," which was one of my old Bromo-Seltzer pieces. Mr. Plesch said: "No!" quite positively. "This Strauss," he told me, "was not only *not* the man who wrote 'The Blue Danube'; he was a man who *never* could have written anything so trivial, however innocent and pleasant. This Strauss was a new David fending off the attacks of the musical Philistines. He was a revolutionary and was suffering the fate of all innovators. Wagner, too, had been abused in his time, indeed was still being abused."

Mr. Plesch then talked about art. "Art, like life, is a perpetual struggle. Each generation of true artists has to fight for recognition. It has to destroy the enemy of art, as of life—*tradition*. Tradition, rules, restrictions are the weeds that choke art, just as man-made laws choke life. . . ." Mr.

Plesch poured out words and sentences with passionate ve-
hemence, and I felt caught up in the torrent, not actually
comprehending what he said, but sharing his excitement and
feeling proud of being thought worthy to be taught a philosophy of art and life so idealistic and so uncompromising.
He treated his pupils like equals, desiring only to inculcate in
them his own lofty virtues as man and artist. What a piece of
luck for me that we knew Harry Finkle, and through him this
wonderful man! What an accident all life was! If my father
had not lost his job in the slaughterhouse in Waterbury, we
should never have returned to New York and I should never
have met Mr. Plesch!

It was enough to make one superstitious. I had, of course,
always been superstitious, even when I questioned the existence of God. Undoubtedly powers, strange, mysterious,
and quite beyond mortal understanding, operated in the interest or to the detriment of humans. These powers naturally
expected propitiation, and in the past, when I had desired
something greatly, I had propitiated them by avoiding the
cracks in the sidewalk when I walked in the streets. Not having desired anything greatly for some time past, my superstitions had grown weak. I became careless in avoiding cracks
in sidewalks. Now, with the advent of Mr. Plesch, I realized
that my gratitude must be expressed in some secret acknowledgment of the potency of the powers that brought him to me,
which otherwise might as suddenly take him away from me. I
resumed my avoidance of sidewalk cracks, and for good
measure decided thenceforward to put my left shoe on first
when I dressed in the morning. This procedure I adopted on
the theory that it was a pointed deviation from a universal
routine and could not fail to be appreciated by whatever in-
corporeal agency had charge of my destiny.

I also looked about for a superstition with some reference to
music. It was not easy to invent something unmistakably
suitable, but at last I found one in reaching out with my right

foot to touch the right leg of the piano when I sat down to practice. Superstitions, to be effective, had to be practiced in secret. No one would notice that I always put my left shoe on first, and I soon became expert, when walking in company, in avoiding the cracks in the sidewalks without calling attention to what I was doing. But it required ingenuity to reach out and touch the leg of the piano with my right toe in full view of people in the room without creating the suspicion that I was behaving strangely. I was sometimes obliged to accomplish this quite visible maneuver under cover of engaging someone in conversation at the same time. And soon I was able to practice this superstition as easily and as secretly as all the others.

After my lesson Mr. Plesch would linger a few minutes and talk about music or about me. His gentleness and warmth invited confidence, and it was not long before he knew everything about my family. One day he proposed that I should come out to Bay Ridge on Saturdays for my lesson. There in his home he would be able to give me more time. And as he considered Saturday his day off, he would be *obliged* not to charge me for lessons, all the more so as the round trip to Bay Ridge would cost me thirty cents. Of course I saw through this maneuver, though I didn't let on that I did. I had to turn away to hide my emotion. Mr. Plesch shook me by the hand and said it was a bargain and that he stood more to gain than I, as he would no longer have to make the long journey to 112th Street.

On the following Saturday at eight in the morning I took the Madison Avenue streetcar down to the Brooklyn Bridge, where I changed to another car that went to Bay Ridge. It was a long trip, and I took along a book on the lives of great composers to while away the time. Stimulated by Mr. Plesch's comments on the tribulations of great composers, I got the book in the public library on 106th Street, and I soon knew in detail the gloomier aspects of the lives of Mozart and Beetho-

ven. Though I shed tears at their misfortunes, I felt that perhaps misfortunes were necessary to their development as
artists, especially Beethoven's, for Beethoven's music really
expressed his battles with adversity. The music of Mozart,
at least the sonatas Mr. Plesch gave me to learn, did not appear to square with the unhappy facts of his short life. As for
Haydn, whose music I did not know at all, I thought him the
most disappointing, as a man, of all the great composers in the
book. He was pictured as a jolly person who had few troubles,
wrote music easily, enjoyed a great reputation, and died full
of honors and years. I could not believe that so fortunate a
man could write great music expressive of the sorrows and
joys of humanity.

Riding on the streetcars to Bay Ridge, I felt exalted at the
thought of a new and closer intimacy with Mr. Plesch in his
home, and I reread the life of Beethoven, hoping to find a
similarity between the great afflicted composer and my
teacher. Mr. Plesch was also a composer, though thus far he
had showed me only one of his compositions. This was a song
published at his own expense, a setting of a German poem with
the noble title *"Lied eines Jüdischen Sklaven"* ("Song of a
Jewish Slave"). The words spoke of the historic sad plight of
the Jew, and envisioned a time when the shackles of prejudice
and hate would be struck from him. The music, appropriately in the key of D minor, made vivid the agony of the Jew
and, if I recall rightly, also appropriately burst into D major
at the final words of hope. It was heartening that Mr. Plesch,
a Christian, could be so concerned about the plight of Jews.
This very fact lent credence to the promise of deliverance in
the song. Possessing a heart so overflowing with compassion,
Mr. Plesch, I thought, could with propriety be compared with
Beethoven the man. And it was not beyond possibility that in
time he might also be compared with Beethoven the composer.
Both men were lovers of mankind, honest, truthful, un-

worldly, and both regarded music as a means to banish unhappiness from the world.

Mr. Plesch's house stood in a country setting, very much
like our house in Waterbury. Inside it was palatial. A maid in
a white apron let me in (not since I had dined at Mr. Harris's
in London had I again come face to face with a servant in any
house), and as I waited in the parlor I thought it the richest
and pleasantest front room I had thus far seen. Beautiful,
heavy, convoluted chairs and a sofa, all thickly padded and
soft, were artistically arranged round the room. And in an
alcove, in front of a bay window, stood a grand piano of
polished walnut. It had florid, curved legs, and on its top was
spread a large flowered Spanish shawl of many colors, its
long silky fringes almost reaching the floor. An open cabinet
close to the piano held music books, both in paper covers and
bound. On the walls were large framed pictures of great
musicians, among whom I recognized Beethoven, Mozart,
Handel, Bach, and Haydn (I resented the frivolous Haydn
in such august company). The dining-room, which adjoined
the parlor and had no doors, was also richly furnished. Low
over a circular dark table hung an elaborate gas chandelier,
its shade a large half-globe made of innumerable pieces of
differently colored glass. The walls were paneled in dark
wood and were completely ringed toward the ceiling with two
tiers of built-in bookshelves. I craned my neck to read the
titles of the books, and for a moment I felt as if I were again
peering through the window of Malkin's bookstore on East
Broadway. I read familiar names—Dostoievsky, Tolstoy,
Hugo, Emerson, and Turgeniev. One entire shelf held books
with intriguing titles unknown to me—*Memoirs of a Revolutionist, Exile in Siberia, The History of Anarchism in Europe,
Anarchism in America, The Philosophy of Anarchism, The
Anarchist Movement.* In our house "anarchism" was a word to
be avoided, like the name Jesus Christ. "Anarchists" meant

assassins and persons who believed in "free love," and "free love" was the negation of honorable, civilized passion. Could Mr. Plesch be an anarchist? At any rate, the books testified to his interest in the subject.

Mr. Plesch and a lady came into the parlor. He shook hands with me and introduced the lady as Mrs. Plesch. Obviously he was no anarchist, as there *was* a Mrs. Plesch! Mrs. Plesch was a tall, large brunette with a prominent bosom and a high pompadour. Mr. Plesch looked small indeed beside her. I regretted noticing it, for he appeared, for that moment, to have lost in my eyes some of his importance. Mrs. Plesch said that Mr. Plesch had spoken favorably of me and that she was glad to see me. She then left the room, and Mr. Plesch proceeded to give me my lesson. I was awed by the grand piano, and my fingers faltered at first. But Mr. Plesch, with his usual kindness, said I was not to worry, that I would soon get used to the "animal."

I must have had a very long lesson, for Mrs. Plesch, looking stern, came in to announce dinner. I put my music together preparatory to leaving, but Mrs. Plesch said that I was expected to stay for dinner. During my lesson the dining table had been laid with a lovely white cloth, as if it were Friday night. Real silver-plated knives, forks, and spoons were set at each one's place, and the moment we sat down the maid came through a swinging door carrying a cut-glass pitcher gleaming like a huge diamond, and filled our glasses with ice water. I felt ill at ease and ate little, for fear of revealing my ignorance of good table manners. And at one point I was completely put out by Mrs. Plesch's asking me why I didn't butter my bread. I felt ashamed to tell her that it was forbidden to eat butter with meat. So there was nothing for me to do but butter my bread, which I did, and for the first time in my life I ate as indiscriminately as any Christian.

I could hardly wait to get home to describe the grandeur of Mr. Plesch's house. My mother said she hoped that I would not get too accustomed to luxury, and I said I should always be happier at home than anywhere else. I lied, for I was even at that moment looking forward to my next visit to Bay Ridge. It surprised me how rapidly one did get accustomed to luxury. After a month of Saturdays I felt at home with the padded furniture at Bay Ridge and sat at dinner (I had a standing invitation for dinner) as unselfconsciously as I did in my own house. I ate my meat with butter, never once giving a thought to the probability of divine retribution. And one momentous Saturday Mr. Plesch asked me at table how I would like to stay the night when I came the following week. I could hardly answer him for joy. Instinctively I looked up at Mrs. Plesch for confirmation. She said nothing, but looked hard at Mr. Plesch. Mr. Plesch blushed and said: "I'll be able to have more time with him on Sunday. And I think he could do with some fresh air, don't you, dear?" Mrs. Plesch said, after a long pause: "Yes, I suppose he could." So it was settled, and again I was impatient to rush home and tell the great news.

In preparation for my first weekend visit, I accompanied my father to the Russian bath on Friday afternoon. There I ran the gantlet of the three temperature-graded steam rooms, and after several hours of drastic soapings and washings emerged pink and exhausted, feeling virtuously spotless. I had on clean underwear, socks, and a shirt that my mother had hurriedly washed for me. The next morning I set out for Bay Ridge in the most sanguine frame of mind and with a sense of physical elation.

It was a beautiful April day, and on my walk from the car-stop to Mr. Plesch's house I sang out loud the themes of an imaginary sonata that I had in mind someday soon to compose. Mr. Plesch greeted me affably. But Mrs. Plesch dampened my feeling of elation by asking me why I had not brought along a nightshirt and "*a change*"! I told her, with some embarrassment, that I had forgotten both at the last moment, and I tried to arrive in my mind at what a nightshirt might be and what was implied in "a change." Mr. Plesch quickly said it was time for my lesson, and eased me into the parlor.

After lunch I was left to my own devices and I took down Turgeniev's *Smoke* and lost myself in the portrait of the fascinating, worldly, beautiful and unprincipled Irina. She was a new type in my ever-expanding gallery of women.

After supper, visitors began arriving, both men and women. I was introduced as if I were a grown-up, and I solemnly shook hands with everybody. There was only one married couple, a Mr. and Mrs. Posnick. The latter was very free with me and took me off to a corner. She asked me my age and whether I was in love, and on my looking troubled she said one was never too young for love, that she herself must have been around my age when she had her first love affair. She was not actually beautiful, yet there was an uneasy excitement in the way she looked at one and in the boldness of her questions and confidences. She reminded me in some ways of Irina.

I was asked to play, and Mr. Plesch explained that I was still in the formative stage. He asked his guests to bear that in mind. I played an early Beethoven sonata and a Rondo by Weber. When I finished, I was applauded and made much of. Mr. Posnick's disturbing wife took me in hand again and told me I had a great future in music. She led me on to talk about myself. I told her about my childhood in Russia, about my family, my ambitions, and my love and admiration for Mr. Plesch. "Have you been to any of our meetings?" Mrs. Posnick abruptly inquired. "What meetings?" I asked, and she looked surprised. "Hasn't Tibor [Tibor was Mr. Plesch] taken you? No? Well, then Posnick and I will." I had a sudden illumination. I thought of the many books about anarchism on the shelves in the dining-room. "Is Mr. Plesch an anarchist?" I asked apprehensively. "But of course," Mrs. Posnick replied wonderingly. "You didn't know? We all are. And you must be one soon."

Mrs. Posnick must have told the Plesches about our conversation, for when the guests all had left, my teacher and his wife talked to me at great length about anarchism. I asked many questions, and Mr. Plesch unhesitatingly answered them all, revealing an extraordinary knowledge of history. He traced society from its crudest origins to the present day, and asked me to consider the phenomenon of human exploitation, which ran like a thread through his story. Man-made gods, priests, kings, presidents, capitalists were all different manifestations of a single evil, the will of the powerful few to enslave the simple-minded, fundamentally "good" majority. I ventured to put forward socialism as a corrective for the evils in the world (whose existence I could not deny). Mr. Plesch said he was glad that I mentioned socialism, for many people of good will had been taken in by its philosophy. The truth was that socialism negated the essential goodness and probity of the human spirit even more than capitalism did. "No, my friend," Mr. Plesch continued, leaning toward me (I experienced a momentary delicious feeling of equality with my teacher at being called his friend), "socialism puts an even greater faith in laws and restrictions than capitalism. Anarchism *alone* can save the human race. Anarchism *alone* believes that people are essentially noble and good. Let me ask you" (Mr. Plesch obviously valued my opinions!), "do *you* require laws to prevent you from stealing, from inflicting pain, from murder?" I shook my head. "Of course you don't!" Mr. Plesch went on. "Nor does anyone who is not driven to it by hunger, or by senseless ambition. Let us dismiss all rulers, all legislators, all priests. Let everything be free, and no one will take more than he needs. . . ."

Mrs. Plesch interrupted to say that it was getting late. For my part, I could have listened all night to Mr. Plesch. But he said: "Yes, it is late. We must let him go to bed." He went into the dining-room and came back with a book, which he put in my hand. "Please read a little in it, and we'll talk about it in the morning." Mrs. Plesch showed me into a small bed-room, brightly furnished and looking immaculate. On the bed lay a long white garment. "One of Tibor's nightshirts," she said, following my gaze. They said: "Good night," and left, shutting the door behind them. It was clear that the Plesches did not sleep in their underwear, and that they assumed that no one else did. I undressed and donned the nightshirt. It was too big and too long for me, and I had to laugh when I caught sight of myself in a wall mirror.

I got into bed and opened the book Mr. Plesch had given me. *Looking Backward* was its name. It read like a fairy tale, except that the characters were real people. The time was some very distant future, the place Utopia. I began to under-stand what Mr. Plesch had been only hinting at. For I myself was exactly the questioning, doubtful person in the book, familiar only with the materialistic, capitalistic civilization of the present, and astonished and bewildered by the behavior of the people in Utopia. Mr. Plesch had spoken of such a future for the human race in the broadest terms. But the author of *Looking Backward* dramatized this future and was painstak-ingly and delightfully specific. For example, my counterpart in the book goes into a shop to purchase tobacco for his pipe. The clerk, genial and polite, brings out a large selection of tobaccos. The visitor makes his choice and inquires the price. The clerk is bewildered at the question. There is no price. There is no such thing as money, though he believes one could find specimens of it—the relics of an ancient barbarous age— in the local museum. One simply takes what one requires. If one needs shoes, one gets fitted in a shoe store. If one is hungry, one will find plenty of food in shops and restaurants.

But what does one do in return for this largess, the visitor from the present-day barbarous world inquires? The answer is delightfully simple. One works at what one is best fitted to do. The musician composes or plays and sings, the carpenter builds houses, the tailor makes clothes. Everyone has what he needs. There is, consequently, no such thing as crime, judges, lawyers, jails, or punishment. There are no laws, none being required. As for love, it is as free as everything else. Women here being the equals of men, they no longer need sell themselves in marriage in exchange for economic security.

I read until my eyes ached. Reluctantly I put out the gas and tried to sleep. I had been given a glimpse of a beautiful new world that had no resemblance to the one I knew. Yet it was actually a more *rational* world, certainly one within reach of well-meaning people. I would dedicate myself, like the Plesches and their interesting friends, to building such a world. I must make haste to enlist Hannah and Molly in the Cause. In my dreams that night I was showing my sisters and my mother around a beautiful city and taking them into shops and anticipating with delight their pleased astonishment at being able to "buy" everything without money.

In the morning I breakfasted with Mr. and Mrs. Plesch, and they seemed pleased with my enthusiasm for the book. When we rose from the table, the maid came in and whispered to Mrs. Plesch. Mrs. Plesch then turned to me and asked me to accompany her to the room I had slept in. She looked angry and stern, and I felt a nameless fear as I walked upstairs behind her. Mr. Plesch inquired what was wrong and, getting no reply, followed us into the room. My bed looked only partly made, as if the girl had been called away before she could finish. Mrs. Plesch drew back the covering with a spasmodic jerk and pointed dramatically at a tiny, red, immobile object on the sheet. I did not have to look closer. I knew what it was. Mrs. Plesch wheeled round to me in a fury. "There's never been a bedbug in this house before," she screamed. "*You* brought it!"

I could not believe she was telling the truth. I had never heard of a house that had no bedbugs. And why should she accuse *me* of having brought it? And even if I had unknowingly brought it, why should she create a fuss about it as if I

had committed a crime! At the same time I felt ashamed before
Mr. Plesch. Mr. Plesch was regarding me with compassion
and murmuring: "Please, dear, stop this. You are being unjust,
dear . . . don't, please!" Mr. Plesch was kind, but he appeared to share his wife's horror at the presence of a single
bedbug on the bed. I burst into tears and sobbed that I wished
to go home.

Mr. Plesch led me downstairs and took me for a long walk
out in the country. He begged me not to take his wife's outburst too seriously. He explained that she was scrupulously
clean and took pride in her house. He told me that I must forget the incident, as he was certain Mrs. Plesch eventually
would. When we returned to the house, he closeted himself
with his wife, while I sat dejected and nervous in the living-
room, not feeling guilty, yet wondering whether I had been
too complacent about the presence of vermin. At last Mrs.
Plesch came downstairs and told me that she hadn't meant to
hurt me, but that one couldn't be too careful or one would be
quickly overrun. I took my lesson and was persuaded to remain for lunch; but my pleasure in being in the house had
evaporated.

I left Bay Ridge in the early afternoon. My indignation
(and secret shame) grew with the journey back, and I arrived
home desperately unhappy. I hated Mrs. Plesch for her in-
sensitiveness, but in relating the story at home I spoke passionately and resentfully of having to live in poverty and uncleanliness, thus in effect blaming my mother for the misfortune that had overtaken me that morning. If my mother
understood the wicked implication of my hysterical outburst,
she gave no sign. Instead, she lashed out at Mrs. Plesch,
apostrophizing her scornfully as a Bay Ridge "all-right-
nick" who pretends to faint at the sight of a bedbug—a *single*
bedbug! She thought *that* was putting on airs with a vengeance. No one, of course, *wants* bedbugs. But to scream and
shout and insult innocent guests (my mother called attention

to the fact that for once I had gone to Bay Ridge as clean as a whistle) because of one little bug was just a calculated exhibition of snobbery. I had not transported the bug—of that she was sure. But if I had, she was glad of it.

In this fashion my mother went on until her anger was played out. Yet the incident was not without its effect on her. She engaged more frequently in housecleaning. I would find my underwear and socks removed after a single week's wear and fresh things substituted. And before my departure for Bay Ridge on Saturdays she would give me a last-minute going-over with an extra-coarse clothesbrush.

In music Mr. Plesch steered me in conservative directions. My fingers having been strengthened by the *Pischnas*, little and big, and my sense of musical form stimulated by the classical examples of Clementi and Kuhlau, I was given next the Inventions of J. S. Bach. Mr. Plesch explained to me the importance and influence of counterpoint and fugue in the development of music. The Inventions were finger-breaking; but when I had mastered them, I found in them an unusual pleasure, a satisfaction that I could not relate to the world and its pleasures and woes. They seemed pleasurable for themselves alone, like Hannah's baby or the brook near Mr. Plesch's house in Bay Ridge.

Mr. Plesch could not, when I asked him, explain to me the *meaning* of the Inventions, as he could explain, for example, the *"Pathétique"* of Beethoven. His explanation of the sonata was complete in its symbolism, and flattering to me because it made clear my own secret conception of what I thought Beethoven had meant to convey. Mr. Plesch identified the second theme of the first movement as a dispute between a male and female principle, and I eagerly concurred, for I had thought along the same lines. The adagio, nobly sad, needed no explanation. But except for its prevailing minor cast, the rondo would have left me at a loss to explain so indecisive a resolution of the battle proclaimed in the first movement. Mr.

Plesch "explained" the rondo as the decision of the composer *not* to resolve the battle, to let the issues hang, so to speak, in the air. This seemed strange for a composer so generally *positive* as Beethoven was. But Mr. Plesch said that I would find no end of positive resolution in Beethoven's later works when I got to them. Indeed, I discovered sooner than I expected how positive Beethoven could be.

To save car fare, I sometimes walked home from the English lessons I gave downtown. One night, passing Cooper Union, on Eighth Street and the Bowery, I saw on a poster on the building an announcement by "The People's Symphony Society" of a concert for the following night. The program featured Beethoven's Fifth Symphony. The price of admission was ten cents. This was something I was now able on rare occasions to afford. I invited Hannah to accompany me, and the next evening we took the Madison Avenue streetcar (Hannah paid the fare) and got off at Eighth Street. The concert hall was in the basement of Cooper Union. On the stage sat a large number of instrumentalists clad in white tie and tails. They were tuning up extravagantly and testing their instruments with scales and arpeggios and bits of melody, each player intent on himself and quite ignoring the efforts of his colleagues. The hall resounded with a fascinating conglomeration of sounds. When the conductor emerged from somewhere in the rear, the great disharmony ceased suddenly, as if by magic. The conductor, a tall, thin, stoop-shouldered man dressed like his players, waited awhile as if for inspiration. Then his stick descended with force, and I was engulfed in the opening movement of the Fifth Symphony.

This was a battle indeed! Compared with it the syncopated turbulence of the *"Pathétique"* seemed small in scale and lacking power. I became aware of a similarity in form in the first movements of both. But I was hardly prepared for the relentless insistence of the bold, naked motto from the beginning to the end of the movement. Not for one moment did the onslaught on my ears, on my nerves, and on my intellect and my imagination waver, not even during the brief, hopeless, futile "gesture" of a lonely oboe cadenza, upon which the orchestra suddenly fell, tooth and nail.

The end left me in a state of epic disturbance and with the feeling that I should never again be at peace. But a moment later the cellos began the andante and I was suddenly at peace. I remembered a sentence in the Bible: "Is there no balm in Gilead?" The furtive scherzo, with its elephantine interlude by the basses, set me on edge again, for during its course there came at first secret tappings of the fateful motive of the first movement, later obtruding brashly with almost joyful insolence. I felt that anything could happen, that something tremendous was *brewing*. Then out of an eerie silence created by the soft, rhythmic tap of a kettledrum there arose a fast-gathering crescendo, like the rapid inflation of a tiny storm-cloud, like a genie swiftly released from a bottle, and trumpets rent the air with brassy exultation. I recalled Mr. Plesch's prophecy. No music could be more "resolved" than the finale of the Fifth Symphony, and this grand revelation of the power and scope of music compelled me to revalue everything in music I had liked heretofore.

I told Mr. Plesch about my memorable experience in Cooper Union, thanked him for having planted the seeds of my conversion to Beethoven, and hinted at my loss of interest in all other composers. He agreed with me about Beethoven's unique position in music, but he would not go along in outlawing the other, for him, "important" composers. And he told me with a friendly smile that I was in a transitional stage, and that I might experience still another change of faith when I came to know the great music dramas of Wagner and the tone poems of Richard Strauss. In the light of Beethoven's Fifth Symphony I could not but be skeptical about the possibility of transferring my allegiance to the two later composers. My business now, however, was to find out all I could about Beethoven and his music. In this Mr. Plesch helped me out. We played together four-hand arrangements of all the symphonies and the overtures. And I set myself to learn those sonatas which were within my technical reach, and one, the *"Appassionata"* (for its name), which wasn't. It was at this point in our relationship that Mr. Plesch, through kindness and affection and, I believe, sympathy for my musical awakening and juvenile daring, made the great error of indulging me in my desire to reach into certain compositions regardless of their technical and interpretive difficulties. And so I swept through the *"Appassionata"* with tremendous fervor but lagging fingers and aching wrists and Mr. Plesch did not chide me. I was, in effect, resurrecting the old "Freedom method," now less brash in its pretensions because of certain technical benefits I had gained from the discipline of the two *Pischnas*.

My introduction to Wagner came unexpectedly. To celebrate the payment of a new installment on her husband's "big job" Hannah took me one Saturday night to the Metropolitan Opera House. Saturday-night performances were given at popular prices, and general admission to the gallery was fifty cents. Around four in the afternoon we joined a queue that already stretched from Fortieth Street halfway around the opera house on Seventh Avenue. At seven thirty the doors opened and Hannah and I raced up endless flights of stairs to the very top of the theater. We were already too late to be among the first-row standees. We made our way, however, to a place near an aisle, directly overlooking the orchestra pit. By stepping out in the aisle when the usher wasn't looking, I could see everything in the theater.

Its size and lavish beauty took my breath away. The two tiers of boxes, with their damask-red interiors, the immense orchestra floor, fanning out in raised platforms on either side, the dizzy height from my position to the floor five stories below, the great lighting fixture depending from the ceiling, the deep gold curtain hanging in graceful, generous folds, and, above all, the vast orchestra pit, into which an endless stream of musicians was now filing—I hardly knew where to look. I heard the same sounds of tuning-up I had heard in Cooper Union. Yet these sounds were different, rarefied as if through the alembic of the great upward distance they traveled to reach my ear. From that distance, too, the instrumentalists looked like an assembly of tiny animated mannikins.

When the lights went out in the theater, the orchestra pit remained illuminated, and a string of red, white, and blue electric bulbs stretching across the front of the stage (I could see them) threw a ravishing warm glow on the curtain. The conductor appeared and climbed onto a high chair in front of the players. A hush fell over the house, and the warm glow on the curtain changed to a bleak gray. In a whisper I had time to ask a man in front of me what the opera was and he whispered back: "*Die Walküre*—Wagner."

From the pit rose music like the patter of rain—a rhythmic patter, tense and malevolent. It grew steadily in volume, and suddenly there were rhythmic crashes of thunder and I *heard* lightning. Then the curtain rose on a rude hut. A large tree trunk stood in the middle of the room, which was lit up by a flickering fire on a great hearth at the extreme left. I could not see the whole stage from where I stood; but now and again I stepped out into the aisle, stooped down, and caught fleeting glimpses of the scene and the personages in it. I heard everything, however, though I understood nothing except that the music and the action were on the grandest scale imaginable. In the second act there took place, amid the sound and sight of thunder and lightning, an epic duel on a high crag, the combatants bathed in a red light. And in the final act dazzling maidens in shimmering armor and feathered helmets ran about the stage brandishing long spears, shouting war-cries in massive harmony spurred on and abetted by an orchestra that

neighed and *snorted* and *whinnied* and emitted brassy yelps so
real, grandiose, and powerful as to wipe out my memories of
the finale of Beethoven's Fifth Symphony.

All through the opera there came long stretches of inaction
on the stage. During these I abandoned my efforts to obtain a
view of the scene and gave all my attention to the extraordinary sounds from the orchestra. But toward the last a hissing
effect as of the escape of steam alerted me to the stage. Cran-
ing my neck into the aisle, I saw little flames springing up all
around the stage (I remembered the forest fire on the stage of
Poli's Theater in *The Ninety and Nine*). Then the orchestra,
having crackled and hissed and spat for many preliminary
measures, broke into a melodic *vizualization* of a self-contained, many-hued conflagration at the very same time that the
fire on the stage assembled its scattered forces and coalesced
in a solid ring around a crag on which the chief of the warrior
maidens lay as in sleep!

Early on the following Monday I went to the library and
took home with me a book on the stories of Wagner's music
dramas, and I learned in detail about Siegmund and Sieglinde,
Hunding, Wotan, and the Valkyries. Knowing this necessitated learning the tale of the Nibelungs from the beginning.
Indeed, in a few hours I knew the plots of all the Wagner
operas from *Rienzi* to *Parsifal*. Notwithstanding my instant
absorption in the imagery and plots of the stories, it was their
ethical and moral implications that raised them above anything I had encountered in books. And the vivid memory of
the music of *Die Walküre* enveloped these implications in a
throbbing dramatic light.

Here was a world of music that dealt not in abstract ethical
concepts, but in men and women and their tremendous problems in life! These personages were of grand proportions, yet
I could relate them, through the music, to myself and the
people I knew. The good and the evil they embodied were out
of proportion to the good and evil I knew, yet fundamentally

they were the same. What else, for example, was the Ring the Nibelungs stole from the Rhine Maidens but the very thing that Hannah once called "that dreadful metal," the pursuit of which embittered the lives of the innocent and good and drove the weak and greedy to cruelty, injustice, and crime.

The battle between good and evil was clearly the basic theme of all the Wagner music dramas. But more important to me was the hidden weakness in most of Wagner's heroes. Though they were all high-minded and generous (like myself), they were (also like myself) a prey to temptation. With the exception of Lohengrin, who belonged to the heavens and was above the battle, the heroes were all only myself on a grand scale! Tannhäuser, especially, seemed like a portrait of me. Though I had never met Venus, she was a reality for me, and her image sometimes stood in the way of the life I longed to dedicate to art and the love of a pure woman. The dallying in the Venusberg made corporeal a situation I often confusedly imagined. How did it come about that Wagner understood so well *my* nature and its problems? But of course it was really himself he understood and expressed in poetry and in music. In so doing, he understood and expressed sensitive souls like myself.

That there were pure and noble women in the world I knew at first hand. But that they existed for the redemption and solace of vacillating, erring (albeit essentially noble) men was a discovery I owed to Wagner. Except for Elsa, who faltered in her loyalty, the others were not only entirely dedicated to the men they loved, but they loved *only* men who *required* salvation. Elisabeth should have loved the pure and noble Wolfram, and a lesser artist than Wagner would have so arranged it. But Wagner knew that the Wolframs of the world were morally self-sufficient—they did not need salvation, as Tannhäuser and I and (I presumed) Wagner himself needed it.

Notwithstanding her imperious pride, her tantrums, her will to destruction, I counted Isolde a pure and single-minded woman. She was indeed, in a way, a more *complete* woman than Elisabeth, perhaps on account of those realistic traits she stormily exhibits in the first act, that touch of Venus in her, which at first made me hesitate to place her beside Wagner's *immaculately* good heroines. She soon became, though secretly, my favorite Wagnerian woman (I felt that her utter self-abnegation and tenderness in the second and third acts absolved her of her first-act weaknesses and her later deception of King Mark). So completely, in fact, that in contemplating her mentally, I quite forgot what I considered the mainspring of my existence—the pursuit of art. And I understood that the death of Tristan was no accident of dueling, Isolde's "Love-Death" no consequence of heartbreak. Tristan and Isolde simply could not expose their searing, utterly exclusive passion for each other to an everyday world. There was no place in the world for such a love. Death, I agreed with Wagner, was their only possible future.

Mr. Plesch received my new enthusiasm for Wagner with pleasure, but again refused to abet me in outlawing all other composers, reminding me of the existence and eminence of Richard Strauss, whose works I had yet to know. Would I, he inquired, be inclined to throw Wagner overboard when I got to know and admire Strauss? I could not imagine such a thing. "Well, then," Mr. Plesch counseled, "don't be hasty. Cherish *all* great men, though I have nothing against your having a favorite." Mr. Plesch then lent me his volume of Liszt's Wagner transcriptions for the piano.

In my eagerness to learn Isolde's "Love-Death" I began to neglect my regular technical studies and the suites of Bach, on which I had only recently embarked. Mr. Plesch, protesting mildly, let me have my way. From Mr. Katz I purchased the vocal score of *Tristan* on the usual long-term arrangement. From the library I took home every book by Wagner or relating to him. The music of Wagner, his life, his ideals, even his polemics— I read *Judaism in Music* without distaste (how could Wagner be wrong?)—now filled my life. And to my astonishment and delight, Bernard Shaw's *The Perfect Wagnerite* officially identified the *Ring* dramas with the philosophy of socialism. This made Wagner complete from every angle, and all other composers superfluous.

I walked the streets as if on air. And my behavior at home reflected my consciousness of having finally matured, of having found at last the right key to art. This time I did not even wish to explore my new enthusiasm with Hannah or Molly. How could I convey to anyone except a perceptive musician and humanitarian philosopher like Mr. Plesch (who of course already knew it) the stature of Richard Wagner as artist and seer? I believe I comported myself at home and in the houses of friends with the air of one who was privileged to know something of great consequence, the esoteric complexity of which prevented him from sharing it with anyone not endowed by nature with special faculties to comprehend it. I was very happy.

CHAPTER FIFTEEN

🌿 *A Paradise of the Rich*

IN KATZ's music store one day I was introduced to I. Jacobs. I. Jacobs was well known on the East Side as a promising young pianist and teacher. The I stood for Israel, but he preferred to be called I. Jacobs, and even had cards printed with the initial for a first name. It was rumored that I. Jacobs contemplated giving a formal debut recital at Mendelssohn Hall the following year. People spoke of his good looks, his charm of manner, and his attraction for women. These reports seemed to be well founded. I. Jacobs was a handsome man of about seventeen, tall and rather plump, with a round face, blue eyes, a sharp nose, and delicate skin. His hair was blond and wavy, curled up at the ends and combed pompadour fashion. His hands were small, his fingers short and pudgy. His hand-clasp was warm, and his manner so friendly with a stranger like myself that I fell under his reputed spell at once.

I had never met a man so at ease and at the same time condescending, but condescending in a charming, inoffensive, generous way. He talked about music and the problems of the piano, and illustrated some technical points he was making with a nonchalance that I found captivating and greatly envied. I felt I was in the presence of both an artist and a man of the world. And the accuracy of his fingerwork in the snatches he played brought home to me my own inadequacy in that department. I watched him with awe; and I thought he resembled Lord Byron (a patrician poet, handsome, generous, and condescending, whose biography I had read) or, better still, Steerforth! So Steerforth must have appeared to the admiring gaze of David Copperfield. I could well understand that women found I. Jacobs irresistible.

We left the store together and walked up East Broadway. In the course of conversation I. Jacobs mentioned that he spent his summers in the Catskill Mountains at the Grand View Hotel on Kiamesha Lake. In return for playing the piano an hour or so each evening, he received board and lodging and a handsome weekly stipend, the size of which he did not divulge. It was, he said, the pleasantest way of going on vacation, and he advised me to do the same. Of course, his was an unusual job. He played solos only (there was a special band for dancing). But that was because the Grand View was the most expensive hotel on the lake and he was a particular friend of the proprietor's wife. The less expensive hotels engaged a violinist and a pianist who played for both entertainment and dancing. The violinist Rashkin, who was a friend of his (Rashkin was an esteemed virtuoso on the East Side), had the job at the Cedar View Hotel, a short distance from the Grand View; and Jacobs would be pleased to recommend me to him as pianist. I wondered aloud at his wishing to recommend me without hearing me play. I. Jacobs said that he had heard about my playing from Mr. Katz, and what was good enough for Mr. Katz was good enough for him. I was melted by his

kindness and trust in me, and I hardly knew how to express
my gratitude. At his request I gave him my address, which he
noted down on one of his professional cards extracted from a
brown leather wallet, and I left him at the stoop of a fine three-
story brick house, near Gouverneur Street, where he resided
on the second floor in an apartment that ran the entire length
of the house! A brass plaque on the outside of the house announced: "I. Jacobs, pianist and teacher."

I dared not hope that a job in the Catskills would ma-
terialize from a chance meeting with this amiable and humane
artist. But I. Jacobs was as good as his word. A few days later
I was summoned by letter to Mr. Rashkin's house on Jefferson Street for an interview. The letter threw our house into a
turmoil. It marked, in a way, my acceptance by the world as a
professional musician, and confounded my father's doggedly
held belief that music, however ornamental an accomplishment, could not offer a serious, lucrative way of life. It
promised an easement of the summer slack, which was now
upon us with full force. But it also brought up the alarming
consequence of my having to be separated from my family for
the first time in my life. I wondered how I would endure such
a parting. At the same time I was eager to see the fabled
Catskills and the renowned Kiamesha Lake, where only rich
people might sojourn, and to play for their delectation.

Though I knew Mr. Rashkin by reputation, I had never
seen him. He lived in a basement apartment, and a plaque on
the door read: "Sol Rashkin, violin virtuoso and teacher." I
was somewhat taken aback by his looks and speech, neither of
which was of the superior kind I had expected in a violin
virtuoso. Sol Rashkin was short and eel-like, with a swarthy
yellow face and coarse hair. He looked about twenty, but I
knew he was not more than seventeen. I could see he was
obliged to shave often, for his chin and the sides of his face almost to the eyes and his upper lip showed up bluish over the
basic yellow of his skin. He was startlingly hirsute. Hair grew

wherever it could, on the back of his hands, in his nostrils and
ears, and low down on his forehead. A coarse, curly strand of
hair protruded from an opening in his shirt where a button
was missing. His voice was truculently husky, and he spoke
without refinement. I could not help comparing him with
I. Jacobs, whose appearance and speech bespoke the musician
and gentleman. Could this be the Sol Rashkin whose tone on
the violin was (I'd heard) of melting sweetness, and whose
mournful double-stops in *Zigeunerweisen*, his showpiece,
clutched at one's heartstrings!

Rashkin asked me if I had played summer jobs before. I
said I hadn't. He then wanted to know if I read well at sight,
and I replied that I did (as I believed), but he did not ask me
to play. The pay, he said, was six dollars a week. Laundry
would be my only expense—the management stipulated a
change of shirt three times a week. I was to meet Sol at the
Courtland Street ferry the following Monday at eight in the
morning. The interview over, I wondered if I might ask him to
play. But his matter-of-fact references to music seemed to
imply a strictly commercial consideration of art, and I
refrained from asking him. I left with the impression that he
was not the man to play the violin for pleasure alone.

The news of my summer engagement was greeted at home
with a mixture of pleasure and sadness and a burst of activity
from my mother. I was in need of an outfit to meet the
sartorial standards of the Playground of the Rich. Our
finances, however, were, at the moment, at their lowest ebb
since we had left Waterbury, and my mother's resourcefulness was severly taxed to negotiate a loan. First she outlined a
possible wardrobe. This included a lightweight dark-blue
suit for formal occasions, two extra pairs of socks (I already
owned two), four shirts (I owned two), four starched collars,
and half a dozen handkerchiefs (I owned three). This array,
apart from the suit, was necessitated by the Cedar View
management's exaggerated laundry-mindedness.

On sober second thought, the new suit was abandoned as an extravagance, as the jacket of my old blue suit was in fair condition, though the pants were shiny (at night, when I should wear them, the pants would shine less brazenly). Instead, a pair of white pants was substituted as constituting, with a dark-blue jacket, the more stylish outfit for formal evening wear. The cost might be around six dollars. Hannah would have gladly raised with her ring more than the needed sum, but the "stone" was "out" just then, having relieved a friend from a threatened eviction. Every suggestion from Molly or me of a source for borrowing the money was vetoed by my mother as one she had only recently tapped. But the next morning my mother returned from the grocery store downstairs with a load of provisions *and six dollars!* The grocer had not even been mentioned by us, as being quite outside the bounds of possibility. Yet my mother had talked him into lending her the money, though he had filled an entire notebook with sums we had owed him for over a month! I could only guess at the exaggerated story she told him about my summer prospects; for he greeted me, when he next saw me, with unwonted deference, and said he hoped I would return in the fall a rich and celebrated artist.

The day before my departure was a scorcher, hardly to be borne. It was even too hot to practice. But my mother, after finishing her household work late in the evening, mended my old shirts, socks, and underwear and set them to boil in a tin basin on the stove. I sat on the stoop talking with Molly until my mother had hung the wash on the clothesline. Then, redfaced and perspiring, she summoned us to bed. Long before I rose next morning, she had ironed my things and packed them in an old, unsteady valise. She was unusually silent and went about her work studiously avoiding looking at me. I, for my part, watched her with emotion. As the time approached for my leaving, I grew panicky, and considered, for a wild moment, canceling the trip.

Hannah came down to bid me good-by. Molly, who had little control over herself, broke into sobs. I felt my heart aching unbearably with love for these three, and even for my father, who left his breakfast unfinished and hovered self-consciously in the background. But my mother kept doggedly busy and aggressively dry-eyed. At a certain moment every-thing seemed ready. My mother glanced at the small round tin clock that stood on the window ledge in the kitchen. "Finished," she exclaimed, tying a string around a paper bag in which she had packed my lunch of hard-boiled eggs, rolls, a tomato, and some salt in a tiny paper cone. I felt I must leave the house at once or I would break down. Hannah and Molly saw me off on the streetcar at the corner. I looked back at our window for a final glimpse of my mother. Only my father was there, waving his colored handkerchief in my direction.

The Cedar View Hotel was a large, sprawling wooden structure, three stories high, with a wide veranda halfway around the ground floor. Sol Rashkin and I were given a narrow, elongated room on the third floor. A small window offered a breath-taking view of a lake and great mountains in the not too far distance. On the four-hour train journey I had given myself up to feelings of loneliness and yearning for home, and had been obliged several times to seek refuge in the toilet to vomit or to cry. But when I looked out from our bedroom window at the panorama before me, I forgot, for the moment, my home and my family. The air was so clean that the pines on the side of the mountains stood out solid in dark velvet-green. They seemed so near to me that I thought a leap from the window would set me down in their midst. The lake, too, pellucid and emerald-green, seemed within hand-reach, though I knew it to be several hundred yards away. Some people were rowing boats, and I thought I could even make out their features. I had never imagined any part of the world to be so lovely.

Sol was either too familiar with the scene or congenitally indifferent to lakes and mountains, for he busied himself unpacking his valise and hanging up his clothes on pegs screwed into the wall, never once looking out the window. Besides a bed and two chairs, the room held a tin washstand with a pitcher and bowl. Two shelves on a wall served as a dresser. When we had disposed our things and shoved our valises under the bed, Sol took his violin case and his music and we went down into the dining-room to rehearse. It was late afternoon, and waiters and waitresses were setting the tables for dinner. I sat down at the upright piano with trepidation, never having accompanied anyone before.

Sol warmed up with a few scales and passages, which he tossed off with terrifying confidence and ease. I struck a few chords tentatively, but my fingers were cold, though the dining-room was oppressively warm. "Let's try *Zigeunerweisen*," Sol commanded. I picked out the music and placed it on the rack. It began with a few introductory solo bars for the piano. My hands trembled as I played. A moment later Sol came in with the same theme. The rich sound of his tone and the sureness and boldness of his fingers and bow were in startling contrast with the sound of the tinny piano and my uncertain playing. I counted four in a bar under my breath, so that I might not rush forward or lag behind the violin. But to my discomfiture Sol played freely, paying no heed to the directions in the score. His style was improvisational, as if he thought up the music as he played. His throbbing tone and arrogantly erratic phrasing gave to his performance the stamp of authenticity.

I accompanied him with difficulty. I could not anticipate the vagaries of his tempi and phrasing. Repeatedly he upset my calculations and did something I was not expecting. Several times I was hopelessly lost, and Sol stopped playing and said huskily: "Let's take that again." And there was that in his voice which warned me that he was impatient and displeased, and which in turn unnerved me so that I lost control of my fingers and my wits. The rehearsal was abruptly terminated. Sol stopped in the middle of a phrase, put his violin in its case, and, muttering obscenities, strode from the room. I gave way to tears. Yet I could not blame Sol, and I remained in the dining-room till near supper time, practicing my part of *Zigeunerweisen* and some other pieces that Sol intended to play that evening.

At half past six Sol came into the room carrying his violin case. He tuned perfunctorily while a waiter opened the double doors of the dining-room. We struck up the *Double Eagle March*. At the first notes, a horde of guests streamed in and hastily made for their tables. By the time we had played the march half through, the room was full of chattering men, women, and children. Even the strong tone of the violin was unable to penetrate the din, and before we had come to the end of the piece Sol motioned me to stop. Waiters came running in bearing large platters of salted herring cut in big chunks, great bowls of vapor-breathing, extra-large boiled potatoes, immense heaps of large, aromatic sliced onions, young scallions with tender white bulbs and maturer scallions with large, graying, peeling heads. Into wicker baskets on the tables they dumped fat slices of rye bread thick with caraway seeds, and chunks of chaleh which had been torn out by hand.

Though the march had gone rather well, the piano part being only a succession of chords, I was grateful for the respite, and divided the time between going over mentally the tricky places in *Zigeunerweisen* and envying the clamorous and enthusiastic diners. Sol thought it would be useless to resume playing before the guests had been somewhat appeased by the seemingly inexhaustible succession of appetizers that kept arriving from the kitchen. He said the advent of soup would be our signal. And at the appearance of the huge tureens we played a Polish piece, *Krakowiak*. The din had by now subsided and *Krakowiak* was audible, though it had an added accompaniment in the sound of a mass intake of soup. It was not until the arrival of the double dessert of stewed prunes and watermelon that Sol pointed his bow at the music of *Zigeunerweisen*.

He had chosen the proper moment for this powerful number. The diners were now tired out and in a semi-comatose or, perhaps, a reflective condition. The moment I sounded the introduction, there was absolute quiet in the room. I played with more confidence than at our rehearsal. Indeed, I was about to give myself up to the enjoyment of Sol's sensuous tone when he suddenly hurried the repetition of a phrase that he had formerly taken quite slowly, and I found myself a bar or so behind him. Sol moved closer to me and began pointedly accenting some notes in the hope that this would help me find my place. But his proximity only aggravated my nervousness, and for a while we were distressingly at odds. At the height of my panic the violin broke off and I stopped automatically. I turned around anxiously to Sol for directions, but he was looking at the crowded tables. Pointing his bow backward at me, he demanded throatily: "What's the son of a bitch doing?" I was overwhelmed with shame, and I wheeled back to the piano for refuge. "From beginning!" Sol commanded. With tear-dimmed eyes I began the introduction again. This time Sol curbed his penchant for musical license, and the piece went off without serious mishap on my part, and elicited great applause.

Thereafter I took care to learn all violin as well as piano parts of Sol's repertoire; and Sol, who did not like to rehearse, thought it wiser to go over the pieces frequently with me. These rehearsals were sad events, though I recognized the need for them. Sol's sarcasm was biting, and his use of profanity (I had not heard such words since my street-gang days, when I, too, used them, but without realizing their meaning) shocking. Afterwards I would run to my room and seek and find solace in the volume of Shelley which Mr.

Plesch had given me on my birthday. The book contained a portrait of the poet. I gazed often at the sparse, feminine, delicate features, so different from Sol's swarthy, vulgar face and ferret-like eyes. Yet when he played, Sol, too, was a poet. I was disturbed by an inconsistency so glaring. I deplored the apparently haphazard way in which nature scattered its endowments. Why was not I, whose face, as I saw it reflected in a mirror, was delicate and spiritual (though not so incandescent as Shelley's), outfitted at birth with the genius and the power of a Shelley or a Sol Rashkin to move men's hearts?

For consolation and advice I walked over in the afternoons to visit I. Jacobs at the Grand View Hotel. I refrained, of course, from telling him about my disappointment in the character of Sol Rashkin. But I did confess the handicap of my inexperience as an accompanist. I. Jacobs understood, and was touchingly sympathetic. He undertook to show me what he referred to as the "tricks of the trade." These, he assured me, were well known among professionals and practiced by the best pianists, himself included. The "tricks" were, in effect, simplifications of difficulties, to be employed in certain contingencies, such as excessive nervousness, mental depression, or physical indisposition.

"For example," I. Jacobs said, seating himself at the piano to illustrate, "you see in your piano part a long, difficult technical passage. Perhaps you haven't practiced it, or if you have you suddenly feel nervous about it and *know* you will not do it justice. So you look at the passage harmonically and you see that it is all in, let us say, C major. Well, you certainly can play, for instance, arpeggios in C major, can't you? So you make a fast decision, forget all about the passage as it is written, and play instead a series of C major arpeggios. Now, supposing that you are even too nervous to play arpeggios. In that case, forget about them and play C major chords instead. Since the harmony is all right, there is no harm done. No one (except the person you are playing with) will be the wiser."

He added: "But whatever you do, do it with confidence. Confidence is half the game." And, indeed, he himself was the personification of that attitude. If confidence were contagious, I should have returned from my visits with I. Jacobs the boldest of pianists. But whatever optimism I rubbed off from I. Jacobs, Sol Rashkin speedily erased. I found that only hard practice could provide me with the stamina essential to a musical collaboration with Sol Rashkin. It was only many years later, when I collaborated with more humane, far greater artists than Sol Rashkin, that I was able, in critical moments, to employ some of the tricks I. Jacobs so generously taught me.

Even more searing to my sensibilities than his cavalier and unfeeling treatment of me was Sol's unromantic, indeed lascivious approach to women. He was often late in going to bed. I would be awakened by his lighting the gas-jet and the noise he made in undressing. And as I turned, now wide-eyed, to the wall, pretending to be asleep, he would spell out the details of the night's adventure. The musician who only a few hours earlier had filled my heart with pure feelings of joy and tenderness now described his sordid conquests with depraved relish. I was relieved to find that his paramours were Polish and Irish chambermaids. I could not bear to think that Jewish girls could succumb to his coarse blandishments.

He derided everything I cherished, and took delight in shocking me with obscene jokes and stories. I kept to myself when we were not playing together, so as to avoid his confidences. One of the guests, a young girl, delicate and pretty, and generally silent, smiled at me one evening as she left the dining-room with her parents. I had noticed her before, and her beauty and modesty brought vividly before me the figure of Elsa von Brabant in *Lohengrin*. I decided to love her, though she should never guess my passion. Indeed, she looked so fragile that I could not imagine her loving any man in an earthy sense. And when she gave me a passing smile, I felt that it was more than I could hope for or deserved. To my horror Sol caught the smile and saw my ecstatic face. He followed her out of the room with an appraising eye. "I suppose you like that kind of thing," he remarked with a sneer. "Thin as a rail—nothing anywhere"—and he made all too vivid gestures with his hands. I turned away and weakly said: "I don't know whom you mean."

The intensity of my love grew hourly. I caught glimpses of her in the dining-room, rocking on the porch, or sitting on the lawns. I walked in the pine woods hoping that I would encounter her and that she would notice me and smile again; or I sprawled on the grass, pretending to be absorbed in my volume of Shelley and praying that she might pass by and ask me what I was reading and I would tell her about my favorite poet and read her *The Sensitive Plant* (which she so resembled) or "I arise from dreams of thee," and so convey obliquely my love and my torment! But she never came close enough, and I had to content myself with watching her slim figure from a distance.

When I lay down in bed at night, I would invoke her image and say to her: "You will stand before me the whole night through, and when I arise it will be from 'dreams of thee.'" And every night she stood in front of me the moment I shut my eyes, and in the morning I awoke with thoughts of her only, as if I had not slept at all. Sometimes from my window I would see her walking toward the lake, as if she had only just left my dream and emerged into the reality of mountain air and sun-reflecting water. All this Sol never suspected. Nor could he have understood it if he had.

One late afternoon, an hour before supper, when the guests either had not returned from walks or mountain-climbing or were napping or preparing themselves for the evening meal,

I went down to the lake, got into a rowboat, and idly rowed close to the shore, watching the cloudless, darkening sky and absorbing the gray quiet. Then I became aware of a figure coming down the path from the hotel, and my heart stopped beating. It was *she*. Not a soul else was about.

She walked as if in thought, with her eyes on the ground, and saw me only when she reached the water's edge. She was dressed for the evening in a pale-blue silk dress, and she looked touchingly slight and insubstantial. When she saw me, I was a few feet from the water's edge. She stood quietly, and her eyes left mine and rested on the far mountains. For a while everything looked transfixed, as if absolutely nothing was occurring, not even time. Then I felt a new and strange emotion. I was *seized* by courage. "Would you," I called out suddenly and boldly, "care to go for a row?" She said: "Yes," distinctly. I rowed to the shore, close to where she stood. I let go the oars and, leaning forward, stretched out my right hand, which she took. I permitted myself a momentary awareness of her touch (this feeling I instantly laid aside as something to examine in detail and savor at some other, less crucial time). She placed one foot in the boat. But as she did so, the boat moved lightly away. Before she could put her other foot into the boat, the distance between us widened. Instead of releasing her hand, I held it tightly, expecting to draw her into the boat. This did not happen. As the boat drifted silently away, her legs separated alarmingly. I still clung to the hope that she would, at the final moment, make the leap. Then a sudden movement of the boat tore our hands apart and she fell like an open pair of scissors into the lake.

I sat in the drifting boat quite drained of all feeling. Like a disinterested spectator, I watched her submerge and rise, scramble up the bank, and stand there irresolutely, dripping and disheveled, her silk dress clinging to and outlining her body. The sight of the figure, grotesque, unromantic, even comical, brought back my senses and my will, and I seized the oars and hastily made for the shore. But by then she was running toward the hotel, and when I tied up the boat to the dock she was nowhere in sight.

She did not come down to supper. When I got into bed I went through my accustomed ritual and summoned her image to appear to me. But the only image I could evoke was the pitiful, ludicrous one I had last seen. I brooded during most of the night over the stupidity, the enormity of my behavior, and wondered how I could ever face her.

But I was destined never to see her again. For the very next day, just before lunch, Sol was summoned to the manager's office, accused of improper behavior toward a female guest, and told that we must leave at once. Sol called the manager names and invited him out on the lawn to fight, a summons that the manager, unfortunately for himself, accepted. I watched the battle from the window of my room. The manager, though plucky, was no match for Sol, who felled him with a blow and left him senseless on the ground. Sol was for remaining until the next morning so as not to miss supper, but a constable was summoned to hasten our departure. So we left Kiamesha Lake after a bare two weeks' employment at the Cedar View Hotel.

My unexpected arrival home caused a great commotion, as if I had been away for years, and I was hugged and made much of, and it was some time before I could tell my story. I had had no supper and my mother commanded Molly to go down to the grocery store for a tin of herring in tomato sauce and some rolls. Molly's hesitation to go to the grocer's brought back to my mind the precarious nature of the family's credit situation. I reached into my back pocket, pulled out my two weeks' wages in eleven crinkled dollar bills (I had spent one dollar for laundry), and gave them to my mother, who counted out six of them into Molly's hands and told her to give them to

the grocer on account and to say nothing of my return. I did
not doubt that my mother herself would have something
plausible to tell him by morning.

Later Molly and I took a walk on Madison Avenue and I
was brought up to date on matters pertaining to our family
and friends. I learned that Molly had broken with the Plesches!
In the first week of my absence Mrs. Plesch had written
asking her to come to Bay Ridge for Sunday supper, and
Molly, greatly flattered, had gone. There she had been introduced to Mr. Cartwright, an Englishman of middle age, who
thereafter never left her side. He expounded in great detail the
philosophy of anarchism, with special emphasis on its effect
on the relations of the sexes. He had asked permission to see
her home, and when he said good-night on the stoop of our
house, he had invited her to a concert and ball in Webster
Hall on the following evening. Molly had consulted Hannah on
the propriety of accepting an invitation from a man she had
only just met, but Hannah thought Mr. Cartwright's friendship with the Plesches guaranteed his respectability. At any
rate, she saw no harm in going to a concert and ball.

At the ball, as they were waltzing, Mr. Cartwright had
made Molly the extraordinary proposal that she should
accompany him to his apartment near by. Molly left him then
and there in the middle of the dance, and arrived home alone
in a state of bewilderment and shock. She had not breathed a
word of this to anyone but me. But the incident had cooled
her toward anarchism and all its exponents. She absolved
Mr. Plesch from any blame for the behavior of his friend, but
she thought Mrs. Plesch might have conspired with Mr.
Cartwright in the attempt to introduce her to the rites of free
love. Because of the unsavory episode Molly was now inclined
to question the basic philosophy of anarchism, which rested,
so it appeared to her, only on the *assumed* natural goodness of
people. She discovered little natural goodness in Mrs. Plesch
and certainly none in Mr. Cartwright. She was even inclined

to question the natural goodness of Emma Goldman, Johann Most, and other great figures of militant anarchism.

Still smarting from my fortnight's intimacy with Sol Rashkin, I could not but share Molly's disillusionment with the human race, and I wondered again whether socialism, with its curbs on the evil and predatory instincts of people, rather than anarchism, was not perhaps the best hope of the future. As for Mr. Plesch, I hesitatingly permitted myself to appraise him anew in the light of Molly's experience with Mr. Cartwright and my own with Sol; and I arrived at the conclusion that he was a weak, good man who mistakenly endowed humanity with his own virtues. I also began to see him in a new perspective as a pedagogue—a weak idealist, unable to maintain discipline and prone to be indulgent where his affections were involved. I realized that at my time of life I should be playing the piano with the assurance and command of an I. Jacobs, and that I would never acquire these qualities except under the pressure of the strictest discipline. I revealed to Molly these doubts and my reluctance to continue my studies with Mr. Plesch. She agreed with me that it was time for a change. In both our minds was the desire to divorce ourselves completely from anarchism and anarchists.

CHAPTER SIXTEEN

Sergei

Now again as in the old days on the East Side our flat was never without guests from overseas. Friends and relatives from Russia came to us in an unbroken stream and stayed until they found jobs and suitable lodgings. The rate of the turnover varied. Sometimes a visitor remained only a week, when he was summoned to a distant town by some closer relative. Sometimes he lodged with us for months.

I recall a lengthy tenure by a very distant relation who brought with him a man he had met on the voyage over. They slept in the windowless room next to the kitchen. The distant cousin was naïve to the point of being a simpleton, and his continual inconsequential chatter amused me, though it annoyed the rest of the family. He and his friend were unfailingly cheerful and childishly optimistic about their prospects in New York. Both were tailors, and they soon found work in a sweatshop. They did not seem to mind the long hours, the lack of light and ventilation, and the unfeeling attitude of the foremen and boss. They hoped someday to own a sweatshop of their own. In the meantime they showed no inclination to leave us, and offered to pay us something for board and lodging. In our impecunious state such an offer was tempting. But the pair were unsanitary to a degree that exceeded the laxity permitted to persons in our economic station. My cousin and his friend were cheerfully indifferent to the vermin that, hidden in their clothes and belongings, had left Russia with them and accompanied them to America; and my mother, who was not inclined to be over-finicky in such matters, was obliged to speak out and to urge them to seek lodgings elsewhere.

I believe our visitors found our house congenial, for they made a valiant attempt to meet my mother's hygienic requirements. Many nights when everyone but I was asleep they would stay up and painstakingly explore the seams of their undergarments and clothing, prattling the while in a subdued but cheerful undertone about quite alien matters. Indeed, the men were so pathetically eager to remain that they would eventually have sufficiently deloused themselves to overcome my mother's objections. But their hopes were dashed by a letter my father one day received from his first cousin in Russia, announcing the imminent arrival in New York of the cousin's son Sergei Drasin and *his* friend Joseph Cohen. One's obligation to a first cousin took precedence over that to a cousin of lesser rank, and my mother now succeeded in dislodging the amiable boarders by means less controversial than a charge of uncleanliness.

At the moment I was deep in the novels of Turgeniev, and the name Sergei and what I could learn of his history led me to identify my cousin with some of the revolutionary heroes of my favorite author. My father hinted that Sergei had been a thorn in his family's side in Russia. Though brought up in strict orthodox Jewish fashion, he had early been beguiled by

Christian learning. He had dropped his Jewish studies and prepared himself for Gymnasium (Russian high school), where he had been accepted as one of the small quota of Jews. More grievous still, he had joined a band of revolutionaries! ("Heathens! Anarchists! Nihilists! God knows what!" my father called them)—and had in due course been apprehended by the authorities and confined in prison for nine months. Having only recently been released, Sergei had given in to the pleadings of his mother to flee the country before he got into worse trouble. My father added grudgingly that Sergei was not really evil at heart, only weak in character and, in consequence, an easy prey to evil influences.

When Sergei entered our house, followed by his friend, a pock-marked, short youth, both of them wearing long Russian blouses and belts, I instantly saw them as Bazarov and his disciple Arkady, the hero and his acolyte straight out of *Fathers and Sons*! Sergei, in truth, had a mild, kind face, but I chose to read into it the haughtiness and disdain with which Turgeniev had endowed Bazarov. I could hardly believe that I stood in the actual presence of a fighter for Russian freedom who had just emerged from solitary confinement in a tsarist dungeon (later I learned with sorrow that Sergei had been one of a large company in a large cell). At bedtime I begged him to take my bunk on the top of the tin bathtub, but he refused, saying it didn't matter to him where he slept, and he and his friend retired to the windowless room of their predecessors.

I longed to be of service to Sergei, and offered to show him the city. This would give me the chance to be alone with him, to draw him out on the subject of his heroic past and to get his opinions about literature and life in general. Like Bazarov, Sergei to my satisfaction showed little enthusiasm for anything. He accepted my invitation politely, yet in the manner of one conferring a favor, at least so it seemed to me. We rode on the Second Avenue elevated. He still wore his

Russian blouse and smelled of "ship," and he looked every bit the revolutionary. I felt proud to be seen with him. He was twenty-three, and I was fifteen and a half, so I hastened to impress him with the maturity of my intellect and ideas. I asked him if he knew *Hamlet*, and he looked at me with surprise and embarked on a long speech in Russian which, by its rhythm and magniloquence, I took to be a famous quotation from that tragedy. I probed him on all intellectual subjects. His knowledge of Russian literature seemed vast. He quoted poetry, which surprised me in a revolutionary. Bazarov, I recalled, had contempt for poetry as a form of sentimental distraction quite unrelated to the harsh realities of the revolutionary struggle, as he had contempt for Arkady's father's addiction to the cello.

"Was Lermontov the Russian Byron?" I asked, and Sergei repeated the Russian poet's own modest disclaimer: "I am not Byron." As he talked, I was obliged to make a quick revision of my mental picture of a revolutionary. After all, Bazarov was a fictional revolutionist; Sergei was the real thing, fresh from incarceration. Sergei had kind eyes and a deep, disarming dimple in the very middle of his chin, rather disconcerting characteristics in a Nihilist. Bazarov was physically and ideationally granitic, Sergei not so. Sergei looked as if he could never be ruthless, as Bazarov was. Which type was the better equipped to liberate Russia? I could not tell. Sergei's eyes hinted at a character too humane for the carrying out of the impersonal measures of general destruction which would clear the way for the advent of the Brotherhood of Man.

I probed Sergei on religion. He revealed himself a dogmatic atheist. Religion, he stated flatly, was another name for superstition. I agreed. But I secretly hoped that he meant superstition in a theological sense, not the small superstitions I practiced to ward off evil and to bring me good luck. We got off at Fourteenth Street and walked westward, talking all the

while. I took Sergei into Siegel Cooper's store and showed him
the celebrated fountain. We then walked downtown to
Grand Street, and I pointed out well-known shops and theaters. But Sergei exhibited little interest, as befitted a serious
revolutionary. By the time we returned home on the streetcars, Sergei and I were on a delightfully friendly footing. He
did not exactly make me feel like an equal, but he did not
treat me with the intellectual superiority with which Bazarov
had treated Arkady. That was gratifying, in a way. Yet it had
the effect of diminishing Sergei's stature as a revolutionary.

For some weeks Sergei enjoyed leisure; that is, he did not
look around for work, but devoted all his time to studying
English with the aid of an English-Russian grammar. I offered
to help him and felt honored by his acceptance. His progress
was extraordinarily rapid, for, aside from his diligence, his
knowledge of Latin (he could quote pages of Cæsar's *Commentaries* and Virgil) made English easy for him.

In the evenings I would invite him to walk with me in the
privacy of Central Park. Sometimes at my insistence Molly
would accompany us. I shared all my enthusiasms with her,
and I wanted her not only to get the benefit of Sergei's
revolutionary opinions and beliefs, but also to take account
of the extent of my intimacy with him. To my surprise, Molly
showed no especial interest in my cousin—he was really no
relation of hers. On our walks she always managed to place
me between herself and Sergei. This pleased me, as in that
way I had Sergei all to myself and we could converse without
interruption. I was all the more astonished when one evening,
on returning from an errand my mother had sent me on, I
found that Sergei and Molly had gone for a walk without
waiting for me. I went to look for them in the Park, but they
were not in any of the lanes we usually walked in. Nor did
they return until quite late. I could not help feeling piqued
that Sergei could dispense with my company for so long a time.
I felt sure that Molly, notwithstanding her vitality and charm,

could hardly be an adequate substitute on a two hours' walk for a passionate intellectual like myself.

In less than two months Sergei spoke and read English fairly well. At that point he and his friend applied themselves to finding jobs. And after weeks of answering want ads in the *New York World* and the Jewish dailies, they were taken on as apprentice painters at twelve dollars a week in a railroad yard in Westchester. Thither they were obliged to move, to my regret, for I could now see and talk to Sergei only on Sundays, when he came to spend the day. But even these Sundays were less rewarding than I had expected. For when dinner was over, Sergei and Molly would manage to disappear without saying a word to me while I was practicing the piano or otherwise employed. Sometimes I would catch up with them in the Park. But I failed to draw Sergei out as I had used to do.

I became a prey to the horrid suspicion that I was not wanted, that Sergei preferred Molly's company to mine. But Molly's behavior in Sergei's presence always reassured me. She appeared to be indifferent and offhand, and almost always suggested our return home the moment I joined them. Anyway, were she to feel anything about my cousin, I felt sure she would tell me. She had never hesitated to talk to me about her suitors. I, in my turn, confided in her, even going so far as to acquaint her with my recent passion for the delicate, unfortunate young lady at Kiamesha Lake. Whatever Sergei felt about my sister, it was plain to me, by her silence, that she was not in love.

Yet, though my reason reassured me, I could not shake off a recurring feeling of vague dissatisfaction, of hurt pride, of vexatious discomfort. Between the two something was going on to which I was not a party. Sergei was often kind and informative, but I no longer felt the elation of being singled out. Once, when the three of us were walking on Madison Avenue, Sergei gave me a nickel to buy myself a soda in an ice-cream parlor we were passing. It was a warm Sunday, and I enjoyed the soda. But when I emerged from the parlor, Sergei and Molly were nowhere in sight. After a futile search of side streets, I went home, but it was more than an hour later when they appeared, Molly complaining that *they* had looked for me everywhere, even in the Park, and could not imagine what had become of me! This could hardly be the truth. I was taken aback by her duplicity. But Sergei's silence smote me to the heart. Bazarov would never have stooped to deceit, even tacitly. If Sergei loved Molly, why didn't he come out with it like a man and a revolutionary? I recalled the passage in *Fathers and Sons* in which Bazarov discussed with Arkady his passion for Madame Odintsova, and even confided to the peasant coachman who was driving them his chagrin at having been outsmarted by that unfeeling lady! Bazarov hid nothing from his friend. With bitterness I told myself that Sergei was not the *real thing*.

My fears proved to be only too well-founded. My mother and father spoke in my presence unfavorably of the intimacy of the pair, my mother because she foresaw a life of poverty and drudgery for her daughter, my father because of his congenital hostility to the happiness of his stepchildren. And one night Molly herself dispelled all doubt by announcing her engagement to Sergei. To my mother's reasoned objections she opposed a passionate stubbornness for which her former simulated indifference had not at all prepared us. She countered my father's cold opposition with a bold declaration of love for Sergei. "She *loves* him!" my father mimicked scornfully. "What kind of nonsense is that! They *love!* They don't *love!* At home [meaning in Russia] one never heard the word 'love'! One loved *after* marriage, not *before*. Sergei is my sister's child, and I had a duty to befriend him. But he is a *heathen*. He holds nothing sacred, neither God nor Tsar! Do you have to love *him*? Can't you love somebody else?"

But it was all to no avail. At Molly's behest Sergei no longer visited us on Sundays. But they met in the Park, where they walked about all day and took shelter in ice-cream parlors when it rained. Without relaxing her opposition, my mother sent me after them to the Park with a paper bag full of hard-boiled eggs and buttered rolls. The three of us sat on the grass and ate our lunch. By then I had become a confidant and ally. Molly had asked my forgiveness for her evasions, and Sergei, in his trouble, turned to me for advice. This at once restored my former esteem for him, and the contemplation of his future dual relationship of cousin and brother-in-law gave me pleasure.

They could, of course, easily resolve their difficulties by eloping, a method that Molly herself suggested. This, however, Sergei, much to my astonishment, opposed. Instead, he suggested conciliation. (Bazarov would have frowned on marriage itself as a bourgeois institution. He would have lived openly with Molly, defying my mother and father and the whole world, if need be!) Sergei held the opinion that in time my mother would give way. If that should happen, my father could not hold out much longer, for, owing to my economic ascendancy, his power in family matters was waning perceptibly. Faced with a united front of my mother and me, he would eventually be forced to capitulate or else himself seek another home, an alternative most unacceptable to him. I could see the force of such reasoning. After all, things were different from the days when I would be sent by my mother to Zalman Reich's with a peace-offering of gefilte fish and chaleh to plead with my father to return home.

Sergei's counsel, though regrettably wanting in revolutionary defiance, bore fruit. I was delegated to work on my mother, which I did earnestly and with great enthusiasm. I painted Sergei as a man awakened to reality and its responsibilities by love, and I went so far (with, indeed, a heavy heart) as to hint that, once married, he would lose his revolutionary ardor and aims and devote himself exclusively to wife and children. I also added that Sergei had had an offer of a steady house-painting job in Waterbury at fifteen dollars a week. There being no more desirable suitor at hand, my mother was unable to withstand the logic and passion of my intervention. Furthermore, she found herself in the indefensible position of siding with my father against her children (Hannah had, of course, joined our faction). She capitulated. And to soften the blow of her defection to "our" side, she made the suggestion that my father should be invited by Molly to officiate at the wedding ceremony. Realizing now that further opposition would be futile, my father very sensibly accepted both the situation and Molly's invitation to him to preside at her wedding. So Molly and Sergei were married, and removed to Waterbury.

Before a year had passed, Molly gave birth to a son. At my suggestion the infant was named Walt Whitman, whose poetry both Molly and I constantly read. Naming a child after anyone but a deceased relative was unheard of among respectable Jews. I was therefore obliged to pretend to my father and mother that Whitman was the Anglicized form of Velvel, the name of a deceased relation of Sergei's in Russia. Fortunately my father could recall some such relative, and no more was said about the matter. I nicknamed my new nephew "Whitty," and only his parents, Hannah, and I knew the secret of its origin. I hoped that the child would grow up to be a poet like his namesake, or, at the least, a good-hearted, well-read, sensitive man.

In the meantime Whitty's father had settled down, as I had promised my mother he would, into a kind and devoted husband, industrious to a degree. His resemblance to Bazarov grew less and less distinct, and I felt more and more that I was his intellectual equal. As the application of a proper chemical reveals words that have been written in invisible ink, so marriage had brought to the surface Sergei's orthodox virtues, and I recognized their beneficent effect on Molly's comfort and peace of mind. Had Sergei been a Bazarov, he might not even have fallen in love with Molly, who, though a girl of spirit and charm, possessed neither the challenging maturity and cynicism of a Madame Odintsova nor the intellectual and moral passion of that ideal revolutionary mate, Elena, the dedicated, self-sacrificing soul-mate of the proud Bulgarian revolutionary Insarov, in Turgeniev's *On the Eve*. I loved Sergei for Molly's sake and later on for his own. Yet often I recalled that he had had it in his power to be different, and I rather wished that he had had the strength to resist his passion for a simple girl like my sister. His marriage and its restrictive consequences had perhaps cut short an important revolutionary career. It had certainly robbed me of a hero and an ideal.

CHAPTER SEVENTEEN

Debut

M OLLY's marriage once more disrupted our household economy, which now called for a move either to increase the family's earning power or to lower its living costs. From a commercial point of view, Madison Avenue had been a disappointment. The Jewish elite had not bombarded my father with requests to perform marriages and circumcisions, and most of what money I earned came from the lower East Side. In a family council in which for the first time I participated as an equal, we weighed the advantages of a move to the scenes of my childhood, the lower East Side. For one thing, I should no longer waste hours in traveling; and my being always on the spot and immediately accessible to prospective pupils from the neighborhood must certainly result in an increase in my earnings. My father, too, was sure to benefit from a move to a less "high-toned" part of town.

Most of his friends and acquaintances lived on the lower East Side. He might gather a brand-new clientele from among *their* friends and acquaintances. Then there was Mr. Beylinson, his former pupil and more recent benefactor. Mr. Beylinson resided close to his ice-cream factory on Grand Street. Proximity to Mr. Beylinson was desirable in the event of sudden financial emergencies. In fact, he had once hinted to my father that if "one" lived closer to him he might be in a position to "throw him something" once in a while.

Immediately after Molly's marriage my father, at my mother's instigation, called on Mr. Beylinson to explore the nature of that "something" and to acquaint him with our resolve to move downtown. By good fortune the "something" was immediately available to my father. It related to the weekly collection of sums owed Mr. Beylinson's ice-cream factory by numerous ice-cream parlors in New York and its environs. It was a part-time occupation, and could be disposed of in two days a week. It required no knowledge of English. My father would be given duplicate bills in Yiddish. The salary was five dollars a week and car fare.

My father did not immediately accept. Bringing home the momentous offer, he asked us, and himself, whether bill-collecting was consonant with the dignity of the profession of shochet and mohel? We could not, in honesty, say it was. My mother, however, hit on a solution of the delicate problem. My father was to accept the job and after a token collection or two turn it over to me, first obtaining, of course, Mr. Beylinson's consent. On hearing the suggested compromise, Mr. Beylinson acquiesced, confessing that he, too, had worried about the question of propriety involved in my father's acceptance of a commercial task that had no religious connotation like, for example, the sale of matzoth and Passover wine.

We moved into a four-room tenement on Rivington Street at the corner of Gouverneur. The rent was twelve dollars a month. Our upstairs neighbor on Madison Avenue, Naomi

Finkle, the schoolteacher, entered into an arrangement with my mother whereby Naomi, who taught in a school close to Rivington Street, would eat lunch at our house five days a week for six dollars a month. This, my mother figured, would, in effect, reduce our rent to seven dollars. She minimized the cost of feeding Miss Finkle, alleging that she was a tiny person (as she was) who ate "like a bird." Thus, when we were settled in Rivington Street, our economy presented approximately the following picture per month:

INCOME:	Ice-cream collections	$20
	Piano lessons and lessons in English	20
	Sale of matzoth and Passover wine (on the average)	2
	Sarah's contribution from wages	16
	Miss Finkle's lunches	6
	Weddings, circumcisions, slaughtering of chickens, etc.	6
	Total	$70
OUTGO:	Rent	$12
	Food	50
	Clothing, shoes, gas, and synagogue dues	15
	Total	$77

The imbalance between income and expenditure was not considered improper. Indeed, my mother thought it rather favorable, and claimed that our prospects looked bright for the first time since we had left Waterbury.

If our prospects looked bright, even brighter was my outlook on the world. There appeared to be no limit to my discoveries in the realm of music. Living now within ten minutes' walk from Katz's music store, I established the closest relations with Mr. Katz, and soon the shop became my second home. There I was free to examine the sheet music and the bound volumes reposing in cardboard folders on a sea of shelves behind the counter. Mr. Katz was a married man with two children, and his business sense was of necessity keen. He had been a singer himself, a basso. He had prudently put his savings into this shop, and he had prospered. His love of music and musicians expressed itself in his kindness to enthusiastic, indigent students like myself. No longer was I constrained to buy music. On his small piano I tried out a never-ending series of classic masterpieces; and when, as with the later Beethoven sonatas, I felt the absolute need of possession, Mr. Katz allowed me the same large discount he gave to an eminent pedagogue like Tramonti.

I began frequenting Carnegie Hall and the Metropolitan Opera House. In Katz's store I learned that money was not essential in gaining admission to these temples of music. One of the piano students who, like me, hung around the store wondered that I had not heard the great Polish pianist Vladimir de Pachmann. And on my confessing that I couldn't afford to buy a ticket, he declared a ticket was not necessary, and invited me to accompany him to the virtuoso's next recital.

We gave ourselves time to walk to Carnegie Hall, thus saving twenty cents in car fare. Once there, my friend advised me to stick close to him, and on no account to say anything to anyone. Then, with me behind him, he joined the crowd that, tickets in hand, pressed at the gate of the ticket-taker. When his turn arrived, my friend rushed so quickly past the ticket-taker that the man could barely put forth a restraining hand before I too had passed him. Me, however, he stopped, and demanded my ticket. Whereupon my friend boldly called back: "That's all right! He's with *me*," and drew me forward. The ticket-taker appeared satisfied with this explanation. At any rate, his attention was immediately diverted by the press of impatient ticket-holders behind us, and a second later we were safely inside the auditorium, two anonymous youths among a large group of standees.

The incomparable De Pachmann did not command my entire attention, for I expected the ticket-taker to appear at any moment and order us to leave the hall. But we were safe enough; and toward the end of the concert I felt sufficiently at ease to be ravished by a group of Chopin mazurkas which the pianist played with shimmering coloring and an ease I thought I could duplicate. Yet when I tried out these same muzurkas in Katz's store, I found them not at all easy to play. Nor could I summon the variety of tone-colors De Pachmann had, so to speak, shaken out of his sleeve. Every celebrated virtuoso I listened to invariably sent me confidently to the piano to repeat what I had heard. And, invariably, the music confronted me with difficulties that had not existed for the virtuoso.

My colleague taught me many ways of informally gaining admittance to Carnegie Hall. The Metropolitan Opera House, however, was another matter. There the ticket-taker at the main entrance had once been too quick for my friend, who, his ruse having been instantly discovered, turned tail and fled from the building. But only to rush around the corner to the gallery entrance on Fortieth Street. On the way he picked up a discarded ticket envelope and in it placed a quarter. Climbing the staircase to its very top, he handed the envelope to the ticket-taker at the gallery gate. That practical employee, feeling the coin in the envelope, acknowledged what was then a time-honored practice by calmly admitting my crafty friend. I too came to employ this ruse, and the frequency of my visits to the Metropolitan depended only on the number of quarters I could round up. Fortunately for the well-being of my family, I desired to witness only the music dramas of

Wagner. My visits to the Metropolitan were therefore not unreasonably frequent.

The Metropolitan performances were heatedly debated in Katz's store. Each of us had his favorite artists. Mine, of course, were limited to those who appeared in the Wagnerian operas. The majority of the vocal students and teachers who gathered in the store to voice enthusiasms and exchange opinions espoused only Italian and French opera and the artists who appeared in them. I could not understand their bias for what I believed to be a perversion of opera, whose true function only Richard Wagner fully understood. In my ignorant childhood I had loved the music of Verdi and a few other *melodious* Italian composers. But that was before I came to know the music dramas of Wagner, which were based on lofty ethical ideas and noble emotions, which in turn gave birth to a kind of *endless* melody that could not exist apart from them. Compared with this kind of music, how tawdry and meaningless were the collections of tunes that constituted Italian opera!

I heard endless talk at Katz's about Italian *bel canto*. For myself I scorned the idea of vocalism as an end in itself. Of what use was beautiful singing of music that had neither validity nor importance? I could not care that Madame Sembrich sang trills, roulades, arpeggios, and scales with the precision of an instrumental virtuoso. With all her vocal resources she could never convey the nobility of Elisabeth in *Tannhäuser*. Nor did she even wish to portray that self-sacrificing, tender virgin; preferring instead to please the groundlings with the coloratura fireworks of an allegedly insane Lucia di Lammermoor. Another example of misguided ambition was Enrico Caruso, the "golden-voiced" tenor who had become the financial mainstay of the Metropolitan. His voice was exceptional, that I freely admitted. But to what base uses was he putting it three or four times a week! Not for him

the mystical, virtuous Lohengrin, the erring and later repent-
ant Tannhäuser, the noble Siegfried, the love-ravaged Tristan.
For him (the more the pity) the sensual Duke in *Rigoletto*,
the clown in the melodious *I Pagliacci*, the one-dimensional
Faust in Gounod's musical travesty of Goethe's tragedy.
Most of the disputants in Katz's store were partisans of
Caruso, and I battled unaided. Had the quality of Caruso's
voice been controversial, my attack on the tenor as an artist
would have been successful. My opponents untiringly insisted on the sensational beauty of his voice. "I agree," I said
at one particularly stormy session; "Caruso is like a man who,
possessing the most beautiful handwriting in the world, uses
his penmanship in forging checks." This neat retort was
admired for itself. But it convinced no one.

The low musical taste of the majority of the habitués of the
shop was something that I could bear, for I felt that time was
on my side, and that eventually everybody must realize the
supremacy of Wagner. What really disturbed me was the
indifference of the musicians and music-lovers around me to
the moral values of art. Indeed, in argument, many of them
denied that art, especially music, possessed moral values.
Music, they contended, was *music* and nothing else. As for the
interpreters of music, it was absurd to expect them (as they
knew I did) to be more moralistic than ordinary people. I
insisted that morality and idealism were implicit in the libret-
tos and music of the operas of Richard Wagner, and that the
interpreters of these operas must in turn become ennobled by
them. I was ridiculed for holding these opinions. But Mr. Katz
indulgently said that such beliefs were understandable in one
so young as I.

Mr. Katz was of a mundane disposition, though he would
not deny the importance of Wagner. He was given to telling
off-color jokes and stories, which I pretended not to hear. On
the subject of Wagnerian singers he held that they were no
better morally than the artists whose specialty was Italian or

French opera. It was common knowledge, he said, that Herr —— (one of the tenors of the Metropolitan's German wing) was an unmitigated lecher (Mr. Katz hastened to add that he himself had nothing against persons so disposed). I spoke up in defense of Herr ——, whom, of course, I did not know. But I had seen and heard him as Lohengrin, and I could not believe that an artist who so convincingly expressed the pure emotions of that supernatural being could be a sensualist privately. More distressing was a casual remark Mr. Katz made one day after he returned from a matinee performance of *Tannhäuser*, which I had also witnessed. I had been exalted by the artistry of my favorite Wagnerian soprano, Madame ——, in the role of the saintly Elisabeth. Mr. Katz agreed that she had given an excellent performance. Then, as an afterthought, and as if to himself, he said something so destructive to my attribution of purity and innocence to Madame —— that tears came to my eyes and I was obliged to turn away to hide them. "She wouldn't be bad," Mr. Katz said, "in *bed*."

Not all of Mr. Katz's customers were worldly, over-sophisticated, or morally callous. Some of the younger students were receptive of my philosophy of the close interrelation of art and life. If they lacked the boldness to abet me in the ideational disputes that raged in the store, I was nevertheless aware of their sympathy for me. I became friendly with two of these mute and timid adherents, Mike Dorf, a cellist, and Hymie Fink, a violinist. Mike lived in Cherry Street, a neighborhood once strictly Irish, but now more than half Jewish. He was thirteen years of age, a thin, lanky, long-faced boy in short pants. He lived with his widowed mother and earned his board and keep by playing odd jobs at weddings and balls. He himself had free lessons from a famous cellist who sat in the fifth cello stand in the Philharmonic Society Orchestra and lived uptown. Hymie Fink was a youth of about my own age, one of a large family of brothers and sisters. He had a round, absolutely untroubled face and wore his hair in a pompadour. He was extraordinarily agreeable, never voicing objections to anything I or anyone else proposed.

At my suggestion the three of us undertook to play chamber music. Mr. Katz kindly lent us a volume of trios by Reissigger, and one auspicious day we met at my house and essayed the first trio in the book. The session was both exciting and amusing. Not having practiced our parts individually, we frequently found ourselves helpless before intricate and difficult passages. We had ruled against taking time out for correction of individual mistakes, and we only stopped when one of us had lost his place. The resulting cacophony made us laugh, and drove my father from the house. Though I knew that chamber-music players abhorred leadership, I was, for once, in the gratifying position of being the guide of our trio. With the score before me, I could spot mistakes, advise my colleagues that they were behind or ahead, and call for repetitions of passages in which we sounded at odds. As I played, I could not help contrasting my present decisive position with the abject secondary role I had played during my brief partnership with Sol Rashkin. If only Sol Rashkin were around to hear me call out: "F sharp, Mike, not F natural," or "Hymie, you are two bars behind."

Down at the Educational Alliance there was unusual activity. A children's theater had been started by a rich uptown lady, and performances of *Snow White and the Seven Dwarfs* had been scheduled for the auditorium. In addition, the celebrated violin virtuoso, teacher, and conductor from uptown, Sam Franko, was forming an Educational Alliance string orchestra, with the twofold object of providing incidental music for the performances of the children's theater and giving several orchestral concerts during the season. Mike and Hymie at once applied for membership in the orchestra and, after an audition by Mr. Franko, were admitted to the class.

After the first rehearsal they came to me with awesome tales of Mr. Franko's musicianship, his iron discipline and terrible temper. In fact, all they had done that evening was to play over and over again some scales in unison at a very slow tempo. It was, in effect, a free lesson, if one did not mind the abuse Mr. Franko heaped on practically all of the players. Sarcastic admonitions and downright insults had filled the room. Miss Yetta Garbash, the spinster lady from uptown who had created the children's theater and invited Mr. Franko (for the magnificent remuneration, it was reported, of twenty-five dollars each weekly session!) to form the orchestra, had been present at the rehearsal and, unable to bear the conductor's terrifying fulminations, had retreated from the room.

At around ten thirty p.m., however, when the ordeal was over, Mr. Franko became affable, fraternized with the members of his orchestra, and invited all who cared to do so to walk with him to the Third Avenue el on Grand Street, where he would board a train for his home uptown. Mike and Hymie and eight or ten other players accompanied him to the el. Mr. Franko was in an expansive mood and, as he walked, spoke about eminent musicians he had known in the past and knew now. He himself had been a child prodigy and had traveled much in the civilized world. He had many positive ideas about music, among them the belief that mastery of scales was the true foundation of instrumental virtuosity.

At the second rehearsal, a week later, Mr. Franko told the class that he required a young pianist to fortify the cello section, which consisted of Mike only, and to add harmonic body to the strings. Mike Dorf thereupon recommended me, and Mr. Franko asked him to bring me along the following week.

The rehearsals were held in a high-ceilinged room that served as an art studio in the daytime. Its walls were covered with water-colors, oils, and drawings of East Side scenes and figures. Mr. Franko questioned me about my musical background, and gave me a piano reduction of Schubert's "Unfinished" Symphony to read. I must have read to his satisfaction, for he said nothing. After putting the orchestra through a few slow scales, he said we would try the Schubert symphony. Mr. Franko was watchful and thorough to a degree I had never encountered in a teacher before. He stopped us incessantly, suggested fingerings for tricky passages, and had them played in very slow tempo a number of times, accelerating the speed as the orchestra played more cleanly. Sometimes he would seize some player's violin and show how he wanted a passage or a phrase to sound. I was rather taken aback by the tone he produced. It was straight and dry, not at all like the lush, heartbreaking sounds Sol Rashkin used, with slow vibrato, to coax from his violin. Yet his playing was impressive for its precision and rhythm, though its want of sensuousness seemed to me a denial of the genius of the instrument.

The Schubert symphony after a while began to take recognizable shape. I had never before heard it. It did not resemble any symphonies I knew. Its alternations of pure lyricism and violent drama were altogether novel. The oboe melody at the beginning was mine to play, and the effect of the melancholy phrase over the figuration in the strings was ravishing. I also helped out the cello with the lovely second theme. Mr. Franko found much fault with the intonation of the orchestra, which did not quite agree with the piano. He shouted a good deal and ordered everyone to tune to the piano A, which I boldly sounded. At length the ordeal (the evening had been an ordeal, notwithstanding the acute pleasure the music gave me) was over. Mr. Franko now assumed a pleasant benignity and invited us to walk with him to the elevated. I strode next to him. He said I read music fairly well, and asked the name of my teacher. When I confessed that I had none, he said he would speak to his sister Jeanne about me. Jeanne Franko, he told us, had been a great pianist in her time and was now devoting herself to teaching.

When we neared the elevated station, Mr. Franko suddenly announced that he craved a glass of beer and a sandwich and invited us to join him. We were eight boys and one girl, nine in all. It seemed incredible that anyone should undertake the expense of such a generous invitation. Mr. Franko took our silence for assent, which it was, and marched us into Lorber's famous restaurant on Grand Street, directly opposite the Grand Street Theater, the very restaurant where the stars and actors of the Jewish theater supped nightly after performances. I had often in my childhood stood in front of it in the hope of catching a glimpse of Mr. and Mrs. Adler, Mr. and Mrs. Thomashefsky, Mr. Kessler, Mrs. Lipzin, and, best of all, Miss Bertha Kalich, whom I then secretly loved.

Mr. Franko seemed to feel quite at home in Lorber's. At his behest waiters joined together three tables, around which he then disposed us, himself at the head. He ordered *ten* beers and *ten* Swiss cheese sandwiches! We drank and ate, following his lead. He spoke about conductors he had known and played under, about the great violinist Joachim and other luminaries, about the musical supremacy of Berlin and Vienna over New York. To these superior capitals he repaired each summer to relax from his winter labors and to immerse himself in the main stream of music. I listened, fascinated, and hoped he would stay till midnight; for apart from my interest in him and the European musicians he described, I wished to see at close hand the thespian celebrities who would arrive about that time. But this was not to be. For at eleven thirty Mr. Franko, after inquiring whether we would like something more to eat and drink—which we politely refused—called for his bill. This he examined carefully, even, to my embarrassment, disputing some items. Sitting immediately on his right, I could see for myself how costly the party had been. Finally

Mr. Franko gave the waiter two dollar bills and told him to keep the change!

The following week, on our now accustomed walk to the elevated, Mr. Franko told me he had spoken with his sister about me and had made an appointment for me to play for her the next day. Madam Franko lived on the first floor of a brownstone house on Madison Avenue between Sixty-first and Sixty-second streets. She opened the door to my ring and led me into a large, pleasantly furnished room. A light-colored upright piano stood against a wall, and above it hung numerous framed photographs of musical celebrities, each one personally inscribed to Madam Franko.

She looked middle-aged and was rather stout. Like her brother, she was brusque in speech and manner. After a few inquiries about my studies, she asked me to play. I played the Liszt transcription of the *"Liebestod"* from *Tristan*. When I finished, she made no comment about my playing, but offered to give me lessons. I told her that I was in no position at the moment to pay her, and she said that she was prepared to give me a scholarship. But I must play Wagner sparingly and concentrate on the "old, good composers" and acquire a solid technique. My first assignment was to be Bach's Organ Prelude and Fugue in A minor in Liszt's arrangement. Madam Franko then went to the piano and played the composition from memory, with beautiful finger accuracy and a matter-of-factness that I could not help liking, though it gave the performance an air of aloofness foreign to my own approach to music. However, I read into her restriction on Wagner an animosity to that supreme composer and, for all I knew, to modernism itself, and I found myself resenting her lack of musical perspective. There could be, of course, no question of my abandoning Wagner. But my need for a solid technique was apparent to me too, and I accepted the scholarship gratefully. Before I left, Madam Franko asked several direct questions about the economy of our household. And as I bade her good-by she said that if I practiced hard and followed her directions faithfully she could prophesy a fine musical career for me.

Riding home on the streetcar, I gave myself up to visions of the future thus opened to me. How soon would it be before I would walk onto the stage of Carnegie Hall like De Pachmann and be greeted by the applause of a packed house? I visualized my inscribed photograph among those of the celebrities on the wall over Madam Franko's piano.

At home the news of Madam Franko's sponsorship and her hopes for my future created a sensation. And some weeks later an event occurred which confirmed Madam Franko's interest in me. When I reached home one afternoon after a long, heated argument at Katz's on the subject of Wagner contra Verdi, my mother told me that Madam Franko herself had just paid her a visit. They had managed to converse, Madam Franko in German, my mother in Yiddish, and they had understood each other! Madam Franko had said that I was gifted but undisciplined, and that I held stubbornly to certain revolutionary opinions about music and society. Furthermore, I paid no attention to dress and had no manners, and much of an artist's success depended on dress and deportment. She had noticed that I wore no *gloves*, and had bought me a pair, which she hoped I would accept and wear. The gloves were of beautiful, soft brown leather and bore a much-advertised trade-mark. I was not sure that I should accept so personal a gift as an article of dress. But because the gloves were symbolic of my artistic possibilities, I decided to wear them, like a decoration.

Under Madam Franko's tutelage my technique began to improve. Along with the music of Bach, now extended to include the first book of *The Well-Tempered Clavichord*, she gave me the least difficult preludes and waltzes of Chopin, and (I presumed as a conciliatory gesture) the Liszt arrangement of the Spinning Chorus from Wagner's *Flying Dutch-*

man. Madam Franko intimated that she had nothing against Wagner's earlier works. They were, in the main, melodious. When it came to operatic lyricism, however, the Italians for her were supreme.

For practice in sight reading, Madam Franko gave me a book of overtures arranged for four hands. Together we played the overtures to *The Magic Flute*, *The Marriage of Figaro*, *Fidelio*, and Bellini's *Norma*. When we finished playing *Norma*, Madam Franko challenged me to cite any music of Wagner that could compare with it in beauty and nobility. I promptly cited *all* the music dramas of Wagner and said heatedly that I found the overture to *Norma* neither noble nor beautiful. It was "barrel-organ music," and hardly fit to be mentioned in the same breath with the very least of Wagner's works. Madam Franko thereupon grew angry and called me an impertinent and ungrateful boy. I burst into tears and ran out of the house. I swore to myself that rather than abandon Wagner I would give up Madam Franko. But that evening when I arrived at the Educational Alliance for the orchestra rehearsal, Mr. Franko gave me a sealed note from his sister. "I will not permit your bad manners and ignorance to interfere with your work," it said. "I shall expect you at the usual time." I was relieved to receive what was obviously an apology. For in spite of my determination not to abandon Wagner, I could not bear the thought of abandoning my career as well.

At my next lesson Madam Franko refrained from making any reference to Bellini. She talked about the progress I had made, and hoped that in a few months I would be ready to play for some of her influential friends. To prepare me for that event she would work with me on a recital program, and when I had mastered it she would arrange "an evening" at some "rich" house. The idea both attracted and repelled me. I saw the importance of a private concert as a test of my abilities. At the same time I felt an antagonism toward

Madam Franko's rich friends and resented the power she ascribed to them. I esteemed Madam Franko as an artist and pedagogue, but her social philosophy filled me with distaste. I was sensible of her kindness and appreciated her interest in me, but I suspected a condescension in her manner toward me. My mother, who had been impressed by Madam Franko's visit to Rivington Street ("She came all the way from up-town," my mother told Mollie Finkel with pride), her smart suit and elaborate hat, called her a "practical guardian angel" and entreated me not to offend her, but obey her in every-thing, as she meant everything for my good.

For some time after the Bellini-Wagner episode nothing occurred to disturb our peaceful relations. I mapped out my day to the best advantage. It was my first attempt at self-discipline, and it afforded me a conscious pleasure. I practiced three hours in the morning, then walked the streets for an hour, reading a volume of Shelley as I walked and looking up only when I came to a crossing. People whom I bumped into as I read were invariably kind and polite when I apolo-gized. I lunched at home with Naomi Finkle. Naomi was well-read, but her taste in music, notwithstanding her brother's musical eminence as a member of the Metropolitan Opera House chorus, was lamentable. Like Madam Franko she loved the old-fashioned music of Verdi and Donizetti and regarded the music dramas of Wagner, even the early ones, as so much noise. Her favorite aria was *"Ah, fors' è lui"* from *La Traviata*. I tried to expose its inanity by singing and playing it with mock pathos and exaggerated high spirits in the manner of a celebrated Metropolitan Opera coloratura soprano, but Naomi only laughed and reminded me that when we had first moved to Madison Avenue I, too, had loved Verdi and favored this very aria.

Twice a week I embarked on my father's ice-cream "route," traveling as far afield as Brownsville and Rockaway Beach. I took books with me to read on the streetcars, and the

in the novels of Tolstoy, Turgeniev, Dostoievsky, Gogol, Zola, Flaubert, Thackeray, and George Eliot. Yet I never missed a rehearsal of the children's theater, even when the orchestra was not required to play.

Sitting in the empty auditorium, I felt I *was* the velvet-clad Fauntleroy. I could never call my mother "dearest" instead of "mother" as Fauntleroy did his, but only because mine, though just as lovable, was not as gentle and refined. The cruelty visited on Sarah Crewe affected me deeply; and the wonderful scene in which her benefactor transforms with rich hangings her shabby little attic room into a princess's bower always brought tears to my eyes. While it was inevitable for justice and mercy to triumph, the triumph was also beautifully unexpected, like the startling C major opening of the finale of Beethoven's Fifth Symphony. So, too, the denouement of *The Prince and the Pauper* was æsthetically, morally right *and*, at the same time, surprising.

At the opening performance Mark Twain himself sat in the front row. Dressed all in white, his wavy hair a yellowish white, he looked pleasantly old and vividly handsome. After the performance he came backstage and we were all presented to him. He seemed to me very much at ease for so celebrated a man. I had expected him to behave somewhat haughtily, as I would have done in his position. But he spoke to us as to equals. I could not help feeling let down.

Many celebrated people from uptown came to see the productions of the children's theater. The climax of these visits was undoubtedly the arrival, one Sunday matinee, of the great Jacob Schiff. We had received word of his forthcoming visit some days before and were concerned to be well prepared for the honor. But it was hard to believe that we would eventually see Jacob Schiff in the flesh, for Jacob Schiff was a legend among Jews everywhere in the world, and especially on the East Side of New York. To my father his name was the supreme symbol of Jewish affluence, power, and orthodoxy. It eclipsed, for him, such Old World representatives of the Jews as the Rothschilds, the Herzels, the Baron Gunsbergs. Among the things that Jacob Schiff proved, my father maintained, was the compatability of business success with religion. Avoiding doing business on the Sabbath, Jacob Schiff had yet been able to amass many millions. He could be the leading banker of the world without forgetting his obligations to his coreligionists. He was indeed a rarity. And it was not hard to understand why God continued to shower prosperity on him.

The Sunday matinee finally arrived. A few minutes before the curtain went up on *Snow White and the Seven Dwarfs*, there was a commotion in the auditorium, and Jacob Schiff and his party, followed by the top dignitaries of the Educational Alliance, entered and took their seats in a row that had been roped off for them. The performance went unusually well. The actors and the musicians had never acted and played so well. After the play Jacob Schiff came on the stage and congratulated the artists. He was short and had a small beard and looked imposing, and, unlike Mark Twain, he seemed to know his importance. I had never before met a millionaire, and I half expected to see on his person some evidence of his wealth. My father, too, must have had some such illusion, for that night at home he questioned me closely about the appearance and habiliments of Jacob Schiff. My mother, on the other hand, seemed more interested in Mrs. Schiff, of whom I had little to relate, my own attention having been entirely centered on Mr. Schiff.

My father made great social capital out of his son's "meeting," as he called my handshake, with the great man, as indeed I myself did in the houses of our friends and relatives. I believe I embroidered the "meeting" even more than my father did, going so far as to retail a conversation I had with Jacob Schiff *alone* in a sequestered corner of the stage, on the subject of his refusal to lend the Tsar of Russia a large sum of money because of the pogroms that had occurred in Kishinev and other Russian cities. The newspapers had played up Jacob Schiff's humanitarian decision, so I felt myself on pretty safe ground.

Mr. Franko's orchestra played a secondary role in the representation of the children's theater. However, it was his plan, when we should have become fairly proficient as an ensemble, to demonstrate our progress by a concert of our own in the auditorium. He now declared that we were about ready to appear in public. Our orchestra had given one public concert in the Educational Alliance auditorium. But that was in the nature of a public rehearsal, and no admission was charged. One of Mr. Franko's best students, a girl of fourteen, had been the soloist, playing the first movement of Mendelssohn's Violin Concerto. There being no printed reduction of the orchestral accompaniment to the concerto for a string ensemble like ours, Madam Franko offered to accompany the young lady on the piano. Now, the piano "tuttis" of the Mendelssohn are extremely difficult to play, and on the day of the concert Madam Franko, veteran though she was, succumbed to justifiable nervousness. When the concert was about to begin, she took me aside and commanded me to sit out front during the concerto and applaud vociferously the moment the piano came in with a tutti, and to keep on applauding until the next entrance of the violin. This I did zealously, the audience following my lead, so that all of Madam Franko's solos were drowned in the tumultuous noises out front.

The proposed concert before a *paying* audience assumed an immense significance for me when Mr. Franko designated me as the soloist in Mozart's D minor Concerto, which I was then studying with Madam Franko. Mr. Franko had discovered a reduction of the orchestral portion for strings. I was, then, to make my public debut accompanied by an orchestra! Nothing could have been more gratifying. Most of the great artists before the public had made their debuts with orchestra, and from that springboard had leaped into fame and gone on to triumphal recital appearances. Besides the implications of such a debut, there was for me the anticipation of playing *over* our orchestra instead of *under* it, as I had been doing. Three months were to elapse before I would take my place at a grand piano placed at the edge of the stage, with the orchestra behind me—certainly a long interval to endure with patience, but, I felt, a necessary one if the professionalism Mr. Franko desired was to be attained. Besides my concerto, the orchestra had a long program to learn. Among the purely orchestral numbers were Gluck's overture to *Iphigenia in Aulis*, the first movement of Schubert's "Unfinished" Symphony, *Loin du Ball*, a sonata for strings by Pergolesi, Grieg's *Peer Gynt* Suite, *Heart Throbs*, and an arrangement of Sinding's *Rustle of Spring*. My solo would come before the intermission.

In preparation for the great event, Madam Franko arranged for me to practice on a grand piano at the Steinway Building on Fourteenth Street. I had not played a grand piano since my last visit to Mr. Plesch's house in Bay Ridge, now so long ago, and I was surprised and annoyed at the intractability of the elongated ebony instrument that was assigned to me in a large back room of Steinway Hall. I was further disconcerted by the sounds that issued from other rooms, where unseen players were testing pianos—sounds of pearly scales, impeccable octaves, and snatches, professionally executed, of familiar passages from Chopin and Liszt. My competitors seemed to be all over the building, and my heart sank at the distance I still had to travel to match their proficiency. There was something malevolently human in the resistance of the piano keys to my fingers. The sounds I expected to hear I could not, try as I would, coax from them. The scales and passages that I played with ease on my upright piano at home refused to emerge at the level of my accustomed pressure. I had to dig into the keys to elicit any semblance of a respectable tone. I voiced my despair and frustration to Madam Franko, who offered no false consolation and said that a good grand piano was a beast that had to be tamed.

Madam Franko thought it prudent to prepare at least two encores, which she thought the public was sure to demand after my performance of the concerto. I myself had doubts about the necessity for encores, but there was that in the manner in which she made the suggestion which assured me the necessity would arise, regardless of the success or failure of the concerto with the audience. I thereupon selected Chopin's Nocturne in F sharp and Mendelssohn's "Spinning Song" to play in that order—a slow piece to follow the rapid finale of the Mozart concerto and a very fast piece before, bowing and smiling and helplessly stretching out my arms to the audience, I retired to the wings for good. (I had taken note of the behavior of soloists with the Philharmonic Society Orchestra.)

Madam Franko had induced the Steinways, with whom she appeared to be on the most intimate footing, to ship my practice piano, which I was also to use at the concert, to the Educational Alliance a whole week in advance, so that I might get used to its sound in the auditorium and make what modifications of tone the participation of the orchestra might, in rehearsals, necessitate. In three months I had, if not conquered the "beast," at least managed to tame him to the point that I no longer feared him. Still, when at the first rehearsal of the concerto with the orchestra I took my seat in front of the piano, its lid raised high up on a stick, I was again gripped by fear of what it might attempt against me at this crucial moment.

The orchestra finished the first *tutti*. From his podium Mr. Franko looked down at me critically. Madam Franko watched me from a seat in the front row of the auditorium. I rubbed my hands together as I had seen soloists do before starting. They were damp. The huge instrument, massive and sullen, challenged me. Mr. Franko tapped his music stand impatiently with his baton and said: "Well?" I could hesitate no longer, and I began the lovely quiet first theme. The smallness of the sound that came back to me was disconcerting. In the room in Steinway Hall my tone had at last grown ample. From the corner of my eye I saw Madam Franko making signs to me to put weight into my fingers. I proceeded to bear down more heavily on the keys, and the signs subsided.

Suddenly I felt at ease. The orchestra had come in with the introductory theme very softly, and my fingers were weaving a musical embroidery over it. Both piano and orchestra grew louder, more intense. I experienced a joy I had never before known. I was a craft sailing on an unpredictable sea. At one moment the sea was turbulent, at one moment calm, but the bark was strong and flew along confidently. When the orchestra ceased on the chord that was the signal for my cadenza, I did not feel the nervousness I had anticipated for the moment when, unaided, I must plunge into a maelstrom of scales, arpeggios, and trills. The cadenza *went!* And at the end of the movement the orchestra put aside their instruments and applauded. Mr. Franko nodded approvingly and Madam Franko smiled.

That very day, emerging from the Educational Alliance, my heart almost stopped beating as I beheld my name on a painted sign announcing the concert. There it was, in large, bold letters:

SOLOIST
SAMUEL CHOTZINOFF
INTERMISSION

I could not tear myself away from the sign. And, indeed, I managed to pass the Educational Alliance several times each day, in the company, if I could manage it, of some friend or acquaintance. I took my mother to see it, and she in turn invited relatives and neighbors to view it with her.

As soloist I was entitled to four complimentary tickets for the concert. Our auditorium had no boxes, else I should certainly have been given one. I had heard that each soloist with the Philharmonic Society Orchestra was given a box at Carnegie Hall. One ticket would go to Molly, who had long before been apprised of my forthcoming debut and had made plans to leave Waterbury on the morning of the concert and return in the evening. The day being a Sunday, her husband would be at home to look after Walt Whitman. Hannah would leave her child in the care of Jacob. My other two tickets I reserved for my mother and father. My father had showed an unusual interest in the concert, and had even been seen pointing out my name on the painted sign to his cronies from the synagogue. My sister Sarah *bought* two tickets for herself and her bosom friend, Ella, a young lady who, though unprepossessing in appearance, was one of my most devoted admirers as a pianist. The sale at the box office, where I made frequent inquiries, was gratifying. Children under ten were admitted free if accompanied by a ticket-holder; in consequence the concert attracted many mothers who could not leave their infants unattended at home.

Early on the morning of the day of the concert I awoke violently from a dream in which, sitting at a grand piano in Carnegie Hall with the Philharmonic Society Orchestra behind me, I lost all memory of the composition I was about to play and was quite unable to begin. Relieved to find it only a dream, but still apprehensive, I ran in my underwear to the piano to test my memory. I probed the concerto for elusive spots, and to my almost hysterical relief I played it through without flaw or hesitation. Madam Franko had warned me to practice only sparingly on the day of the concert. I had heard that artists like De Pachmann, Paderewski, and Hofmann contented themselves with running through a few scales on the day of *their* concerts. Like them I must conserve my powers for the actual performance. Yet I was unable to hold to this resolve. For suddenly, several times during the morning, I recalled my dream, and panic seized me, and I could not remember what passage followed a certain modulation. Until the moment of my departure for the hall, I was constantly at the piano. Even as I left the house I was assailed by misgivings and ran back for a final look at the music.

I was escorted to the Educational Alliance by an honor guard consisting of Mike Dorf and Hyman Fink. They, realizing that I was nervously going through the concerto in my mind, kept respectfully silent, taking care to steer me safely through the Sunday crowds on the streets, for I stared into space as I walked, seeing only notes before my eyes. Though the concert was still two hours away, when we reached the Educational Alliance there was a line of people that began at the East Broadway entrance and stretched around the corner into Jefferson Street. Young people, mothers with babies in their arms, old men and women were pushing and shoving to get into the hall, for there were no reserved seats. No one appeared to recognize me, though my name on the poster stared them in the face! I wondered at that as I entered the building and made my way to the stage. The curtain was down, but I could hear the noise and clamor of the people rushing for seats. I sat down at the piano and began to practice softly. A moment later (so it seemed) the members of the orchestra appeared and took their places and I was asked to sound the A. Somebody clapped his hands for silence, the curtain went up. Mr. Franko emerged from the wings to great applause, bowed stiffly, turned to us, and gave the downbeat for the overture to *Iphigenia in Aulis*. Next came Schubert's "Unfinished" Symphony. My time was drawing near. My hands felt quite cold. Why hadn't I thought of soaking them in hot water as Josef Hofmann always did before he came out to play?

Mr. Franko went into the wings after the Schubert, and three violinists and I shoved the piano down front to the very

edge of the stage. Then I raised the lid. There was a burst of
applause as I sat down and began adjusting the height of the
stool. As I did so, I glanced at the auditorium and saw everyone I knew or had ever known. In that frightening moment I
recognized members of my family—Molly, Hannah, my
mother, my father in his shiny stovepipe (evidently he considered my debut a serious occasion), Chaie Rive Flayshig and
the twins (my mother must have bought her a ticket), Zalman
Reich and his wife, Mr. and Mrs. Gold of Passaic (how did
they know?), the Finkle girls, and Harry Finkle from the
Metropolitan Opera House chorus. More formidable, and
disturbing to me, were Miss Taffel, my very first piano
teacher, Montana, the celebrated pedagogue, the baritone
Beniamino Burgo, Mr. Katz, I. Jacobs, and Sol Rashkin, the
violinist and my erstwhile tormentor. Unlike my family and
friends, they would be highly critical. And there sat Madam
Franko in the middle of the first row, right below the piano,
stony-faced, grim, alert. For comfort I shifted my gaze to my
mother, Hannah, and Molly. They looked back at me eagerly,
smilingly. Evidently they did not realize what was at stake. I
shut out all other thoughts and concentrated on the loving-
kindness they signaled to me with their eyes.

Mr. Franko returned and stood on the podium a little in
front of me to the left. An ominous silence fell on the auditorium like a pall, made more terrible by the sudden cry of an
infant calling "Mamma! Mamma!" Mr. Franko turned his
head sternly toward the disturbance and waited. Silence again
became painfully palpable. After an eternity Mr. Franko
raised his stick. After another his arm descended and from
behind me came the soft opening syncopated D minor chords
of the concerto. I played at the right moment, a little timidly.
My fear about not coming in at the right moment had been
groundless! The broken octaves in the left hand went better.
I began to grow confident. My playing *sounded*. I could hear
the full round tones as they glanced off the raised polished-

ebony sounding-board of the piano. Long before the cadenza, I felt at ease. And as the orchestra swung into the preparatory tutti, I boldly looked down at Madam Franko and read approval in her eyes. I was conscious, in the midst of the intricacies of the cadenza, that I was feeling *pleasure*.

Nevertheless, the vociferous applause that greeted the end of the movement caught me unawares. I looked down trying to remember whether an artist bowed after each movement or only after the last. The applause persisted, and I glanced at Madam Franko for guidance. Madam Franko's eyes were puckered shrewdly, and she was applauding with the rest. She was, in fact, leading the applause; for when it showed signs of abating, she clapped wildly and infectiously, and everybody followed suit. It was at the height of this demonstration that she motioned me to rise and bow, and when I did she led the crowd into an even more shattering outburst.

Thenceforward I was in full command of myself. At the end of the concerto I did not forget to rise and shake hands with Mr. Franko as I had been told to do by Madam Franko. I had also been told to insist on Mr. Franko taking several bows with me. But that was not necessary, for Mr. Franko *volunteered* to accompany me from the wings three times. He then sent me out alone to play my encores. These, too, came off well, and at Madam Franko's insistence I was obliged to add the "Minute" Waltz to the C sharp minor Nocturne and the "Spinning Song." When I took my final bow, my sister Sarah advanced to the stage and held up a bouquet of four roses wrapped in a Jewish newspaper. I was completely taken by surprise. I had, in the excitement, quite forgotten the hope I had cherished that someone would give me flowers over the footlights. I would have bent down and kissed Sarah for her kindness and extravagance (nobody ever *bought* flowers). But the stage was too high from the floor of the hall for me to make the attempt.

Later, after the end of the concert, I kissed Sarah backstage, and on learning that the bouquet was a joint offering of herself and Ella, I also kissed her plain but generous friend. But I had little time to devote to them, for the stage was filled to suffocation with my friends and relatives, the friends and relatives of the orchestra, and some smartly clad uptown people who had come as the guests of the Frankos. Madam Franko took me aside, shook my hand, and said that she was glad her work had not been in vain, and that I must never minimize the importance of thinking things out in advance in the building of a career. Even applause, she whispered, must not be left to chance. Mr. Katz slapped me on the back as if I was a man of his own age, called me a credit to his store, and asked me to drop into his shop in the evening, where we could further discuss the momentous event of the day. He had also invited Burgo, Montana, I. Jacobs, and some others.

I was congratulated on all sides. The celebrated Montana spoke in broken English about the beauty of my tone, and I. Jacobs threw his arms around me and said we must play four-hands together. Even Sol Rashkin made his way to me through the crowd and said: "Why didn't you play like that in Kiamesha?" in a very loud voice. Sarah had whispered to me that the rest of the family had gone on home to greet the many friends and relations who were coming to congratulate me and partake of refreshments. When I had spoken to everyone on the stage I knew, Mike and Hymie hurried me out of the building and led me triumphantly home. Unlike our previous journey to the Educational Alliance, this return was filled with talk and laughter all the way to Rivington Street.

The house was full of people and had the festive air of a wedding. I learned to my sorrow that Molly had waited for me until the last moment and had just left in time to catch the train for Waterbury. My father solemnly kissed me and introduced me to three bearded old men from his synagogue. The look on his face said plainly that he recognized the prestige I had created for him, but was dubious about its ultimate practical value. My mother and Hannah were restrained in their attentions to me, for which I was grateful. My mother herself was the recipient of congratulatory embraces. People came up to her, nodded their heads toward me, and said succinctly: "*Nu?*" and my mother, easily grasping the flattering implication, smiled radiantly, showing her dazzling white rows of false teeth and echoing the exclamation affirmatively.

Pesach wine and *taeglech* were passed around. Someone broke into a Chassidic song of a jolly nature. It was a tune well known to everybody, and soon others joined in, clapping their hands in rhythm. One of the bearded men, overcome by the Pesach wine and his own emotions, executed a Chassidic dance, vainly trying to force my mother to be his vis-à-vis. All at once I felt a longing to be at Katz's store in the company of fellow musicians, to drink in knowledgeable words of praise, to bask in the adulation of colleagues, to be a part of the *real* world. The longing was like an ache that throbbed with increasing intensity. Did I dare leave the house at this moment? My mother would grieve. The guests would not understand. I would be like a groom stealing away alone in the midst of the wedding festivities.

But Hannah understood when I told her how I felt. She agreed to make up some plausible excuse and urged me to go at once. I ran down the stairs two at a time. On the way to East Broadway I began to feel ashamed of what I had done, and thought of returning before my absence could be noticed. But when I opened the door of Katz's music store and beheld the familiar company leaning against the counter, the diminutive form and shrewd, eager face of the proprietor behind it, and heard voices loud in argument about music, I forgot my home and all the people in it.

A NOTE ON THE TYPE

The text of this book was set on the Monotype in JAN-SON, a recutting made direct from the type cast from matrices made by Anton Janson. Whether or not Janson was of Dutch ancestry is not known, but it is known that he purchased a foundry and was a practicing type-founder in Leipzig during the years 1600 to 1687. Janson's first specimen sheet was issued in 1675. His successor issued a specimen sheet showing all of the Janson types in 1689.

His type is an excellent example of the influential and sturdy Dutch types that prevailed in England prior to the development by William Caslon of his own incomparable designs, which he evolved from these Dutch faces. The Dutch in their turn had been influenced by Garamond in France. The general tone of Janson, however, is darker than Garamond and has a sturdiness and substance quite different from its predecessors. It is a highly legible type, and its individual letters have a pleasing variety of design. Its heavy and light strokes make it sharp and clear, and the full-page effect is characterful and harmonious.

This book was composed, printed, and bound by KINGSPORT PRESS, INC., Kingsport, Tennessee. Paper supplied by S. D. WARREN COMPANY, Boston, Massachusetts.